ANCIENT DAMASCUS

ANCIENT DAMASCUS

A Historical Study of the Syrian City-State from Earliest Times until its Fall to the Assyrians in 732 B.C.E.

by

Wayne T. Pitard

EISENBRAUNS
Winona Lake, Indiana
1987

Library of Congress Cataloging-in-Publication Data

Pitard, Wayne Thomas.
Ancient Damascus.

Bibliography, p.
1. Damascus (Syria)—History. I. Title.
DS99.D3P58 1986 956.91′4 86-24360
ISBN 0-931464-29-3

CONTENTS

ACKNOWLEDGMENTS

This book had its beginning as my doctoral thesis at Harvard University, which was completed in 1982. It has since been substantially revised, with a number of improvements.

Throughout the long period that I have been involved with the subject of ancient Damascus, I have had the benefit of advice and counsel from a number of people who have left a significant imprint on this work. Foremost I would like to thank Prof. Frank Moore Cross, my thesis director, who steered me into this subject to begin with and whose deft comments and observations during the course of my work on the thesis were acutely valuable. Dr. Michael D. Coogan, a member of my thesis committee, also took much time to read the rough draft of the thesis and to make numerous helpful comments and suggestions. Dr. William L. Moran assisted me especially with regard to the large amount of Akkadian material which had to be digested. Dr. Thomas O. Lambdin, also a member of my thesis committee, provided me with a number of helpful suggestions. I would also like to thank Dr. Irene J. Winter, who read and commented on the thesis, and Dr. Jack Sasson, who provided a number of insights to me when he reviewed a section of the thesis that was published separately. Much of what is good in this book is due to these people.

I would like to thank Jim Eisenbraun and the Eisenbrauns staff for their help in the preparation of the book for publication, in matters ranging from editing to helping in preparation of the maps. I am particularly grateful that I was allowed to make significant revisions to chapter 5 as a result of my examination of the Bir-Hadad stela in Aleppo during the late summer of 1985, even though that chapter was already in the galley stage.

My colleagues at the University of Illinois, especially Drs. Gary Porton and Bill Schoedel, have provided much encouragement and stimulation during the process of revision. I cannot fail to record here my thanks and love to my parents, Cecil and Ruby Pitard, whose support has been unfailing. And most of all, I must thank my wife, Angie, who has continuously encouraged me onward, even though I suspect she has long since found ancient Damascus to be less than the most exciting subject that we could talk about. It is to her that I dedicate this book, since it is she and our daughter Sarah who have provided the impetus to see the project through.

ABBREVIATIONS

AAAS	*Les Annales archéologiques arabes syriennes*
AfO	*Archiv für Orientforschung*
AION	*Annali dell'istituto orientali di Napoli*
BA	*Biblical Archaeologist*
BASOR	*Bulletin of the American Schools of Oriental Research*
BSPF	*Bulletin de la Société Préhistorique Française*
CBQ	*Catholic Biblical Quarterly*
CRAIBL	*Comptes rendus de l'Académie des inscriptions et belles-lettres*
EI	*Eretz-Israel*
HUCA	*Hebrew Union College Annual*
IEJ	*Israel Exploration Journal*
JAOS	*Journal of the American Oriental Society*
JARCE	*Journal of the American Research Center in Egypt*
JBL	*Journal of Biblical Literature*
JCS	*Journal of Cuneiform Studies*
JEA	*Journal of Egyptian Archaeology*
JNES	*Journal of Near Eastern Studies*
JSS	*Journal of Semitic Studies*
MDOG	*Mitteilungen der deutschen Orient-Gesellschaft*
OLZ	*Orientalische Literaturzeitung*
PEQ	*Palestine Exploration Quarterly*
RA	*Revue d'assyriologie et d'archéologie orientale*
RB	*Revue biblique*
RSO	*Rivista degli studi orientali*
UF	*Ugarit-Forschungen*
VT	*Vetus Testamentum*
VTS	*Vetus Testamentum Supplement*
WO	*Die Welt des Orients*
ZA	*Zeitschrift für Assyriologie*
ZAW	*Zeitschrift für die alttestamentliche Wissenschaft*
ZDMG	*Zeitschrift der deutschen morgenländischen Gesellschaft*
ZDPV	*Zeitschrift des deutschen Palästina-Vereins*

INTRODUCTION —— ONE

THE CITY OF Damascus is located on the edge of a large basin at the foot of the eastern slopes of the Anti-Lebanon range, at the foot of the massif of Mt. Qāsiyūn. On the border of the great Syrian Desert, it is in a location where at first one might hardly expect to find what is today Syria's largest city, a city which has had many eras of greatness.

The climate of the Damascene basin is arid. The twin mountain ranges of the Lebanon and the Anti-Lebanon deprive it of the winds from the sea and of the rain that comes with them. Damascus receives only a third of the average yearly rainfall that Beirut gets (250–300 mm. as opposed to 850–930 mm.). It is a land of short winters and long, hot, dry summers. But Damascus was provided by nature with the attributes necessary to make it one of the great oases of the Near East. It is located where the only perennial river in the area, the Baradâ, flows down from the mountains onto the plain. With this water the inhabitants irrigated the rich soil of the basin and so created one of the richest agricultural regions in the Near East, called the Ǵūṭah by the Arabs today. In Muslim tradition, the Ǵūṭah is one of the three earthly paradises and is sometimes said to have been the location of the Garden of Eden.[1]

The area of the Ǵūṭah is not very large, but fanning out around it is the Merj, a wide area of pasture and farm land. Today all of the arable land in the basin, including the Merj, does not extend more than 20 km. east of the slopes of Mt. Qāsiyūn. Past this point, the desert begins.[2]

[1] On the geography of the Damascene, see Wirth 1971: 403–7; Elisseeff 1965a: 277–78; 1965b: 1105–6; Sauvaget 1934: 425–29.

[2] See Elisseeff 1965b: 1105.

The richness of the area is greatly dependent on the extremely complex irrigation system. No one knows when people first began manipulating the waters of the Baradâ, but written sources dating back to the first millennium B.C.E. already mention the extraordinary gardens and orchards of Damascus. But the system certainly goes back far earlier than these references.

The irresistible attraction that the waters of the Baradâ and the rich soil held for the early inhabitants of Damascus is clearly evident when the serious disadvantages of the location are considered. Because of the abundant water, much of the Damascene has always been marshy, leading to problems with diseases such as malaria and typhoid. There was no location on which a city could be built that possessed any natural defenses against military attack, nor was there abundant local stone for building purposes. These factors were outweighed, however, by the richness of the oasis.[3]

There has been a long tradition that Damascus is the oldest continuously occupied city in the world.[4] Josephus in his *Antiquities* (I: 145) attributes the founding of Damascus to Uz (Ουσησ), son of Aram, son of Shem, son of Noah—very early indeed. This is a pleasant tradition, one probably related to the tradition of Damascus as the location of Eden, but in fact no one knows how long the city has been occupied. No excavations, even to Iron Age levels, have been undertaken to date, and thus virtually nothing is known of the city during its most ancient periods except through written sources and archaeological discoveries at other sites.

A few things may be deduced from the present topography of the site and from information about the city of the Roman Period, most notably the likely location of the chief temple of ancient Damascus. It is highly probable that it occupied the area where the Umayyad mosque now stands, in the northwest quadrant of the Old City. This site is known to have been the location of the Basilica of St. John the Baptist in the Byzantine Period, and before that the temple of Jupiter Damascenius during Roman times.[5] Jupiter Damascenius was the Latin designation

[3] See Sauvaget 1934: 427–28.

[4] Cf. M. F. Unger 1957: 1; Porter 1855: 1, 26; Thubron 1967: 3.

[5] On the Roman Period temple, see Watzinger and Wulzinger 1921: 3–28; Dussaud 1922b: 219–34; and Sauvaget 1949: 315–26.

Figure 1. Topographical plan of the old city of Damascus. Note particularly the hill some two hundred meters to the south of the mosque. From Watzinger and Wulzinger 1921.

for Hadad-Rammān ("Hadad the Thunderer"),[6] the patron deity of Damascus during the Iron Age; the Roman temple almost certainly was built on the ancient site of the temple of Hadad.

In the late 1940s, during some restoration work on the northwest corner of the ancient wall that surrounded the court of the Roman temple, a basalt orthostat, ca. 0.80 × 0.70 m. was found secondarily incorporated into the wall. Carved in relief on this orthostat was a crowned sphinx, stylistically related to Syrian and Palestinian carvings of the ninth century B.C.E.[7] This is the only major piece of archaeological evidence of Damascus from the Iron Age or earlier.[8]

A hill near the center of the Old City, some 250 m. west of the Roman arch on Bāb Šarqî Street and directly to the south of the street, rises some 5 to 6 m. above the surrounding terrain. It is clearly not a natural feature. C. Watzinger and K. Wulzinger, in their study of the topography of the city, suggested that this hill represented the location of a theater or odeion from the Roman Period.[9] However, J. Sauvaget has persuasively argued that it is the location, not of a theater, but of the Hellenistic palace of Antiochus IX Cyzicenus, who ruled from Damascus near the end of the second century B.C.E. He has noted that the area was known as *el-bariṣ*, 'the palace, fortress', during the Middle Ages, although there was no fortress there at that time. He suggests that the palace of Antiochus was erected on the location of the Persian period palace,[10] which in turn was probably built over the remains of the palaces of the Aramaean kings of the Iron Age.[11]

[6] On Hadad-Rammān, see Greenfield 1976: 195–98.

[7] El-Kader 1949: 191–95.

[8] Two other large carved stones have been found in the general area of Damascus, both dating to the Iron Age. One is an orthostat from Tell eṣ-Ṣāliḥiyyeh, 15 km. east of Damascus, with a relief carving of a man or a god and is dated to the Iron II period. The other one is a carved lion found by inhabitants of the village of Šeiḫ Saᶜd to the south of Damascus. It has been dated to the end of the second millennium B.C.E. See Contenau 1924: 207–11.

[9] Watzinger and Wulzinger 1921: 44–46. Evidence for a theater has been found some 200 m. farther west.

[10] During the late Persian Period, Damascus played an important role in the military preparations of Darius in his struggle with Alexander the Great. See Tarn 1964: 24, 35, 41.

[11] Sauvaget 1949: 350–55.

Although there is no way to prove these proposals short of excavating the hill, there are some factors that make the suggestion plausible. This hill is the only really high spot within the area of the Old City, and it is fairly close to the site of the temple of Hadad where the palace would be expected (the hill is some 300 m. south of the present enclosure wall of the mosque).[12] The palace hill and the temple were likely the two poles around which the ancient city was built, similar to the plan of Ugarit in the Late Bronze Age. The western part of the Old City may cover most of the ancient site of Damascus.

It is hoped that sometime in the near future excavations may be undertaken in the Old City so that some of the basic questions about ancient Damascus may be answered.

PREVIOUS RESEARCH ON ANCIENT DAMASCUS

There have been few attempts over the past century to investigate the information that has been preserved about ancient Damascus in a comprehensive and systematic way. This is not too surprising in view of the fact that the sources are so fragmentary that not a single period, not even a single reign of a king of Damascus, may be reconstructed with any degree of completeness; the transitions between periods are even more poorly documented. The earliest written reference to the area of Damascus, from the Middle Bronze Age, is followed by centuries of silence. In the Late Bronze Age, only a few isolated references appear. Only during the ninth and eighth centuries B.C.E. is there something like a connected narrative, and even during these years massive gaps appear again and again. A true history of Damascus simply cannot be written at this point, a fact which frustrates anyone who studies the topic.

The fragmentary nature of knowledge of ancient Damascus has influenced the form in which scholarly investigation of this subject has developed. Most of the research has been done in circumscribed areas; few synthetic studies have appeared. Thus only one book has previously appeared which attempts to deal with the entire history of Damascus down to its incorporation into the Neo-Assyrian empire in 732 B.C.E.—Merrill F. Unger's

[12] The distance between this hill and the much larger enclosure of the Roman Period temple was only some 150 m. See Watzinger and Wulzinger, 1921: Tafel II.

Israel and the Aramaeans of Damascus, based on his doctoral dissertation at Johns Hopkins University and published in 1957. In spite of several weaknesses in interpretation, it has remained the standard resource on Damascus. There are, however, other works which have investigated shorter periods of the history of the city.

Study of the area of Damascus during the second millennium B.C.E., when it was known as the land of ʾĀpu(m), has been minimal. The only attempt to gather all the information available from this period has been the above-mentioned work of Unger. Even Horst Klengel, in his monumental *Geschichte Syriens im 2. Jahrtausend v.u.Z.* (1965–70), did not include a chapter on ʾĀpu; he refers to it only in connection with events concerning its neighbors.

For the first millennium there are several important studies which deal with the kingdom of Aram Damascus within a more general discussion of all the Aramaean states. The dominant role of Damascus takes up a substantial percentage of these historical analyses of the Aramaeans, including Sina Schiffer's *Die Aramäer* (1911), Emil Kraeling's *Aram and Israel* (1918), and André Dupont-Sommer's *Les Aramaeans* (1949). The most detailed and perhaps most influential of these is Kraeling's book. One article has had a major impact since its appearance and should also be mentioned here: Benjamin Mazar's "The Aramean Empire and its Relations with Israel" (*Biblical Archaeologist* 25 [1962] 98–120). Mazar proposed that Damascus came to rule all of Syria as a unified empire during the last half of the ninth century B.C.E., a hypothesis which has been widely accepted.

None of the works just cited are less than twenty years old, and most of them are much older than that. Many developments in the past few decades have rendered much of the material in these books obsolete. *Israel and the Aramaeans of Damascus* appeared a quarter of a century ago and is dated in several areas. A number of hypotheses which Unger supported in his book have more recently been shown to be incorrect; several others are in need of careful reexamination. Besides this, some new inscriptions relating to the history of Damascus have been discovered during the past thirty years.

In this study I will look anew at what is known of the city and the kingdoms of which it was the capital, examining the documents in order to present as clear and correct a picture of this important city as possible. I will also carefully examine many of the proposals that have been made by others who have studied this subject. Because of the nature of the material, it is appropriate to follow a general chronological order, first presenting the evidence of the prehistoric periods, then considering what is known of the Middle Bronze, Late Bronze, and Iron Ages down to 732 B.C.E., the date of the incorporation of Damascus into the Neo-Assyrian provincial system.

THE NAMES OF DAMASCUS AND THE KINGDOMS IT RULED

The Name of Damascus

The etymology of the name has been the subject of considerable scholarly research, but very little consensus has been reached. No one has been able even to show whether or not the name is Semitic. If it is Semitic, as many think, there is no unanimity as to its meaning. There have been many proposals, but none carry compelling arguments.

The city name appears for the first time, as *ta-ms-qu*[13] (written *tỉ-ms-q*ȝ), in the lists of towns conquered by Tuthmōsis III which are inscribed on the walls of the Karnak Temple at Luxor.[14] The same spelling occurs in a list of Amenōphis III from the fourteenth century.[15] In the Amarna tablets, the name appears three times, written ^URU^*di-maš-qa* (197:21), ^URU^*du-ma-aš-qa* (107:28) and ^URU^*ti-ma-aš-qì* (53:63). In another fourteenth century letter, found at Kāmid el-Lôz in Lebanon, but addressed to Zalaia, a king of Damascus, we find it spelled ^URU^*ta-ma-aš-qá*.[16] The Hebrew Bible provides three different versions of the name: *dammeśeq*, the normal rendering; *dummeśeq*, which occurs only in 2 Kgs 16:10; and *darmeśeq*, which occurs four times in 2 Chronicles (16:2; 24:23; 28:5, 23). In Neo-Assyrian texts it appears as ^URU^*di-maš-qa*, ^URU^*di-maš-qi*, ^URU^*di-maš-qu*, ^URU^*dim-maš-qa*, along with a few other insignificant variants.[17] Finally, the name appears in an Old Aramaic inscription as *dmśq*.[18] It is difficult to fit these various forms together etymologically.

[13] For the vocalization of the name, see Albright 1934: 62. See also Helck 1971: 129.

[14] See Simons 1937: 111, #13a–c.

[15] Edel 1966: 11, name #3.

[16] Edzard 1970: 52, line 1. See also p. 55.

[17] For the various spellings and references, see Parpola 1970: 103–4.

[18] The Bir-Rākib inscription, in *KAI*: #215, line 18.

The most common approach has been to understand the name as Semitic in origin. Two distinct paths have been taken by those who have accepted this thesis. The first is to understand the *dālet* of *dmśq* as representing the Semitic demonstrative relative particle *ḏū*, 'the one of'.[19] The other alternative is to take the spelling of Damascus in 2 Chronicles, *darmeśeq*, as the original form of the name and to explain *dar* as 'settlement, fortress', thus making the name mean 'Settlement of *mśq*'.[20]

Suggestions for the meaning of *mśq* have been numerous, but none have gained widespread support. Clay supposed that the name was related to the mountain Mašu, where, according to the Gilgamesh Epic, the sun set. He understood the name of the sun god Šamaš to mean, 'the one of Maš, the god of Maš', and he identified Mt. Maš with Mt. Hermon. Thus the city at the foot of Mt. Maš would have been known as 'the (city) of Maš'. He explained the *qop* as a retention of the Akkadian city determinative KI.[21] All of this is impossible and merits no further consideration.

The most common resolution of the problem has been to locate an etymology that fits the entire final part of the word, *mśq*. Haupt suggested that the name was derived from **šqy*, a root that deals with water and drinking. He translated the name *dār-mašqî* as 'settlement in water-rich surroundings'.[22] While this would be an appropriate name for the city, it has a serious linguistic problem in that the Hebrew and Aramaic forms of the name show that the penultimate consonant is a *śin*, not a *šin*, and thus the consonant group *mśq* cannot be related to *šqy*.[23] Albright

[19] See, for example, Albright 1961: 46; Gordon 1952: 174; Speiser 1951: 257; Kraeling 1918: 46, n 2.

[20] Haupt 1909: 528; Clay 1909: 130–31. Kraeling (1918: 47) takes this form to be the name given the city when the Aramaeans first took over Damascus during the thirteenth century. Both Kraeling and Clay use as evidence for this form of the name a proposal made by W. M. Müller (1893: 234) that a town called *srmsk* in a list of cities conquered by Ramessēs III is actually Damascus. See Simons 1937: 164, #7; cf. also Helck 1971: 235. This identification is impossible, as has been noted by M. F. Unger (1957: 113–14, n 17).

[21] Clay 1909: 123–31.

[22] Haupt 1909: 528.

[23] This etymology, however, has been followed by a number of scholars, including Speiser (1951: 257) and Kraeling (1918: 46). The Arabic form of the name *dimašq*, also reflects the etymological *śin*, since Arabic is characterized by a *śin*/*šin* shift.

derived *mśq* from a word found in Arabic, *mišq*, meaning 'chalky clay'. Thus he rendered the name *d̲ī-mišqi* or *d̲āt-mišqi* (the latter explaining the doubled *mem* of the Hebrew) as 'the (town) of (chalky) clay'.[24]

All of the solutions referred to above assume that the name is Semitic and that it began either with the relative particle or with the word *dār*. But the Egyptian and Akkadian evidence from the second millennium provides no support for the originality of *dār* as an element of the city's name, making it unlikely that it is primitive. In fact, it is difficult to say whether the *darmeśeq* form is any earlier than the Persian Period.

The identification of the *dālet* with the demonstrative is also objectionable linguistically. F. M. Cross points out that the Egyptian transcription, *ta-ms-qu*, does not support this view, since normally etymological *d̲* is transcribed by Egyptian *d̲*, not *t*. He also notes the Aramaic inscription of Bir-Rākib from the eighth century that renders the name as *dmšq*. If the name had been understood by the scribe as *d̲ī-maśqi*, then the name should have appeared in the inscription as *zmšq*, since etymological *d̲* appears in Old Aramaic as *zayin*.[25] Thus it is difficult to accept the understanding of the *dālet* as deriving from the demonstrative.

It is clear, then, that there are serious unresolved problems with the view that the name 'Damascus' is Semitic in origin. It is probably not Semitic at all,[26] and until a convincing Semitic

[24] Albright 1961: 46, n 53. Note that he was a bit reluctant about the etymology. Unger refused to take a stand on whether the name is Semitic or not, but does suggest that the name was originally Meśeq, rather than Dammeśeq. This suggestion comes from his analysis of the vexed verse Gen 15:2. He understands the problematic *ben-meśeq* as a reference to the birthplace of Eliezer, i.e., 'a son of Meśeq = an inhabitant of Meśeq', which is then glossed in the text with the later name Dammeśeq. This verse is extremely difficult since it is unclear whether it is corrupt or simply idiomatic and glossed. See M. F. Unger 1957: 3–4 and 1953: 49–50. Some have felt that the verse is extremely corrupt. See, for example, Ginsberg 1970: 31–32; Skinner 1930: 279. Since the text itself is uncertain, it is unwise to use it to prove any particular point about the name of Damascus.

[25] Cross 1972a: 40, n 17.

[26] This is the opinion of Sauvaget (1934: 435) and Gordon (1952: 175, n 7). One other possibility is that it is a primitive Semitic quadraliteral.

etymology is proposed, it seems preferable to assume a non-Semitic origin of the name.

The Names of the Area of Damascus

Damascus was a major city of a series of kingdoms during the second and first millennia B.C.E. But from the early second millennium until the end of the eighth century, there were only two names (so far as we know) by which these kingdoms were known to their inhabitants—ʾĀpu(m) in the second millennium and Aram in the first. These two names will be examined in some detail.

ʾĀpu(m)/ʾŌpu The name ʾĀpum actually appears prior to the first reference to the town of Damascus. It has been found among the names of the states and towns in the Middle Kingdom Execration Texts discovered at Saqqarah in Egypt. Albright first identified the land called *ỉpwm* in these texts with the area of Damascus[27] and vocalized the name as *ʾāpum*. He identified it with this area based on the fact that the area was called ʾĀpu/ʾŌpu in the Late Bronze Age. All of the other references to the area of Damascus under this name come from the Late Bronze Age. It is mentioned several times in the Amarna tablets in two forms: KUR*a-pí* (EA 197:34, 42) and KUR*ú-pí/ú-pì* (EA 53:57, 59, 62, 63; 189: rev. 12). From Egyptian texts of the period comes the spelling *ỉwp3*, which may be vocalized as *ʾŌpa*.[28] Hittite texts spelled the name of the state *a-pí-na*[29] or *a-pa*.[30]

From these different forms some conclusions about the name may be drawn. The shift of the first vowel from *a* to *o* in some areas of Syria-Palestine and in Egypt during the Late Bronze Age strongly suggests that the *a*-vowel was accented and long and shifted to *ō* in those areas where the so-called Canaanite Shift took place, producing the pronunciation *ʾōpu*. Since the orthography of the cuneiform script of the Amarna

[27] Albright 1941: 34–35. The Execration Texts from Saqqarah are published in Posener 1940. The relevant names are E33 and E34, pp. 81–82.

[28] See Gardiner 1947: 152.

[29] See, for example, Weidner 1923: 14, lines 43–44.

[30] *KUB* XXI 17 I: 18–20. See Edel 1950: 212.

letters had no sign for the *ō* sound, we find it written *ú-pí* (this is the genitive form since it always appears in a construct chain with KUR [*māt*]). Because it is written *ú-pí* in the texts, the name usually has been normalized as Upi, and in the present study we will follow this tradition, except where the form of the name is being discussed. In those areas where the shift did not take place the name continued to be pronounced *ʾĀpu*.[31] Since Egypt had its closest ties to the areas where the shift did take place, Egyptian scribes naturally began using the *ʾŌpu* form. On the other hand, in Ḫatti, with its connection to northern Syria where the shift did not take place, the name retained its long *ā*.

Albright believed that the name ʾĀpum was Semitic and related it to the Akkadian word *apu*(*m*), 'reed thicket, canebrake', which he vocalized with a long *a*. He thought this was quite appropriate for the area of Damascus: "Since the eastern *Ghûṭah* (Arabic name for the Damascene) is full of reed-filled lakes and marshes, which extend for a greater distance than do perhaps any similar marshes in Western Asia, outside of southern Babylonia and Susiana, the name was singularly fitting."[32] This etymology is plausible, although it is not provable.[33]

A number of scholars have connected *ʾĀpu*/*ʾŌpu* with a different root, identifying it with the place-name *Ḥôbāh* of Gen 14:15,[34] but this is impossible. The Egyptian transcriptions show clearly that the first consonant is an *ʾalep*, while the second one is a *pēh* (although this could plausibly shift to *bēt*), and the

[31] It is interesting to note that among the three Amarna letters that mention Upi the one that has the written form *a-pí* is from Biriawaza, the official who had close connections with the country. The two letters that have the forms *ú-pí*/*ú-pì* come from Qadesh and Qatna to the north. The fact that the southernmost letter retains the ʾĀpu form indicates that there may have been other factors which influenced the pronunciation of the name in particular areas, since we would expect the area of Upi to have undergone the *ā* to *ō* shift.

[32] Albright 1941: 35.

[33] The Akkadian word *āpu* does not give any indication of beginning with a long vowel, since it is normally written *a-pu*, and both *CAD* and *AHw* list the word with a short *a*. But long *a* which began a word was rarely marked in the orthography. See, for example, the standard spelling of *ālu*, 'city'—*a-lu*.

[34] See, for example, Sellin 1905: 934; Clay 1919: 122; Haldar 1962: 615–16; Helck 1971: 271.

Egyptian and Akkadian forms all show that *ʾĀpum* was a masculine noun, while *Ḥôbāh* is clearly feminine.[35]

Aram. During at least part of the first half of the first millennium B.C.E. the kingdom of which Damascus was the capital was known as Aram, spelled ארם. This is seen clearly from numerous references in the Hebrew Bible,[36] and these references seem to cluster during the period when it was one of the dominant states in Syria in the ninth and early eighth centuries. But during the tenth century this may not have been the case. 2 Sam 10:9–19 uses the name Aram to refer to the kingdom also called Aram Zobah, an important kingdom that predates Damascus' rise to power. The Bible also refers to a number of states with compound names the first element of which is Aram—Aram Beth Rehob, Aram Naharaim, Aram Zobah, Aram Maacah and, a few times, Aram Damascus.

The use of the name Aram is complex in other sources as well as in the Hebrew Bible. The Zakkur Stela, an Aramaic inscription of the early eighth century, mentions Aram, by which it means the kingdom ruled from Damascus. But the Sefîre Stela I, from the mid-eighth century, refers to "all Aram" and "Upper and Lower Aram" and seems to be indicating the kingdom of Arpad rather than Damascus, although the context does not allow for certainty. The ninth-century Bir-Hadad Stela, with its reference to "the king of Aram," has usually been identified as belonging to a king of Damascus, but a new reading of the inscription, discussed in chap. 5, suggests that "Aram" is to be located in northern Syria. The use of the name Aram for a country becomes even more complex when the Neo-Assyrian inscriptions are examined, for here the name *Aramu* (*Arumu*, gen. *Arimi* in earlier texts) apparently never refers to the kingdom of Damascus, even during the ninth and eighth centuries. The Assyrians had a distinct name for Aram Damascus, KUR ANŠE-*šu* (*māt imērišu*) or KUR *ša* ANSE-*šu* (*māt ša-imērišu*), which will be discussed below. The Neo-Assyrian references to a land of Aram during the tenth and early ninth centuries seem to refer

[35] Some of these objections have already been noted by Albright (1968: 70, n 40).

[36] Every reference to Aram in the books of Kings from 1 Kings 11:25 to 2 Kings 16 is to be understood as referring to the kingdom ruled by Damascus.

to areas in northern Syria.[37] But by the mid-eighth century the Assyrians' land of Aram appears to have changed locations. In the inscriptions of Tiglath-Pileser III, the king who captured and annexed Aram Damascus, what is called the land of Aram is now located on the banks of the Tigris River.[38]

From this jumble of "Arams" a few observations can be made. It is clear from the Hebrew Bible and from the Zakkūr Stela that during the ninth and early eighth centuries the kingdom ruled by Damascus was simply called Aram by the other states of Syria-Palestine. The fact that Aram Zobah in the tenth century, before Damascus became a dominant state, and perhaps Arpad/Bīt-Agūsi in the mid-eighth century, after Damascus had declined in power, were both referred to during their periods of strength simply as Aram suggests that the dominant Aramaean power in Syria was called Aram, without any qualifying modifiers. This was true only while it was recognized as the strongest of the Aramaean kingdoms, and lesser states were referred to with more specific designations (Aram Beth Rehob, etc.). There is as yet too little information about the usage of this name for this proposal to be accepted without question, but it does explain the Syro-Palestinian evidence. It also appears that Assyrian usage of the name was rather independent of the western usage. It is quite clear that the ambiguous occurrences of the geographical name in both Syria-Palestine and Mesopotamia during the first millennium are related to the extensive infiltration throughout the Near East of the ethnic groups known collectively as the Aramaeans.

No satisfactory etymology of the name Aram has been suggested. Some have attempted to relate it to the root *rûm*,[39] but without success. The most common proposal is that it was a geographical name that was associated with a tribe in the area and eventually became the designation of a confederation of

[37] See ^{KUR}*a-ru-mu* in the inscriptions of Aššur-dan II (932–911 B.C.E.), which is apparently located around Carchemish. See Weidner 1926: 152, 156, lines 6–15 and 23–32. The inscriptions of Adad-nirari II also placed Aram in north Syria. See Seidmann 1935: 20, lines 49–54. The forms *Arumu* and genitive *Arimi* reflect vowel harmony that is characteristic of Neo-Assyrian. The original name is certainly *ʾAram*.

[38] See Rost 1893: 1. 42, line 5. Cf. also p. 75, line 24, where the princes of Aram and Kaldu are mentioned together.

[39] Kraeling 1918: 22.

tribes.[40] This solution must be considered speculative for the moment; the etymology of Aram remains unsolved.

Imērišu and Ša-imērišu. As mentioned above, the Assyrians did not use the name Aram to designate the kingdom of Damascus during the ninth and eighth centuries; they used the unusual title, *Imērišu* (KUR ANŠE-*šú*) or *Ša-imērišu* (KUR *šá* ANŠE-*šú* or KUR *šá* ANŠE.NÍTA-*šú*). How the Assyrians arrived at this name is unclear. Its meaning has been disputed for decades, and, in fact, the geographical area that it designated has been disputed as well.

A surprising number of scholars have identified *Sa-imērišu* as an Assyrian variant of the name of the city of Damascus.[41] This cannot be correct, since it refers to the state, not the capital city, and is therefore the Assyrian equivalent to Aram, not Damascus.[42] That this is so may be seen in the context of some of the Neo-Assyrian inscriptions themselves. For example, in Shalmaneser III's accounts of his eighteenth year, Hazael, the king of Aram Damascus, is called [I]*ḫa-za-ʾi*-DINGIR *šá* KUR ANŠE-*šú*, while later in the account Shalmaneser is described as bottling up Hazael *ina* [URU]*di-ma-áš-qi* URU *šárru-ti-šú*, "in Damascus his royal city."[43] In the Kalaḫ Slab of Adad-nirari III, we find the following: *a-na* KUR *šá*-ANŠE-*šú lu-ú a-lik* [I]*ma-ri-ʾi šárru šá* KUR ANŠE-*šú ina* URU *di-ma-áš-qi* URU *šárru-ti-šú lu-ú e-sir-šú*, "To the land of Ša-imērišu I went. Marʾi, the king of Imērišu, I enclosed in Damascus, his royal city."[44] Here the distinction between the state, Ša-imērišu, and the capital, Damascus, is quite clear.

[40] See O'Callaghan 1948: 95–96; M. F. Unger 1957: 41; *KB*, 88.

[41] See, for example, Haupt 1915: 168–69; Clay 1909: 130; Kraeling 1918: 46–47, n 2; M. F. Unger 1957: 3; Speiser 1951: 257; Gordon 1952: 174–75; Cross 1972a: 40, n 16.

[42] See especially Tocci 1960a: 131–33. This was also the view of Pognon (1907: 177, n. 2) and Albright (1961: 47). With only one exception, the Assyrian occurrences of *imērišu* or *ša imērišu* are accompanied by the determinative KUR, 'land'. The exception is [URU]*šá i-ma-ri-šú*, but it dates to the reign of Sennacherib, several years after the state of Aram (*ša imērišu*) had ceased to exist. This is also the only reference to *ša imērišu* after the fall of Damascus in 732.

[43] See Michel 1954–59: 38, lines III:46 and IV:2–3.

[44] The text is published in Rawlinson 1861–1909: I: pl. 35, #1, lines 14–16. See Tadmor 1973: 148–49, for a transliteration of the text.

Confusion about what Ša-imērišu refers to has misled several attempts to understand the meaning of the name.[45] There has been an underlying assumption that *ša*-ANŠE-*šu* somehow must be an Akkadian translation of *dmśq*. The presence of *ša* at the beginning of the name has been taken as proof that the *dālet* of *dmśq* was the relative pronoun *ḏū*.[46] The obvious meaning of ANŠE = *imēru*, is 'ass', and since there is no known connection between *mśq* and any known Semitic word for 'ass', at least two scholars have attempted to explain the problem by assuming that the Assyrian scribe who created the Akkadian form misunderstood the meaning of *mśq* and simply thought that the name had to do with asses.[47] E. A. Speiser took a different approach by asserting that ANŠE = *imēru* in this name was not 'ass' but rather 'windlass, (water) pulley'. Since he related *mśq* to the root *šqy* and understood it as 'well-watered place', he believed that the connection with water that he saw in his definition of *imēru* explained the Assyrian form.[48] It has been shown, however, that it is impossible to derive the etymology of *mśq* from *šqy*; the translation of *imēru* as 'windlass' is not certain, either.[49]

Pognon suggested that the signs ANŠE.ŠÚ ought to be read 'Aram', and that *imēru* was used because it was an anagram of Aram.[50] This proposal must now be discarded, since there are

[45] The confusion has also led to some of the problems concerning the etymology of Damascus, since those who believed *ša imērišu* was equivalent to Damascus tried to use it to explain the etymology of *dmśq*. Note this problem in the discussion below.

[46] See, for example, Goetze 1941: 131, n 39; Speiser 1951: 257.

[47] Gordon (1952: 174–75) explains *mśq* by connecting it with Hebrew *mašqeh*, the cupbearer who serves wine. Then, he suggests, when the Assyrian scribe asked an informant what the name Damascus meant, the informant indicated that it had to do with wine, *ḥămar*, but the scribe misunderstood and thought that the informant had referred to *ḥămôr*, 'donkey'. Malamat (1950: 64) suggests that Damascus was known as *ᶜir*, 'The City (*par excellence*)', and that this word was taken to be *ᶜayir*, 'ass'. These two suggestions are, however, much too speculative.

[48] Speiser 1951: 257.

[49] See both *CAD* I/J, s.v. *imēru*, meaning #3, pp. 114–15; and *AHw*, 376.

[50] Pognon, 1907: 177, n 2.

two texts in which the name is written syllabically as *ša i-ma-ri-šú* and URU*šá i-me-ri-šú*.[51]

There is little doubt that the *imēru* element of the name is to be understood as 'ass', and that therefore the Assyrian designation of Aram should be translated "Land of the Ass," as several have suggested.[52] Albright's contention, that the *-šu* possessive is to be understood as giving the name determinate force is probably correct.[53] But why the Assyrians chose to call Aram Damascus by this name is still unknown. Lewy assumed that the Damascene was the home region of a particular breed of donkeys and that this explains the name. A similar idea was suggested by Albright.[54] This may be correct, but so little is known about such things as the donkey trade that nothing can be stated with certainty. Another possibility is that the name is related to Damascus' important position on several major trade routes, including the two major routes of Palestine, the "Way of the Sea" and the "King's Highway" in Transjordan, as well as the routes to Tadmor in the Syrian Desert, which led on to Mesopotamia, and the route through Qadesh and Qatna into northern Syria.[55] Since Damascus was the point of convergence of so many trade routes, and since donkeys were a prime means of transport in the caravan trade (especially before the domestica-

[51] The former is published in Hulin 1963: 54, line 29. The latter is in Rawlinson 1861–1909: III: pl. 2, #20, line 3.

[52] See Albright 1961: 47. See also Haupt 1915: 168–69; and Cross 1972a: 40, n 16, who opts for "City of asses." Lewy (1961: 72–73) views KUR as *šadu* and renders, "Mountain of its Donkeys."

Recently, E. Gaál (1978: 43–48) proposed that *ša imērīšu* might be a translation of the name Api. He suggested that Api or Apina was a Hurrian name and that the word is perhaps Hurrian for 'ass'. The evidence he adduces for this proposal comes from the Nuzi tablets. He attempts to show that a town in the area of Arrapḫa, called Apina/Apinaš in these texts, was sometimes designated by the Sumerian logograms URUANŠE. However, there is no reason to identify URUANŠE with the town of Apina. The evidence indicates that Apina and URUANŠE were both located in the same district. That the latter town was called Anše rather than Apina is clear from one tablet (HSS XIV 542), which contains the name of the town spelled out syllabically as URU*an-še* (cf. Gaál 1978: 47).

[53] Albright 1961: 47, n 56a

[54] Lewy 1961: 73–74; Albright 1961: 47.

[55] See Aharoni 1979: 53–54.

tion of the camel), it is possible that the name "Land of the Ass" could have referred to the Damascene's commercial importance, in the sense of "The land filled with caravans of asses."

ARCHAEOLOGICAL EVIDENCE FROM THE EARLIEST PERIODS

During the past two decades there have been attempts to investigate the remains of the earliest periods of human occupation of the Damascene and the eastern slopes of the Anti-Lebanon that flank it. Only survey work has been done for the Paleolithic Period so far, and exceedingly little has been published. However, some excavation has been undertaken at a number of Neolithic sites so that from an archaeological standpoint there is more evidence from the Neolithic than from any other period through the Iron Age; regrettably, only preliminary reports have appeared for these sites. The following section includes brief discussion of what is known of the periods from the Paleolithic through the Early Bronze Age.

The Paleolithic Period

The evidence indicates that human beings did not begin to live in the Damascene area until the Middle/Late Acheulean era of the Lower Paleolithic.[56] In fact, as far as has been determined through surface survey none of the inland steppe of Syria was settled before that time.[57] However, during the Middle/Late Acheulean there was extensive occupation, particularly in the hills around the periphery of the Damascus basin.[58] Most of the sites are near the Baradâ and the ᵓAᶜwaj (a river along the southern boundary of the basin). W. J. van Liere believes that the sites in the hills were spread along the edge of the forests that existed in the mountains. In the Damascene basin itself was a large lake, and some evidence of occupation has been discovered near its shores as well.[59]

A few individual sites have been mentioned in the very sketchy reports thus far published. In the 1930s a site was

[56] A fine summary of the Paleolithic in Syria-Palestine is Garrod 1962: 541–46. See also Hours 1975; and Copeland 1975, for Syria and Lebanon in particular.

[57] Hours 1975: 258, 263.

[58] See Potut 1937: 131–32; and van Liere 1966: 25 and fig. 36.

[59] Hours 1975: 263.

found on a terrace overlooking the Wadi Šerkas, and a large scatter of objects from the Middle Acheulean, some 30 hectares in extent, was found at Ašrafiyyeh, near the northern edge of the basin, some 20 km. north of Damascus.[60] Stone tools have also been found along the terraces of the Baradâ and at Berzeh. Although some of the sites have produced tools from the Late Acheulean, there has been no evidence of occupation during the final phase of Late Acheulean, which is well known from the Mt. Carmel caves.[61]

Little evidence of the Middle Paleolithic has been found in the Damascene so far.[62] One preliminary report of a survey, however, does describe finding large numbers of Levelloiso-Mousterian tools at sites near Mezzeh and el-Hāmeh.[63]

There is also some evidence for Upper Paleolithic occupation, although none of it has been published. No sites, only scattered remains, of this period have been located, and all the material known so far has been discovered in the wash of the river beds.[64]

The Neolithic Period

During the 1960s and early 1970s a great deal of work was done on the Neolithic Period of the Damascene by Henri de Contenson, who surveyed a number of sites (with W. J. van Liere) and then excavated at three, Tell Ramād, Tell ᵓAswad, and Tell Ǵureifeh. While the excavations of the latter two were only sondages, the three sites together have provided a sequence of artifacts from the eighth millennium through the first half of the sixth which will be very helpful as study continues on this period.[65]

While investigating the Damascene, de Contenson and van Liere surveyed a few sites which could be dated to the very

[60] Potut 1937: 131–32.

[61] Hours 1975: 264.

[62] Cf. Copeland 1975: 318–36; and Hours, Copeland, and Aurenche 1973.

[63] Pervès 1945: 204–5.

[64] Hours, Copeland, and Aurenche 1973: 266.

[65] On the dating of these sites, see de Contenson 1975b: 184. Important studies of the Neolithic Period in Syria-Palestine and the Near East in general include: Cauvin 1978; 1972; and Mellaart 1975.

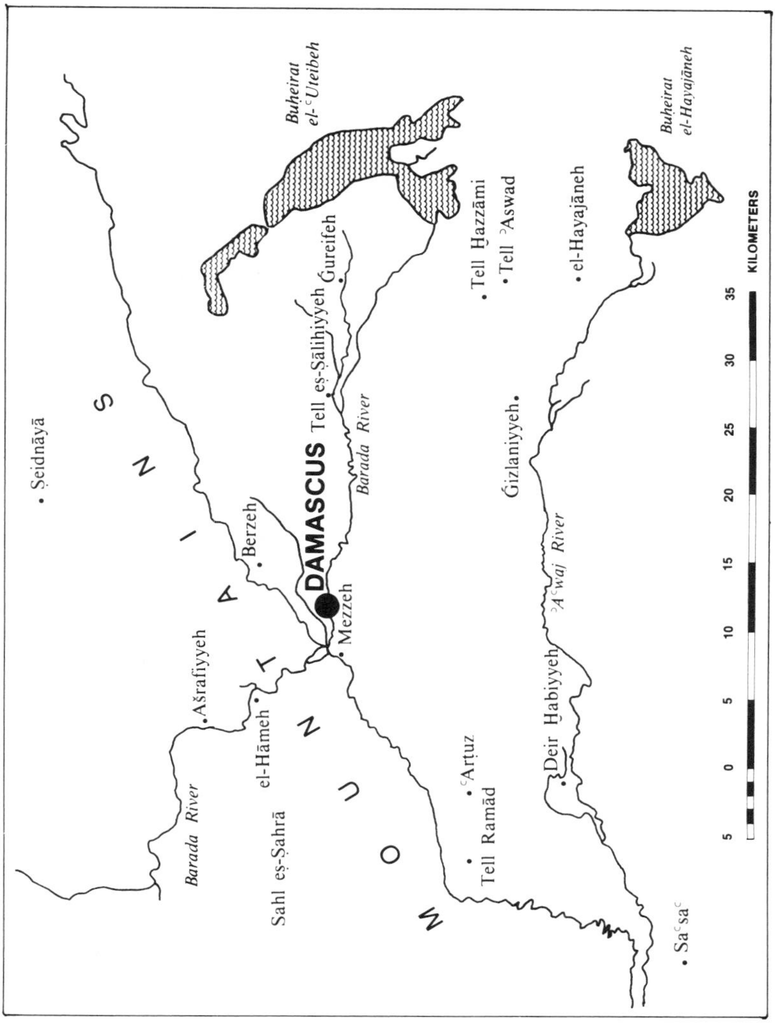

Figure 2. Major archaeological sites in the Damascus region, Paleolithic through Middle Bronze Age.

beginning of the Neolithic Period.[66] The tool industries of these sites had very clear connections with the end of the Paleolithic and the Mesolithic. At Sahl eṣ-Ṣahrāʾ, located between some foothills of the Anti-Lebanon mountains along the edge of the Damascus basin, a number of small villages were noted with a flint industry so primitive that it is difficult to be certain that the sites are Neolithic at all, though the presence of sickle blades and mortars suggests that they are. A small surface site was also found at the source of the Baradâ River. Here the tool industry generally had close ties with the Mesolithic, but the discovery of a polished axe of clear Neolithic style suggests that the assemblage as a whole is of a later date. Finally, a small village which apparently had a protective wall around it was found at Ṣeidnāyā. Again the tools found at the site were very closely related to the Upper Paleolithic and Mesolithic styles.[67]

In contrast with the surface finds, remains from the excavated sites are fully within the Neolithic tradition. The earliest of the three is Tell ʾAswad, a small tell (ca. 275 m. north–south by 250 m. east–west) located east of Damascus, just east of the village of Judeidet el-Ḫāṣṣ.[68] It is situated between two lakes, Buḥeirat el-Hayajāneh and Buḥeirat el-ʿUteibeh, both of which were apparently much larger in antiquity than they are today, so that ʾAswad was quite close to their shores. Two sondages were opened, each a four-meter square, at the highest points on the east and west sides. These produced evidence of two major occupational phases, one from the eighth millennium, the other from the seventh. Very little architecture was discovered in the excavation, although there was evidence of the techniques used to build huts. These were made of reeds from the nearby lakes, probably on top of platforms constructed from hand-made mudbricks. The earliest phase, ʾAswad I, has been divided into two parts, A and B, both on the basis of stylistic variations in the finds and on C-14 dating of charred wood from different levels.[69] The stone industry of Phase IA has strong connections with the Pre-Pottery Neolithic A (PPNA) phase of Jericho and the Mureibiṭ III phase in northern Syria. Phase IB is comparable to Mureibiṭ IVA, and apparently was contemporary with the

[66] Van Liere and de Contenson 1963.

[67] For all of this, see van Liere and de Contenson 1963: 177–79.

[68] See de Contenson 1972; 1977–78.

[69] See de Contenson 1973; 1976b: 199; and M.-C. Cauvin 1974.

break in occupation between PPNA and PPNB at Jericho.[70] Phase II at ᵓAswad is related to the PPNB phase at Jericho and is dated by C-14 to the first half of the seventh millennium. In addition to the stone industry of this phase, a large number of clay figurines were found, including both animals and seated female humans.[71] There are no exact parallels to the style of these human figurines.[72] In a portion of a mass grave from this phase were several skulls (none had been modeled with plaster), a disarticulated skeleton of a child, and an articulated adult skeleton in a contracted position. Throughout the sondages bones of fish and birds associated with the lakes were found, indicating their importance to the inhabitants of the village.[73]

A second site, Tell Ǵureifeh, about 30 km. east of Damascus and 15 km. north of Tell ᵓAswad, overlaps with the last phase of ᵓAswad.[74] Ǵureifeh is about the same size as ᵓAswad, 300 m. north–south × 200 m. east–west, and it reaches a height of 5 m. above the plain at its highest point. The excavations here in 1974 were quite small; only one of the four squares was taken down to virgin soil.[75] The material was divided into two phases, both pre-ceramic, although de Contenson saw no clear evidence of a break between them. Several wall fragments made of unbaked plano-convex bricks were found in the earlier phase. There was evidence here, too, that the superstructure of the houses was made of reeds. A few figurines were also found, as was a good deal of flint (mostly waste flakes, only 4.3% tools). C-14 dates placed Phase I in the first half of the seventh millennium.[76]

In Phase II of Ǵureifeh the flint industry seems to have declined somewhat, with a much higher percentage of arrow-

[70] See M.-C. Cauvin 1974: 435.

[71] That these figurines come mainly from Phase II is not mentioned in the preliminary report, but rather in de Contenson 1976b: 199.

[72] De Contenson 1972: 78. Apparently, the seated female figurines belong to the earlier part of Phase II. See de Contenson 1977–78: 209.

[73] De Contenson 1972: 79.

[74] For this site, see de Contenson 1975a: 17–24; 1976a: 80–82.

[75] In fact, only half of the two-m. square was fully excavated. See de Contenson 1975a: 18.

[76] De Contenson 1975b: 183–84. See also M.-C. Cauvin 1975–77: 295–302, for an analysis of the stone industry and how it fits into the chronology.

heads appearing (31% of the tools as opposed to 14.5% in Phase I) and a much lower percentage of sickle blades (15% as opposed to 31.8% in Phase I). Clay objects were quite rare in this phase. The C-14 samples from Phase II placed it in the latter half of the seventh millennium.[77]

Phase II of Ǵuriefeh is overlapped in its turn by the first phase of Tell Ramād, an important site some 15 km. southwest of Damascus. This tell was excavated in a series of eight campaigns from 1963 to 1973 and has provided the largest sampling of Neolithic material from the Damascene, though the quantity is still quite limited because the excavations have all been very small.[78] Thus far only preliminary reports have been published for this site. There seem to be some problems in the rather complex stratigraphy, but the major outlines of the occupational history of Ramād are fairly clear. Three phases have been distinguished. During the first campaign Phases I and III were thought to have distinguishable subphases,[79] but this idea was later abandoned by the excavators.[80] Three areas of the tell were investigated, but most of the work was concentrated on the eastern part of the site.[81] Most of the information gained so far is from Phase II.

The earliest occupation stratum of Tell Ramād is designated Level I. The houses of this period were ovoid-shaped huts, 3 to 4 m. in diameter, partially sunk into the ground and made of pressed clay (*pisé*). Related to these huts were various domestic installations, such as ovens and silos, made of mud and covered with a lime plaster.[82] In this pre-ceramic phase the flint industry showed an interesting combination of characteristics, with some tool forms having parallels specifically in inland sites, such as Mureibiṭ in northeastern Syria, and also in Palestine (Beiḏāᶜ, Jericho, ᵓAbu Ǵôš, etc.), while other tools were related to those found along the northern coast of Syria at sites such as Ras Shamra.[83] From this phase also come some skulls modeled with

[77] De Contenson 1975a: 20–21; 1975b: 183–84.

[78] The preliminary reports on Tell Ramād are: de Contenson and van Lieve 1964; 1966; de Contenson 1967; 1969a; 1969b; 1970; 1974. See also de Contenson 1971.

[79] See de Contenson and van Liere 1964: 114–15, 119.

[80] De Contenson and van Liere 1966: 168, 171.

[81] See the site map in de Contenson 1974: 22.

[82] De Contenson 1967: 19.

[83] De Contenson 1967: 19–20; 1971: 279–80.

clay, similar to the famous plastered skulls from PPNB Jericho. Several of the modeled skulls have been attributed by the excavator to Phase I and some to Phase II.[84] Unusual figurines were found in assocation with a few of the skulls and were tentatively identified as holders for the skulls.[85] The inhabitants apparently practiced agriculture, since remains of barley, emmer wheat, einkorn, and club wheat were found in the samples from this phase.[86] Hunting provided the main source of meat. Ramād I is clearly contemporary with the PPNB phase at Jericho and Beiḏāᶜ, and the C-14 dates from this level place it in the latter half of the seventh millennium B.C.E.[87]

Phase II is the best known period at Tell Ramād and has been excavated more fully than the other two. The architecture was more substantial; houses were rectangular, with slightly rounded corners, and were single-roomed. A residential area on the eastern side of the site was partially uncovered, exposing four houses, two of them rectangular and two more squarish. A narrow street was also found. Although no distinct function for it could be determined, the southernmost building had much thicker walls than did the other three. The house directly abutting its northern wall had a peculiar walled-in corridor beside its northern wall, running parallel to the street.[88] An important new development in this period was the manufacture of so-called "White Ware" vessels; made from a lime plaster, they were predecessors of true pottery.[89] A large number of figurines of unbaked clay representing both animals and humans were found, as were some modeled skulls.[90] The house styles, the continuation of stone tool techniques, and the modeling of the skulls (if these do not belong with Level I) indicate a relationship with the PPNB sites, but the appearance of "White Ware" indicates that the phase should be dated to a time

[84] See de Contenson 1967: 20–21; 1971: 281–82.

[85] De Contenson 1967: 20–21.

[86] See de Contenson 1971: 279.

[87] See de Contenson 1975b: 184, for a complete listing of the C-14 readings from Ramād.

[88] See de Contenson 1969a: 28–29; 1969b: 32; 1970: 77–78. A convenient plan of the eastern excavation area may be found in Mellaart 1975: 60.

[89] See de Contenson and van Liere 1964: 115–16.

[90] De Contenson and van Liere 1966: 169–70; de Contenson 1967: 20–21.

somewhat later than PPNB Jericho. The C-14 dates from Level II place it early in the sixth millennium.[91]

Level III at Ramād was only found in the western part of the mound, and no architecture has been uncovered. The extensive erosion of the site probably destroyed most of the remains of this period. In Level III true pottery made its first appearance in the form of Dark-Faced Burnished Ware, with parallels throughout Syria, especially at Amuq A, Ugarit VB, Byblos Early Neolithic etc. According to de Contenson, the Ramād pottery is considerably more crude than that found in northern Syria and has a much smaller repertoire of forms.[92] The flint tools of this period are also more crude than those of the previous levels, but it appears that the inhabitants raised domesticated goat, sheep, pig, ox, and dog,[93] reflecting a change from hunting to herding as the major source of meat. Level III has been dated tentatively to the middle of the sixth millennium.[94]

Based on the evidence from surface finds at Tell Ramād, de Contenson has suggested that there may have been an even later occupation of the site which has been virtually destroyed by erosion. Some pottery collected on the surface can be dated to the late fifth or early fourth millennium.[95]

The evidence from the Damascene fits into what is known of Neolithic culture from other areas of Syria-Palestine. Its inhabitants participated in the culture, leaving behind little that might be considered distinctive.

The Chalcolithic and Early Bronze Ages

While excavation in and study in the Damascene during the Paleolithic and Neolithic periods has produced evidence of how this area participated in the developments of those eras, the same cannot be said about the area during the Chalcolithic and Early Bronze Ages. No work has been published dealing with the Damascene during the fourth and third millennia B.C.E. The

[91] See de Contenson 1973: 255; 1975b: 184.

[92] De Contenson and van Liere 1964: 118–19. See also de Contenson 1971: 284, for convenient photos of some of the pottery.

[93] See de Contenson 1971: 285.

[94] See de Contenson 1973: 255.

[95] See de Contenson 1971: 285.

only excavation relating to this period is the salvage excavation of Tell el-Ḫazzami by H. de Contenson in 1967.[96] This site, 25 km. southeast of Damascus, was located on the grounds of the new Damascus airport and was destroyed after the ten-day excavation. It was only 3 km. from Tell ʾAswad. The discoveries there were dated by pottery similar to Pottery Neolithic B and Amuq D styles to the end of the fifth or beginning of the fourth millennium. Houses were built of rectangular, unbaked, mold-made bricks and appeared to have several rectangular rooms. In the East Sondage, doorways between some of the rooms were found.

Apart from this excavation, little else is known about these two millennia. G. Pettinato has stated that the city of Damascus is mentioned in the third millennium tablets from Tell Mardiḫ/Ebla,[97] but publication of the relevant tablets is still pending. In general, the Damascene probably continued to be occupied during these years and participated, at least to a small extent, in the rise of urban civilization that occurred during the Early Bronze Age in Syria-Palestine. W. J. van Liere pointed out, based on a survey he undertook, that there are no tells in the area that compare in size to the great tells of Syria-Palestine. The two largest sites are Tell eṣ-Ṣālihiyyeh and Deir Ḫabiyyeh, but both are fairly small and there is no certainty about when they were first settled.[98] Both of these sites have produced evidence of occupation in the Middle Bronze Age. Van Liere thus believes that there was only a small population in the Damascene during the Early Bronze Age. He believes that extensive irrigation in the Ǵūṭah did not begin this early, and thus large sites did not develop.[99] Whether van Liere's interpretation is correct can only be ascertained when more evidence is available.

[96] De Contenson 1968.

[97] Pettinato 1981: 226. Damascus does not appear in the list of toponyms in Pettinato 1979: 274–79.

[98] Van Liere 1963: 116–17. Van Liere does not mention Damascus itself as a significant tell, presumably since it is difficult at this point to determine the extent of the ancient site.

[99] Van Liere 1963: 116–17.

THE LAND OF ᵓĀPUM IN THE MIDDLE BRONZE AGE ——— *TWO*

IN southern Syria and Palestine the Middle Bronze Age proper begins with the reemergence of town life after an extended period of mostly semi-nomadic existence. Research in the last decade has emphasized the sharp discontinuity between the culture of the full Middle Bronze Age and that of the preceding phase, which has traditionally been called Middle Bronze I.[1] It is now clear that the non-urban cultures between the collapse of the urban civilization of the Early Bronze Age ca. 2300 B.C.E. and the rise of the urban civilization of the Middle Bronze Age proper ca. 2000 B.C.E. have many more links backward to EB than forward to MB.[2] Therefore it is preferable to refer to the intervening non-urban period as Early Bronze IV and to reserve the designation Middle Bronze I for the first period of true Middle Bronze culture, that period which is called Middle Bronze IIA in much of the literature.[3]

The reasons for the renewal of urban life are far from clear, but it seems to have begun with the migration of new cultural

[1] See Dever 1976: 4–6; 1970: 144; Kenyon 1973: 78–82. G. E. Wright (1971: 287) notes some continuity between the periods.

[2] See Dever 1973: 37–63, for an excellent discussion of this aspect.

[3] The terminology for the end of the third millennium and the beginning of the second has been exceedingly confused. On this, see Dever's chart (1973: 38) in which the numerous designations for the period are correlated. Perhaps someday a common and universal designation for the period will be adopted. In this chapter, the following will be used: EB IV = Albright's EB IV/MB I; MB I = Albright's MB IIA; MB II = Albright's MB IIB; MB III = Albright's MB IIC.

groups from northern Syria southward, almost certainly as part of the Amorite expansion which was occurring contemporaneously in Mesopotamia.[4] These people were probably familiar with urban living, for they founded towns, often on the ruins of Early Bronze Age sites, but also in previously uninhabited areas. It appears that some of these new towns were fortified during Middle Bronze I.[5] The material culture of these people was quite sophisticated compared to that of the Early Bronze IV people. Their pottery was superbly made on a fast wheel (in contrast to the mostly handmade pottery of EB IV), and it is clearly related to the styles occurring in northern Syria at the time.[6] W. G. Dever has called this pottery the finest that was made in Palestine during the ancient period.[7] The new towns seem to have quickly absorbed the inhabitants of the EB IV villages. None of the latter have produced evidence of destruction; they were simply abandoned.[8]

Not much is known about the material culture of the MB I towns because there has been little excavation of the pertinent levels. Even where work has been done, the deposits are quite shallow, but this may be due to the fact that this phase was fairly short and was followed by a period (MB II/III) in which extensive building took place, disturbing and destroying much of the MB I material.[9] A few houses were found at Tell Beit Mirsim and Megiddo, built in the styles characteristic of the later MB II and III. One major architectural complex, the so-called courtyard temple has been uncovered at Shechem, but the function of this enclosed group of rooms remains uncertain.[10]

The culture that developed at the beginning of this period thrived throughout most of the second millennium, and there

[4] See Dever 1976: 9–10, 15; and Mazar 1968: 69–71. Gerstenblith (1983) proposes that the changes at the beginning of MB I can be explained without resorting to hypothetical population movements. See esp. pp. 123–25.

[5] For a discussion of fortified sites of the MB I phase, see Kochavi, Beck and Gophna 1979.

[6] For the best discussion of this see Dever 1976: 9–15.

[7] Dever 1976: 7–8.

[8] Dever 1976: 15.

[9] Dever 1976: 8, 20. Dever assigns ca. 150 years to this phase, from ca. 1950–1800 B.C.E. Kenyon (1973: 87) does not require more than fifty years for MB I (ca. 1850–1800). Dever's dates are preferable.

[10] See the discussion in G. R. H. Wright 1968: 2–9.

were a number of continuities and similarities among most of the culture groups from southern Palestine to northern Syria during this time.

Contemporary with the renewal of urban life in southern Syria and Palestine was the reemergence of a centralized government in Egypt and a revival of Egyptian interest in Western Asia. Although the pharaohs of the Eleventh Dynasty reunited the country and extended their control south into Nubia and southeast to the Red Sea, it was not until the rise of the Twelfth Dynasty (ca. 1991–1786 B.C.E.) that Egypt actively turned its interest toward Syria-Palestine.[11] Close relations with Byblos were reestablished, if in fact they had ever been cut off during the First Intermediate Period.[12] Evidence of considerable trade with several areas of Syria-Palestine has been found, both in Egypt and in Asia. From Egypt, for example, there are references to the importation of cattle and slaves from Western Asia, as well as the famous wall painting at Beni Hasan depicting a tribal chieftain and his family arriving in Egypt.[13] In Syria-Palestine a considerable amount of Egyptian material from the Twelfth Dynasty has been recovered. At Byblos, several important artifacts of the period were found in local royal tombs, including a gold pectoral of Amenemḥē III, an obsidian vase inlaid with gold, also of Amenemḥē III, and a gold and obsidian casket with the name of Amenemḥē IV inscribed on it. Sphinxes have been discovered at Ugarit, Beirut, Qatna, Byblos, and Neirab. Statues of two high officials from Egypt have also been found, one at Megiddo and one at Ugarit. In addition to this are numerous smaller objects such as scarab seals, etc.[14]

There has been considerable controversy about whether the Egyptians maintained political control over large parts of Syria-Palestine or whether relations between the two areas were simply commercial.[15] The evidence is unclear, and the nature of

[11] See W. C. Hayes 1971: 476–509.

[12] On this question see Ward 1961: 25–26.

[13] See Posener 1971: 541–44; Helck 1971: 77–81, for more detailed descriptions of finds in Egypt.

[14] Posener 1971: 544–47; Helck 1971: 68–71. Ward (1961: 39–45, 129–36) discusses most of this material, as well as the artifacts found in Egypt.

[15] Ward (1961: 45) takes a fairly minimalist perspective. Posener (1971: 547–50) concludes, on the other hand: "In view of this progressive increase in our knowledge, we shall err less if we exaggerate than

the finds of Egyptian material in Syria-Palestine and of Syro-Palestinian material in Egypt can be interpreted to fit either hypothesis. Unfortunately, few royal inscriptions of the period which might have provided information on foreign affairs are preserved. The one certain reference to an Egyptian military campaign into Palestine is from a stela inscription of a certain Sebek-ḫu, an army officer under Pharaoh Sen-wosre III.[16] The text describes a campaign against the land of *skmm*, perhaps Shechem in central Palestine, and speaks of a battle there, but it does not give enough information to determine the reason for the attack on *skmm* and thus illuminate the position of Egypt in Palestine.

The other major Egyptian documents dealing with Syria-Palestine do not clarify matters either. The Execration Texts, lists of potential enemies of the king written on pots and figurines and then ritually broken in order to break the enemies' power magically, name a large number of towns and areas in Palestine, southern Syria, and the coastal regions farther north, as well as their rulers. But whether the presence of place-names in these lists implies that these potential enemies were at one time under the direct control of Egypt is much debated.[17]

Certainly, during the MB I period in Palestine and southern Syria there was considerable contact with Egypt, whether through political domination by Egypt or through extensive trade and occasional razzia. The Middle Kingdom during this time was characterized by its highest level of activity, and numerous towns were springing up and prospering, presumably with the aid of international trade. The lack of major defensive fortifications in many areas of southern Syria and Palestine during MB I suggests little military activity at the time, but this could be due either to the lack of Egyptian military pressure or to the security of Egyptian military power controlling the area.

While Egypt's exact role in southern Syria and Palestine is unclear, Egyptian documents do provide some insight into the local political situation of the area. The Execration Texts indicate quite clearly that the area was divided into numerous small

if we minimize the hold the Twelfth Dynasty had over Syria and Palestine" (pp. 549–50).

[16] See *ANET*^{3} 230 for a translation. Also see Ward 1961: 39–40.

[17] For detailed discussions of the Execration Texts see Sethe 1926; Posener 1940; Helck 1971: 44–67; and Albright 1941: 30–36.

political units, most of them centered around the newly re-occupied towns. It is also clear, especially from the earlier set of texts (those found at Thebes, dating to the mid-nineteenth century[18]), that there also were many semi-nomadic tribes dwelling around the towns and that their chieftains were often as powerful as the rulers of the towns. The Thebes texts seem to list more tribes than they do towns. They also often name more than one ruler for each place listed.[19] By the time of the second group of texts, found at Saqqarah (early in the eighteenth century[20]), it appears that the towns had gained some measure of control over the semi-nomads, for considerably fewer tribal chieftains are named in these texts. The conditions of the MB I period are well illustrated in the Egyptian story of Sinuhe, set in the time of Sen-wosre I (ca. 1971–1928). The tale graphically describes towns coexisting with numerous tribes of semi-nomadic pastoralists.

Toward the end of the nineteenth century B.C.E. there was an intensification of urbanization with the beginning of large-scale movement toward the fortifying of towns and cities by building massive earthen ramparts, often surmounted by a city wall. It is the development of these fortifications that signals the beginning of the MB II period. The rampart style of fortification was, in the past, viewed as an indication of the arrival of a new ethnic group, the Hyksos.[21] More recent studies have discounted the connection between the introduction of the ramparts and the Hyksos.[22] Instead, it appears that this fortification style was simply a development of the common culture in Syria-Palestine, arising from the necessities of the times.[23]

[18] Sethe 1926. For the questions concerning the date, see Helck 1971: 44–45.

[19] See Aharoni 1979: 144; Posener 1971: 554–55. But also see Helck 1971: 61–63, who suggests that the texts are simply naming deceased rulers of the towns, along with the present ruler, and that the two sets of Execration Texts may not, therefore, reflect a significant change in the political situation of Palestine. Helck assumes that the supposed tribal names are actually town and village names instead, just as in the Saqqarah Texts.

[20] Posener 1940.

[21] See, for example, Albright 1960: 86–87; and Kenyon 1979: 165–66.

[22] See especially Parr 1968: 18–45.

[23] Parr 1968: 42–45.

Much material of the MB II period has been excavated, both in Syria and in Palestine, and it is clear from the similarities in fortifications, pottery types, and temple and house construction, that there were strong cultural ties connecting most of the Levant. There is also a good deal of extant written material from this period. The later group of Execration Texts (the Saqqarah texts mentioned above) reflects the condition at the beginning of MB II, when the newly fortified towns had become the dominant centers of political power as city-states and most of the semi-nomadic tribes had apparently come under at least nominal control of the towns.[24] The city-states in Palestine seem to have been fairly small, but in Syria there were a number of states, known to us from the Mari archives, which held considerable power.

Mari, an important city located along the central course of the Euphrates, had relations with several states in Syria that in some cases were as powerful as any of the Mesopotamian states of the time, most notably Yamḫad, with its capital at Aleppo, Carchemish in northern Syria, Ugarit and Byblos on the coast, and Qatna in central Syria.[25] Yamḫad and Qatna were very powerful kingdoms, as is evidenced by the famous description given by a certain Itur-Asdu in a letter to Zimri-Lim of Mari: "There is no king who is strong by himself. Ten or fifteen kings follow Ḫammurapi, the man of Babylon; as many follow Rim-Sin, the man of Larsa; as many follow Ibal-piel, the man of Ešnunna; as many follow Amut-piel, the man of Qatna. Twenty kings follow Yarim-Lim, the man of Yamḫad."[26]

Yamḫad is the best-documented state in Syria during the Middle Bronze Age, not only from the Mari archives, but also from tablets found at Alalaḫ and Šaǵer Bazar and from Old Kingdom Hittite material.[27] It appears to have been the most powerful state in Syria from at least the early eighteenth century to the latter half of the seventeenth century, when the Hittites began their push into Syria.[28]

[24] Aharoni 1979: 144–46; see also Mazar 1968: 81–82.

[25] For a description of international relations during the Middle Bronze Age, see Munn-Rankin 1956.

[26] This text has only been published in transliteration, in Dossin 1938: 117.

[27] Klengel (1965–70 1.102–11, 136–50) gives a description of the texts relating to Middle Bronze Yamḫad.

[28] Klengel 1965–70: 1.102–74. Also Kupper 1973: 17–19, 30–36.

Qatna was the kingdom south of Yamḫad; it centered around its capital in the plain of Homs (Tell el-Mišrifeh). The capital was a very important trade center, situated along both the major north–south route from Palestine to Aleppo and the east–west trade route from the Euphrates across the Syrian desert via Tadmor (Palmyra) to Qatna and on westward to the Mediterranean through the Tripoli Pass.[29] The Mari tablets reveal an important political alliance between Qatna and Šamši-Adad I of Assyria, as well as later friendly relations with Zimri-Lim of Mari after the collapse of Šamši-Adad's empire.[30] Unfortunately, neither the exact boundaries of the kingdom of Qatna nor the location of its various vassal kings have been determined.

Kingdoms to the south of Qatna are only rarely mentioned in the Mari letters. It appears that the area to the south of Qatna was called Amurru,[31] but it is unclear whether that was a designation for a specific political unit or a general term for the area of southern Syria and Palestine, without specific political boundaries and including several smaller kingdoms. The evidence seems to favor the latter suggestion.

The location of Amurru south of Qatna is clear from an as yet unpublished letter which gives a north–south itinerary as follows: *ma-at ia-am*(!)*-ḫa-ad*^{ki} *ma-at qa-ta-nim ù ma-at a-*[*m*]*u-ri-im*^{ki}—"the land of Yamḫad, the land of Qatna, and the land of Amurru."[32] But that the land of Amurru is not a single kingdom like Qatna or Yamḫad is suggested by another text, which refers to DUMU.MEŠ *ši-ip-ri ša 4* LUGAL.MEŠ *a-*[*mu*]*-ur-ri-i*—"messengers of the four Amorite kings," who are traveling with messengers from Hazor and Qatna.[33] This letter suggests that the land of Amurru covered the inland area from the southern border of Qatna to the land controlled by Hazor and consisted of at least four minor kingdoms, perhaps even including the area of Damascus, which was called ʾĀpum at the time.[34]

29 Klengel 1965–70: 2.96.

30 See Dossin 1954: 417–25; and Klengel 1965–70: 2.96–138.

31 See Dossin 1957: 37–38.

32 The letter in which this itinerary is found has not yet been published. But see Dossin 1957: 38.

33 This text, too, is unpublished. For this passage, see Dossin 1957: 37.

34 For discussions of the extent of Amurru during the Middle Bronze Age, see Liverani 1979b: 14; Malamat 1960: 16–17; Malamat

However, caution must be exercised in drawing conclusions from these Mari references, since too much may be read into them. For example, the term LUGAL.MEŠ *a-mu-ur-ri-i* in the second passage may simply mean "western kings" and have nothing to do with the land of Amurru. It is perhaps significant that there is no KUR or *ma-at* before *a-*[*mu*]*-ur-ri-i*. It seems unwise to attempt to describe the political nature of the state of Amurru from the evidence available; perhaps future discoveries will provide a clearer picture.

At the same time that the towns in Palestine were being fortified, Egyptian influence in Asia began to decline. After the death of Amenemḥē III, ca. 1797 B.C.E., there was a slow but steady disintegration of Egyptian international power and trade. A series of lesser kings and the rise of the weak Thirteenth Dynasty were accompanied by the mass migration of West Semitic groups into the Nile Delta region. By ca. 1720 these groups controlled the Delta, and the period of Hyksos domination began.[35] For the rest of the Middle Bronze Age some trade between Palestine and Egypt continued, but cultural influence apparently declined.[38]

The final phase of the Middle Bronze Age, MB III (Albright's MB IIC), represents a very active phase of MB culture in Palestine, as well as a period of ethnic and political change in Syria. Many of the most impressive fortifications that have been uncovered in Palestine (Shechem's Wall A, Gezer's Middle Bronze fortifications and city gate, etc.) were built during this time.[37] There is evidence that many towns were attacked and destroyed immediately before these new fortifications were installed. B. Mazar believed that these destructions and the new wave of fortifications were the result of the invasion of the Hurrians and Indo-Iranian peoples from the north; there is evidence of their infiltration southward from the Late Bronze

---

1970: 165–66; Kupper 1957: 178–80. Aharoni (1979: 65–66, 149–50) actually includes Hazor within the land of Amurru during the Middle Bronze Age, even suggesting that it might have been the capital city.

[35] See W. C. Hayes 1973a: 42–56.

[36] There is some disagreement about the extent of Egyptian trade with Palestine during this period. Mazar (1968: 86) refers to an "unceasing stream of Egyptian products that flowed into Palestine during MB IIB," while Kenyon (1973: 89–90) says that most of the "Egyptian" material was local imitation.

[37] Seger 1975.

Age.[38] It is not yet possible to make such a connection, however, and the hypothesis relies on the uncertain supposition that the *terre pisé* type of fortification is to be dated to MB II, while the battered wall type appeared only during MB III.[39] J. Seger connects this pattern of refortification with the rise to power of the Fifteenth Dynasty Hyksos king, Ḫayan (ca. 1653–1620) who, he believes, gained control of Palestine.[40] Again, there is not yet enough evidence to attribute the wave of fortifications specificallly to Egyptian intervention.[41]

To the north, new political powers and ethnic groups arose during this period. The kingdom of Yamḫad, which had been the most powerful of the Syrian states, came under the pressure of the rising power of the Hittites in Anatolia during the latter half of the seventeenth century. Although Aleppo was not captured by Ḫattušiliš I, his wars of expansion severely diminished the influence of Yamḫad, and Muršiliš I, Ḫattušiliš' successor, was able to conquer and destroy Aleppo before his famous expedition to Babylon.[42] At the same time, the Hurrians, a non-Semitic people from the area north of Syria, were slowly migrating southward. As early as the eighteenth century the Hurrians had become the dominant force in the kingdoms of Uršu and Ḫaššum, to the north of Yamḫad. During the late seventeenth and the sixteenth centuries many Hurrian groups moved south, gaining political power in several areas by the end of the sixteenth century, most notably in northeast Syria where the kingdom of Mitanni arose.[43] Unfortunately there are no written data from the MB III period furnishing information about the spread of Hurrian influence further southward to such sites as Qatna, even though later, by the fifteenth century, they were a significant part of the population there.[44]

THE AREA OF DAMASCUS DURING THE MIDDLE BRONZE AGE

Little has been discovered to date about the area of Damascus during the Middle Bronze Age. A few general things

[38] Mazar 1968: 90–94.

[39] See Mazar 1968: 91–92. Contrast Parr 1968: 20–21.

[40] Seger 1975: 44*.

[41] For the Egyptian Fifteenth Dynasty, see Hayes 1973a: 60–64.

[42] Klengel 1965–70: 1.157–62.

[43] See Gelb 1961: 39–41; 1944: 62–70; Kupper 1973: 22–23; O'Callaghan 1948: 37–50.

[44] Kupper 1973: 35.

can be surmised on the basis of what was transpiring round about, and there are a few pieces of information gathered from archaeological work in the area that can be of assistance in placing the area into the context of Middle Bronze Syria-Palestine.

It is fairly certain that the land that included Damascus was known as the land of ʾĀpum during the Middle Bronze Age. As described in chap. 1, this was first proposed by W. F. Albright in a study of place-names found in the Execration Texts from Saqqarah.[45] The name, *ỉpwm,* in these texts was related by Albright to the Late Bronze Age place name Api/Upi, and the final *m* was explained as mimation that had disappeared by the fourteenth century. The Execration Text references give some information about the land of ʾĀpum. The relevant passages are numbered E33 and E34 and read as follows: E33—*ḥq*(ꜣ) *n ỉpwm rst* [ ], "The prince of southern ʾApum, [. . .], E34—*ḥq*(ꜣ) *n ỉpwm mḥty ʿḫwkbkb,* "The prince of northern ʾĀpum, Aḫu-kabkabu."[46]

S. Yeivin suggested that the place-names in the Saqqarah Texts are listed in a definite geographical order, along various trade routes through Palestine, and that the names from E25 and E34 are to be located along a route through northern Transjordan to the area of Damascus.[47] This seems quite plausible. At any rate, it is probable that the two ʾĀpums referred to here are to be located in the general area of present-day Damascus. Assuming that this identification is correct provides some small bits of information about the area. The name ʾĀpum clearly designates a region, one large enough to be controlled by two princes, one in the south and one in the north. The prince of northern ʾĀpum, Aḫu-kabkabu, has a clearly Amorite name, as would be expected during this period. The fact that ʾĀpum is mentioned in the Execration Texts indicates that Egypt had significant economic and perhaps political interests this far north. It is quite likely that ʾĀpum was at the northern limit of direct Egyptian influence, since it lay just to

[45] Albright 1941: 35.

[46] Posener 1940: 81–82. Posener reads the name of the prince in E34 as *ʿḫwkꜣkꜣ,* but notes the possibility that it should be read as *ʿḫwkbkb* (p. 82). Albright (1941: 35, n 18) points out that in cursive hieratic the signs for *b* and ꜣ are often indistinguishable. He reads *ʿḫkbkb.*

[47] Yeivin 1956 [Hebrew]. But see the cautions in Helck 1971: 61.

the south of the powerful state of Qatna, which was politically independent and with which Egypt probably maintained trade relations on bases other than political domination. A sphinx representing a wife of Amenemḥē II was discovered at Qatna, indicating that relations of some sort existed between the two countries.[48]

Beyond the Execration Texts there are no other written references to the area of Damascus (see below on the proposed Mari and Assyrian Dream-Book references). Archaeological material from this period is also scarce. The lack of archaeological evidence from the city of Damascus itself, along with the absence so far of the name of Damascus in any Middle Bronze Age sources, precludes determining whether the town was an important trade center at this time, or even whether it yet existed as a fortified town (although it is probable that it did.)

There is some information, however, about a site some 15 km. east of Damascus which was occupied during the Middle Bronze Age. As mentioned in the previous chapter, there are only two substantial tells in the Baradâ-ʾAʿwaj basin besides the city of Damascus, and neither of them is particularly large.[49] The larger of the two is Tell eṣ-Ṣāliḥiyyeh (also called Tell Ferzat), some 15 km. east of Damascus on the north bank of the Baradâ River.[50] Excavations there in 1952–53 reached Middle Bronze Age levels in a trench down the north slope.

Ṣāliḥiyyeh appears to have been the only major town in the Damascene besides Damascus before the Roman Period.[51] During the one season of excavation which took place there, the lowest levels reached were from the MB II period. There is some evidence from the excavation that the site was occupied by an unfortified settlement at the beginning of the Middle Bronze Age, but further excavation would be necessary to confirm this.[52] It is clear, however, that the rampart fortification on the site was built at the beginning of MB II, following the practice

[48] Helck 1971: 68.

[49] Van Liere 1963: 116; Von der Osten 1956: 75–76.

[50] Von der Osten 1956: 1–2.

[51] Von der Osten 1956: 76.

[52] Von der Osten 1956: 36–40, 80. With regard to the previous period, it is not yet sure whether Ṣāliḥiyyeh suffered destruction and/or abandonment at the end of the Early Bronze III phase, as

which appears throughout Syria-Palestine at that time. The rampart was only some 3 m. high, but was built along the edges of the pre-existing mound, which by that time already rose 7 to 8 m. above the level of the plain, thus creating a significant defense work. In a second phase of the rampart, a wall faced with mud bricks was built on top of the rampart.[53]

The location of Ṣāliḥiyyeh was strategic. From the tell it is possible to see all of the major entry points into the Damascene basin, so that enemy troops could be spotted quite early. Von der Osten, the excavator, estimated that the inhabitants of Ṣāliḥiyyeh would have had an eighteen-hour warning of invading troops to prepare for attack and to warn the surrounding villages.[54] It is clear that Ṣāliḥiyyeh at least shared in, if not controlled, the trade that came through the Baradâ Valley, heading north toward Qatna or Tadmor, or south toward Palestine. Too little from the Middle Bronze Age was excavated to provide much information about conditions within the town, but its solitary splendor as a fortified town in the Merj (unless Damascus was also fortified) indicates an important position within the context of the land of ᵓĀpum. Von der Osten proposed that Ṣāliḥiyyeh either controlled or was allied with a series of small fortified sites to the south of the Merj, including el-Hayajāneh, Ǵizlāniyyeh, Deir Ḫabiyyeh, and tells near ᶜArṭūz, Quteibet el-Māᵓ, and Saᶜsaᶜ.[55] All of these presumably fell within the boundaries of ᵓĀpum.

Trade was certainly a very important part of the economic life of the Damascus region during the Middle Bronze Age, although there is very little physical evidence of it. The trade routes known from later times were almost certainly already in existence during this period, and the oasis of Damascus was a vital stop along several of them. One small piece of evidence of trade to the north and east comes from Deir Ḫabiyyeh, the second significant tell in the general area of Damascus, located on the north bank of the ᵓAᶜwaj River, some 20 km. southwest

---

occurred at almost all sites in the area to the south, or whether it continued to exist through EB IV, as many towns did in north and central Syria. I suspect that the oasis shared the fate of Palestine rather than that of the north.

[53] Von der Osten 1956: 37–39, 79–86.

[54] Von der Osten 1956: 75–76.

[55] Von der Osten 1956: 86.

of Damascus. A modern road cuts through the foot of the tell and has exposed remnants of rampart fortifications from the Middle Bronze Age.[56] In 1948, while repair work was being done on the road, an Old Babylonian cylinder seal was found. It is carved with a scene of a goddess and a god standing together, and an inscription on it reads, *^{d}nin-gir-su-ib-ni-šu* / DUMU DINGIR-*šu-ib-bi* / ARAD *^{d}en-ki*, "Ningirsu-ibnīšu, son of Ilšu-ibbi, servant of Enki." This is the only Old Babylonian cylinder seal from the Damascus region whose provenance is certain.[57] Its appearance here is an indicator of trade between Mesopotamia and southern Syria, which is not surprising since the Mari letters demonstrate that there was considerable trade with states even further south, such as Hazor and Laish in northern Palestine.[58]

IS THE AREA OF ʾĀPUM–DAMASCUS MENTIONED IN THE MARI ARCHIVES?

In 1939 Georges Dossin published a preliminary description of the economic documents that had been uncovered in the now-famous archives of the palace of Zimri-Lim at Mari.[59] In this article Dossin provided a preliminary list of foreign kings mentioned in the tablets, who had trade relations with Mari and the cities or states that these kings ruled. Among these names were those of two kings of a land of Abum (Apum), listed by him as *Ḫa-a-ia-a-bu-um šar A-bi-im^{ki}* and *Zu-ú-zu šar ma-a-at A-bi-im^{ki}*.[60]

This was not the first mention of a town or land of Abum or Apum in cuneiform sources. It was referred to in several of the texts found earlier at Kaniš (Kültepe) in Anatolia, in the archive comprising the records of an Assyrian trading colony at the beginning of the second millennium. In particular, the town of Apum was known from a number of itineraries and expense records of tradesmen who traveled from Assyria to Kaniš or vice versa. Stations along the route are referred to in the following texts: *TCL* XIV:57, Apum—Eluḫut(?)—Abrum—Kaniš;[61] *TCL* XX:163, Saduatum—Razamā—Abitiban—Qaṭra—

[56] Von der Osten 1956: 14, 80.
[57] Dossin 1954–55: 39–44.
[58] Malamat 1960: 12–19; 1970: 164–77; and 1971: 31–38.
[59] Dossin 1939: 97–113.
[60] Dossin 1939: 109.
[61] Cf. Falkner 1957: 2; and Lewy 1952: 272–73; 287, n 5; 393.

Razamā—Tarqum—Apum;[62] *CCT* V:44c, Qaṭrā—Taraqum—Apum—Amaz—Naḫur—Eluḫut—Abrum—Ḫaqqa;[63] *BIN* IV: 124, Razamā—Tarqum—Apum.[64] It appears that this city of Apum was located somewhere along the course of the Ḫābūr River in northern Mesopotamia.[65] Accordingly, Dossin identified the kings found in the Mari tablets as rulers of this state in northern Mesopotamia, placing Abum/Apum somewhere near the towns of Ašnakkum and Talḫīyum.[66]

It is clear that there were two areas in Syria known as Āpum (or ᵓĀpum) during the first half of the second millennium B.C.E. The scholarly world has been divided as to which of them the Mari references belong. In 1941, during the course of his discussion of the Execration Text reference to *ᵓipwm*, W. F. Albright identified the two occurrences of *A-bi-im*^ki^ and *ma-a-at A-bi-im*^ki^ in Dossin's list with the ᵓĀpum of the Damascene area.[67] In so doing, he took the kings named by Dossin to have been rulers of the land of Damascus, along with the Aḫu-

[62] There were two towns named Razamā on the route to Kaniš. See Goetze 1953: 65. See also Falkner 1957: 2.

[63] See Wiseman 1953: 109; Garelli 1963: 92.

[64] See Goetze 1953: 65; and Falkner 1957: 2. For general discussions concerning the geography of the route from Aššur to Kaniš, see Bilgiç 1945–51: 22–24; Lewy 1952: 265–92; 393–425 and Goetze 1953: 64–70.

[65] Bilgiç (1945–51: 23) places Āpum near Harran on the Baliḫ. Goetze (1953: 65, 67, map p. 72) places it somewhat south of the Upper Ḫābūr region. Lewy (1952: 272–73) locates it fairly close to the junction of the Ḫābūr and the Euphrates. See also Falkner 1957: 2. The context of the three Mari letters discussed below confirms that Goetze and Lewy are correct in placing Āpum in the Ḫābūr River Valley.

[66] Dossin 1939: 108–9. Dossin arranges his list of kings and states according to what he believed was a geographical order from east to west, along the Fertile Crescent, from Elam to the Mediterranean coast.

[67] Albright 1941: 35. The Mari occurrences should indeed be transliterated *A-pí-im*. This is confirmed by a gentilic form cited in *ARMT* XVI/1 5, as LÚ *A-pa-a-yu*^ki^, but transliterated in a full rendering of the text as LÚ *A-pa-a-yi*^[k]i^. See Bottéro 1981: 1036, line 26.

A word of explanation about the different spellings of the name Āpum in this discussion: although it is probable that the name of the land in northern Mesopotamia and that of the land in the Damascene were identical, the ambiguities of the cuneiform writing system make it impossible to ascertain the initial consonant of the northern state's name. Thus, I have chosen to distinguish the two states by rendering

kabkab of the Execration Texts. But those who have specialized in the study of northern Mesopotamia have tended to identify the Mari references with the location in the north.[68] Albright's suggestion, however, has been widely accepted among biblical scholars and other historians and historical geographers whose areas of concentration have been Palestine and the southern Levant.[69] Because of the greater number in the latter group, Albright's identification has appeared much more commonly in the literature.

It should be noted immediately that Albright's interpretation was based on Dossin's list as published in the 1939 article, not on complete texts. Besides identifying the names *A-pí-im* and *ʾipwm*, Albright gave no other evidence for identifying the Mari Āpum with the state in the Damascus region. In 1968, however, he added another argument in favor of his proposal. In his short discussion on this subject in *Yahweh and the Gods of Canaan*, he recognized that there was a land of Āpum in northern Mesopotamia, but proposed that it could be distinguished from the land of ʾĀpum in the south by reference to two other texts from Mari that he believed do deal explicitly with the northern Āpum. These texts were published only in translation by Dossin in 1958, and describe a land dispute involving a certain Šubram, the king of a town in the Ḫābūr River region called Susā, which was apparently an important town of the land of Āpum, and Ḫāya-Sūmû, the ruler of Ilānṣurā, an important city also in the Upper Ḫābūr River Region.[70] Albright distinguished the northern and southern ʾĀpum's thusly:

---

the northern state and the Mari references to *A-pí-im* as Āpum, while using the form ʾĀpum for the Damascene state, as established above.

[68] See Lewy 1952: 272, n 6; Goetze 1953: 67; Klengel 1965–70: 3.97; Kupper 1973: 21.

[69] Mazar 1968: 79; 1970: 179; Malamat 1970: 166; Aharoni 1979: 149. (In the first edition of Aharoni's book, published in 1967, the author was non-committal about the question: "The Mari tablets do refer to Qatna and perhaps to Apum [Damascus]." See p. 137). M. F. Unger 1957: 6–7; Drower 1973: 431; Helck 1971: 271. Two authors have sought to elaborate on Albright's proposal, but both studies are fundamentally flawed: see Parrot 1953: 2.408–9, and Tocci 1960b: 96–97. On these works, see W. Pitard, *Ancient Damascus: A Historical Study of the Syrian City-State from Earliest Times until its Fall to the Assyrians in 732 B.C.E.* (Dissertation, Harvard University, 1982) 58–60.

[70] Dossin 1958: 388–89.

> In these texts it [the area of Damascus] is called *māt Apim*, 'the land of Apum'. This land, with its kings, is quite different from the land of Apum in the Khabur basin . . . , which was ruled by a chief and elders (G. Dossin, *CRAI*, 1958, 388ff.) Obviously these districts can scarcely be identified in any respect except in the name, which means, 'Land of Reeds'.[71]

This argument apparently is based on making a sharp distinction between the title *šarrum* 'king' and the term *awīlum* 'man'. Albright believed that *awīlum*, when applied to a ruler in the Mari letters, referred to a chieftain and was something quite distinct from a *šarrum*. The two kings in Dossin's list, Ḫāya-abum and Zūzu, have the title, *šar (māt) Āpim*, while in Dossin's translation of the first of the *CRAIBL* texts, there are two references to "l'homme d'Apum," ("The man, i.e., ruler of Apum"), which presumably translate *awīl Āpim*.[72] There are two problems with Albright's argument. First, it has become clear from the additional evidence supplied by continued publication of the Mari tablets that the two terms could be and were used virtually interchangeably when referring to rulers of moderate-sized states. Note, for example, *ARM* XIV 98 7, in which Yaqqim-Addu, the governor of Sagarātum, refers to Ḫammurapi, the king of Kurdā, as *awīl Kurdā*^{ki}, while in ARM XIV 100 6 he calls him *šar Kurdā*^{ki}.[73] Thus, the fact that certain rulers of Āpum might be given the epithet *šarrum*, while others might be called *awīlum*, does not necessitate the proposal that two Āpum's must be distinguished in the Mari letters. However, the second problem with Albright's proposal makes this first one academic. Recent publication of a transcription of the first *CRAIBL* text by J. Bottéro has shown that there is no reference to a ruler of Āpum called *awīl Āpim* in the text at all. Both passages translated by Dossin "l'homme d'Apum" do not refer to a single person, but must be translated in the plural, "people of Apum."[74]

[71] Albright 1968: 65–66, n 30.

[72] Dossin 1958: 389. These two texts have now been published in transliteration in Bottéro 1981: 1034–38, 1041–43. An English translation of the letters has recently appeared in Sasson 1984: 113–14.

[73] On this, also note Klengel 1965–70: 3.143–44; and Buccellati 1967: 32, 64–65, 69.

[74] Bottéro 1981: 1034–38. The lines in question are ll. 26 and 28. Bottéro's transliterations read: line 26, *<a-na>* ^{lú}*A-pa-a-yi*$^{[k]i}$ *a-na qí-iš-tim*

There is no valid evidence that requires the view that the land of Āpum found in the Mari texts must be the Damascene ᵓĀpum. Letters now published in *ARM* XIV allow this question to be reexamined with considerably greater clarity than before. The reading in *ARM* XIV 102 indicates rather strongly that Ḫāya-abum of Dossin's list was a ruler of the northern, not the Damascene, Āpum. It reads as follows:

[a-na b]e-lí-ia qí-bí-ma
[u]m-ma Ia-qí-im-^{d}IM
ARAD-*ka-a-ma*
u$_{4}$*-um tup-pí [an]-né-[e]m a-na ṣe-er be-lí-ia*
ú-ša-bi-l[a]m Ia-wi-^{d}IM *ša be-lí-[ia]*
x x x x x *iš-tu* UD 6 KAM *i-na Aš-na-[ki-im*^{ki}*]*
[x x x *ú-t]a-aš-ši-ru-nim* 1 DUMU *ši-ip-r[i-im]*
[ša Ku-un]-na[m] LÚ *Šu-bat-*^{d}*En-lil*^{ki}
[u 1 DUMU *š]i-ip-r[i-i]m ša I-[ši-im]-*^{d}I[M]
[x x x x] *Aš!-na-ki-im*^{ki}
[a-na Sa-g]a-ra-tim^{ki} *ik-šu-du-nim*
[^{I}*I]a-[w]i-*^{d}IM *ša be-lí-ia*
[ṭe$_{4}$*-ma-a]m áš-ta-al-ma*
[ki-a-am] iq-bé-em um-ma-a-m[i]
[^{I}*Ku]-un-nam a-na ṣe-er be-l[í-šu]*
[ki-a-am i]š-pu-ra-am um-ma-a-mi
[^{I}*Ḫa-i]a-a-bu-um-ma-a* DUMU *Zi-im-ri-[Li-im]*
[ù a-n]a-ku ú-ul ma-ru-šu x x x x x *[i]m?*
x x x *ma-at A-pí-im i-na-[an-na(?)]*
x x x MEŠ *lu-ul-li-ik-m[a]*
[it-t]i a-bi-ia lu-un-na-mi-i[r an-ni-tam]
[^{I}*I]a-wi-*^{d}IM *id-bu-[ba-am-m]a*
[a-na ṣe-er] b[e-l]í-[i]a [aš-p]u-ra-am
[DUMU *ši-ip-ri-im] ša Ku-un-nam*
[ù DUMU *ši-ip]-ri-im ša I-ši-im-*^{d}IM
[i-na Sa-g]a-ra-tim^{ki} *ak-la*
[ša e-te]-qí-šu-nu ù la e-te-qí-šu-nu
[an-ni-tam la] an-ni-tam be-lí li-iš-pu-ra-am
[x x x x] *ma-ḫa-ar be-lí-ia*
[x x x x x D]UMU.ME[Š *š]i-i[p-ri-im]*

---

la id-di-nu-šu, "The people of Āpum did not give it (i.e., the disputed town) as a gift." Line 28, *[2 awī]lu 2 sinnišātu awīl A-pí-im*^{ki} *e-pí-ir ālim*^{ki} *ša-a-ti li-il-qú-ú-ma*, "Let two men and two women of Āpum take the dust of this city."

To my lord say, thus Yaqqim-Addu your servant: On the day I sent this tablet to my lord, Yawi-Addu, (servant) of my lord [ ] after six days at Ašnakkum, [ ] were set free, a messenger of Kunnam, man of Šubat-Enlil, and a messenger of Išīm-Addu [ ] of Ašnakkum arrived at Sagarātum. From Yawi-Addu, (the servant) of my lord I asked a report. Thus he told me: "Kunnam wrote to his lord thus: 'Is Ḫaya-abum son of Zimri-Lim while I am not his son? [ ] the land of Āpum [ ] [ ] let me go and meet with my father.'" What Yawi-Addu told me, I wrote to my lord. The messenger of Kunnam and the messenger of Išīm-Addu I have detained in Sagarātum. Whether they should continue or not continue their journey, one way or the other, let my lord write to me. [ ] before my lord [ ] the messengers. (Two or three lines are lost at the end).

Here is a letter which mentions Ḫāya-abum, the king of Āpum, one of the two kings listed by Dossin in his 1939 article. It is important to note the geographical references in the letter. Yaqqim-Addu, the writer, was the governor of Sagarātum, a town near the confluence of the Ḫābūr and the Euphrates.[75] Kunnam, an Elamite military leader who resided in Šubat-Enlil, a town probably to be located somewhere on the Upper Ḫābūr or somewhat to the east of it,[76] apparently is complaining about some problem in which Zimri-Lim has supported Ḫāya-abum, the king of Āpum, against Kunnam. Kunnam wishes to appear before Zimri-Lim to state his case in person. It is improbable that Kunnam and the Damascene ᵓĀpum would be in conflict. It is much more likely that the dispute is between two nearby principalities, i.e., between Šubat-Enlil and the Āpum located in the Ḫābūr basin. This means that Ḫāya-abum was almost certainly a king of the northern Āpum.

This conclusion is further strengthened by *ARM* II 135, a letter which also probably mentions the same Ḫāya-abum.

a-na be-lí-ia
qí-bí-ma

[75] See ARMT XIV, p. 1.

[76] The most common site identification for Šubat-Enlil in recent years has been Tell Leilan. See Falkner 1957: 25–27, 37; Hrouda 1958: 29–33 and Hallo 1964: 73–74; Weiss 1985: 18–19; 27–30.

um-ma Ša-ak-nu
ARAD-*ka-a-ma*
a-lum I-la-an-ṣu-ra-a^{ki}
LUGAL *Ḫa-ià-su-ú-mu*
ù ṣa-bu-um ša a-na bi-ir LUGAL
be-lí iṭ-ru-dam ša-lim
ša-ní-tam u_4*-um tup-pí an-né-e-em*
a-na ṣe-er be-lí-ia
ú-[ša]-bi-lam
[^{I}*La*]*-wi-la-*^{d}IM GAL MAR.TU
qa-du-um 3 li-mi ṣ[a-bi-im]
[iš-tu/a-na Eš]-nun-na^{ki}
[a-na/iš-tu Šu]-ba-at-En-lil^{ki}
[ú] -ṣi
[pí-qa]-at a-na Aš-na-ki-im
pí-qa-at a-na Šu-ru-ši-im^{ki}
pa-nu-šu ša-ak-nu
ma-an-nu-um lu-ú i-di
ù i-na a-ḫi-ti-ia-ma
ki-a-am eš-me um-ma-a-mi
^{I}*Ḫa-a-ia-a-ba-am iš-ta-lu*

To my lord say, thus Šaknu your servant: [5]The city Ilānṣurā, the king Ḫāya-Sūmû, and the troops which my lord sent me for the fortress are well. Furthermore, on the day [10]that I sent this tablet to my lord, Lawila-Addu, the commander, together with 3000 troops, went forth [from/to] Ešnunna [15][to/from] Šubat-Enlil. Perhaps he is heading toward Ašnakkum, or perhaps toward Šurušim. [20]Who really knows? But within my entourage I heard this: "They have called Ḫāya-abum to account."

All of the people and towns referred to in this letter (except Ešnunna, which is peripheral to the action, as the starting point or destination of Lawīla-Addu's journey) are located in the Ḫābūr River area. It is clear from the letter that Šaknu is located at Ilānṣurā, the capital of Ḫāya-Sūmû (the king spoken of in the *CRAIBL* texts mentioned above).[77] He is reporting the movements of Lawīla-Addu, who is traveling between Šubat-Enlil and Ešnunna with his three thousand troops. The towns to which Lawīla-Addu may go are Ašnakkum, which is to be

[77] See Kupper 1973: 9. Also see Dossin 1958: 390.

located between the Jağjağ River and the Upper Ḫābūr,[78] or Šurušim, which is obviously nearby. But Šaknu has heard that they have "called Ḫāya-abum to account." Whatever that means, it seems clear that if this is Ḫāya-abum, king of Āpum, he too is located by this letter in the Ḫābūr region.[79]

The land of Āpum (and its king, whose name is lost) are mentioned in *ARM* XIV 125 in connection with the towns of Ilānṣurā and Qaṭarā (which was apparently located between Šubat-Enlil and Ekallātum).[80] This letter may refer to an alliance between the king of Āpum (LUGAL *ša ma-at A-pí-im*) and the king of Qaṭarā (LÚ *Qa-ṭà-ra*^{ki}).[81]

[78] Goetze 1953: 59.

[79] Another letter which appears to deal with events described in ARM II 135 and which also mentions Āpum has been published, in translation only, in Jean 1938: 128–30. Certain aspects of Jean's translation will remain questionable until the tablet itself is published, but the main outline of events seems fairly clear. The letter describes a siege of the town of Kurdā by the king of Ešnunna and Qarni-Lim, the king of Andariq, which was broken by the arrival of troops from the land of Ḫana. From Kurdā, the king of Ešnunna went to Šubat-Enlil, where he stayed for about two weeks before leaving for home. But Qarni-Lim traveled to the city of Āpum, where he became involved in some political matters (the nature of which is unclear, since it appears that Jean mistook a personal name, Turum-natki, for a city name, thus creating problems in the understanding of the letter; see ARMT XVI 1 206, under the name Turum-natki.) This letter shows that there were close connections at this time between Āpum, Šubat-Enlil, and Ešnunna. It also makes it clear that Āpum was fairly close to Šubat-Enlil.

One other recently published tablet should be mentioned. Charpin (1983: 58–59) has published a text from Mari which supplies the dimensions of a temple located in Šubat-Enlil, to a goddess called ^{d}NIN-*a-pí-im*. The name of the goddess presumably is to be understood as "Mistress of Āpum." This, too, indicates a close relationship between these two towns.

Lawīla-Addu and his relationship to Ešnunna may also be seen in two other letters, ARM VI 51 and 52.

[80] Goetze 1953: 46. The reference in line 16 to *šarrum* (LUGAL) *ša ma-at A-pí-im* in a context clearly referring to the northern land of Āpum adds further weight against Albright's argument for distinguishing two Āpums in the Mari letters.

[81] On this, see lines 13–19. There are several economic texts from Mari which also mention the city of Āpum. See ARM VII 168 6; 209 9; 210 rev. 2′(?); 211 2; ARMT XXII 1 15 iii 9–10.

In conclusion, there is no reason to identify the land of Āpum mentioned in the Mari letters with the land that included the area of Damascus. It is clear from the letters discussed here that one of the two kings of Āpum that were thought by Albright to have ruled in Damascus, Ḫāya-abum, was a king of the land of Āpum located somewhere along the Ḫābūr River Valley. It is probable that the other king belongs to the same area, although no letters mentioning *Zu-ú-zu* have been published.[82] The distinction drawn by Albright between chieftains (*awīlum*) and kings (*šarrum*) is not valid in this context. There are currently no references to the area of Damascus in the Mari archives.[83]

[82] Jack Sasson has indicated privately to me that *ARM* XIV 125 is probably the text in which Dossin read the name *Zu-ú-zu*. If this is correct, then the northern location for this king is confirmed.

[83] One other text with roots in the Middle Bronze Age, thought to contain a brief reference to Damascene ʾĀpum, is the text known as the Assyrian Dream-Book. For the complete book, see Oppenheim 1956. On a fragment of Tablet IX (Sm 29 + 79-7-8, 94), which lists the meanings of dreams in which one finds oneself in a particular city, one line (y + 11), refers to the town UD.KUŠU$_2$, which is glossed as *ú-pi-e*^{ki} (see p. 312).

It has been suggested that this Upi should be identified with the Damascene land of Upi. See, for example, Malamat 1960: 16, n 19; and Malamat 1965: 371, n 30. The proposal is not a *a priori* impossible, since several west Syrian and north Palestinian names occur in the Dream-Book (for example, Qatna and Hazor are found on the fragment Babylon 36383, lines 13–14, p. 313). Malamat (1960: 16, n 19) identifies the name *La-ba-an*^{ki} which both precedes and follows UD.KUŠU$_2$ in the list, with Lebanon, and thus finds the context for a reference to the Damascene. Aharoni (1979: 149; 186, n 40) disputes the identification of *La-ba-an*^{ki} with Lebanon, since Lebanon is a mountain or region, not a city. He equates it with Lebôʾ(-Hamath) and Labana of the Amarna letters. But neither of these proposals is compelling, and thus the context cannot assure us of the location of this *ú-pi-e*^{ki}.

There are in fact several problems with identifying the Dream-Book reference with the Damascene ʾĀpum. It is true that the Dream-Book originates in the Old Babylonian period, although the tablet fragment in question dates to the Neo-Assyrian period. The gloss, however, seems to be from the Late Bronze Age, if it does refer to Damascene ʾĀpum, since the form *ú-pi-e* (with its *ā* to *ō* shift and its dropping of the mimation) would not have developed during the Old Babylonian period, when we would expect a gloss like *A-pu-um*. The lengthened final vowel does not fit with the attestations of Damascene

A-pí, Ú-pí from other sources, nor does the determinative *ki*, 'city', rather than *māt*, 'land'. Thus, if this reference is to Damascene Upi, it is quite problematic.

However, there was a city, known from texts as early as the Old Babylonian period through the Neo-Babylonian period and later, that was called Upī, spelled *ú-pí*^{ki} in ARM IV 26 12, *ú-pi-i* in a Kassite period *kudurru* stone (see Scheil 1900: 88, line 19); ^{URU}*ú-pi-e* in an inscription of Tiglath-Pileser I (see Weidner 1958: 351, line 46); and as UD.KUŠU$_2$ (or UḪ)^{ki} in the Nabonidus Chronicle (see Pinches 1882: 164, rev. I 12). See also RLA 1.64–65. Upī was located in the kingdom of Ešnunna, along the bank of the Tigris. The identity of the name and the ideographic form shows conclusively that the Dream-Book is referring to this eastern city and not the Damascene ᵓĀpum.

THE LAND OF UPI DURING THE LATE BRONZE AGE ——— THREE

IN THE LATE BRONZE AGE the land of the Damascene continued to be known by the name it had during the Middle Bronze period, albeit in modified form. The land of ʾĀpum came to be known as the land of ʾĀpu in certain areas (the mimation was dropped), while in other parts of Syria-Palestine, where the "Canaanite shift" occurred, the name came to be pronounced ʾŌpu. The traditional practice has been to normalize the name as Upi, following the cuneiform spelling *ú-pí/ú-pì*. Although it is linguistically incorrect, the common spelling will be used in this chapter.

Unfortunately very little is known about the history of Upi during the Late Bronze Age, although its role in international politics is more evident than in the Middle Bronze Age because most of the references to Upi in Late Bronze Age texts come from Egyptian and Hittite sources. The two major powers were seeking to control Syria-Palestine, and references to Upi occur when events there affected one or another of the major powers. Little is known of the internal situation of Upi because sources are virtually silent. The extent of the land is uncertain, and it is not known for sure that Damascus was its chief city. Damascus itself is mentioned for the first time in documents of this period, but these references tell little about events that took place there. Like other towns of the period, Damascus was ruled by a "king," but only two kings from the entire period, Ariwana and Zalaia, are known by name. Most of what can be said about the land of Upi and the town of Damascus during the Late Bronze

Age relates to the historical developments of the major political powers of this period, particularly Egypt, Mitanni, and Ḫatti.

THE FIRST PART OF THE LATE BRONZE AGE

During the second half of the sixteenth century, which may be considered the beginning of the Late Bronze Age, a new political power in northern Syria and northern Mesopotamia emerged, the Hurrian kingdom of Mitanni. At this time Egypt again began expanding its influence into western Asia. Until the middle of the fourteenth century Mitanni and Egypt had a major impact on the development of the smaller kingdoms in Syria-Palestine, and there was a continuous struggle to pull these small kingdoms into the political sphere of one or the other.

In a recent study,[1] N. Naaman has suggested, quite plausibly, that the rise of Mitanni did not come about because of large-scale ethnic movements of Indo-Aryans into northern Mesopotamia, as has been argued previously, but was rather a natural political development of the historical forces operative at the time. Toward the end of the sixteenth century, the Hurrians, who had been migrating into the area for centuries and who had come into power in several small states, began to exercise greater political influence in northern Mesopotamia, leading to the formation of the consolidated kingdom of Mitanni.[2] During the reign of Barattarna, at the end of the sixteenth century, Mitanni spread its control over the kingdom of Aleppo and then expanded in all directions, setting up alliances and vassaldoms among the smaller kingdoms of northern Syria.[3]

To the south of the area controlled by Mitanni, Qadesh, also apparently under a Hurrian ruling party, became the chief state of central Syria, controlling a fairly extensive area, although the exact boundaries are not known.[4] Qadesh was an imposing enemy to the Egyptians when they began to expand into western Asia. The relation of Qadesh to the land of Upi is

[1] Naaman 1974b: 265–74.

[2] Naaman 1974b: 267–71. Also see Drower 1973: 417–23.

[3] See Klengel 1965–70: 1.181–83. See also Drower 1973: 422–23, 436.

[4] Drower 1973: 430–31; Naaman 1974b: 271.

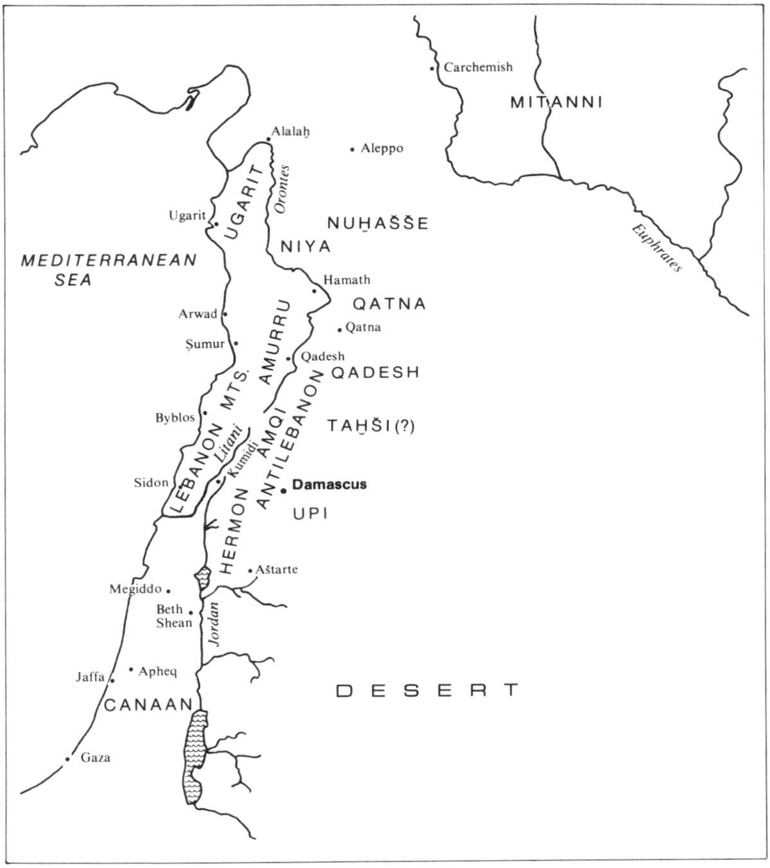

Figure 3. Syria–Palestine during the Late Bronze Age.

unknown, but it is possible that Qadesh controlled Upi as a vassal state toward the end of the sixteenth century.

In Egypt, the movement toward imperial expansion began during the second quarter of the sixteenth century when the kings of the Seventeenth Dynasty, who ruled at Thebes, made a major effort to regain control of Lower Egypt from the Hyksos kings of Avaris. Hostilities began in earnest under Seqenenrēᶜ

Ta^{c}o II, who may have been killed in battle with the Hyksos,[5] and Kamose, his son, whose surviving inscriptions deal with attacks on Hyksos-held areas.[6] Kamose's stelae give little firm information about the incursion he made into the delta region; there may actually have been very little fighting.[7]

It was left to Kamose's brother, ^{c}Aḥmose (ca. 1570–1546), to push the Hyksos rulers out of Lower Egypt. Apparently this difficult task took quite a number of years, but finally the Theban king conquered and sacked Avaris and officially united Egypt once again under single rule. At some time after the fall of Avaris, ^{c}Aḥmose moved through Sinai into southwest Palestine, where he besieged the town of Šarūḥen. With its capture, Egypt's eastern border was made secure, and he then turned his attention for a while to reconquering Nubia.[8] Toward the end of his reign, ^{c}Aḥmose apparently returned to Palestine, but the extent of the campaign is unknown, since it is mentioned only very briefly in the tomb biography of the soldier ^{c}Aḥmose-Penneḫeb—"I followed King Nebpeḥtirē^{c} (^{c}Aḥmose), triumphant. I captured for him in Ḏahy a living prisoner and a hand."[9]

^{c}Aḥmose was succeeded ca. 1546 B.C.E. by Amenōphis I, a ruler about whom very little is known.[10] Although there is no

[5] Hayes 1973a: 73. There is no written account of Seqenenrē^{c}'s death, but study of his mummy, found in the cache of royal mummies at Deir el-Baḥri, shows that he died of wounds to the head, suggesting death in battle. See Harris and Weeks 1973: 122–23. There is also a poem which tells the story of a clash between Seqenenrē^{c} and the Hyksos king Apōpi, which, while of little historical value, may suggest that hostilities began at the time of these two kings. For a translation of the poem, see Simpson 1973: 77–80.

The forms of the names of Egyptian pharaohs used throughout this chapter are those of Gardiner 1964.

[6] For convenient translations of these texts, see *ANET*^{3}: 232–33, 554–55.

[7] On this, see James 1973: 290–93.

[8] For a translation of the pertinent text, a tomb biography of one ^{c}Aḥmose, son of Eben, an officer in the navy during the reigns of ^{c}Aḥmose I, Amenōphis I, and Tuthmōsis I, see Breasted 1906: 2. ##4–16.

[9] Breasted 1906: 2. #20. See also James 1973: 294–95.

[10] A complete listing of the known material from his reign may be found in Schmitz 1978: 240–62.

reference to any campaigns into Syria-Palestine during the reign of Amenōphis I, there is evidence from a stela set up at Tumbos near the Third Cataract of the Nile in Nubia by Amenōphis' successor, Tuthmōsis I, indicating that Amenōphis did indeed enlarge on the success that ᶜAḥmose had had in western Asia. This stela, dated to the second year of Tuthmōsis I, describes the boundaries of Tuthmōsis' empire as extending from Nubia to the Euphrates.[11] If this claim is to be taken seriously, even if only as an indication of the extent of military expeditions that had been undertaken by that time, then Amenōphis I must have made some efforts to increase Egyptian influence in Syria-Palestine before Tuthmōsis came to the throne. The Egyptian penchant for exaggeration in royal inscriptions, however, must be taken into consideration, and the evidence from this stela cannot settle the problem.[12]

By the time of Tuthmōsis I (ca. 1525–1512), Egyptian domination of western Asia as far as the Euphrates was a goal held by all New Kingdom pharaohs. From this time onward, through the Eighteenth and Nineteenth Dynasties, the image of Egypt was that of a predominantly military state whose royal ideal was the king as "the great warrior." The campaigns of these New Kingdom pharaohs became the subject matter of numerous reliefs and inscriptions in Egyptian temples, now the major source of information about Egypt's role in Syria-Palestine.

Early in his reign, Tuthmōsis managed to march all the way to the area of Carchemish, where he set up a victory stela at the Euphrates. The stela was still there when Tuthmōsis III returned some sixty years later.[13] If the Tumbos stela, which gives the Euphrates as the northern boundary of the empire in Tuthmōsis' second year, does indicate the extent of the campaign of that year, then presumably the Egyptians met with little resistance along the way.

Precisely which areas of Syria-Palestine came under Egyptian influence at this time is unknown. The beginning of large-scale Egyptian military campaigns into this area, coupled with the opposing influence of the rising state of Mitanni, meant that Syria-Palestine, including Upi, became increasingly embroiled in a great power struggle between north and south. Great burdens

[11] See Breasted 1906: 2. ##67–73, esp. #73.

[12] See Schmitz 1978: 182–86, and James 1973: 308–10.

[13] Breasted 1906: 2. #478.

on the population resulted, both from the repetitive warfare throughout the region and from the tribute and imposition of often corrupt foreign administrations over the areas affected. The land of Upi was located at approximately the northern extent of regular Egyptian control and at the southern edge of Mitannian and, later, Hittite power, so that it sustained considerable pressure from both sides in the struggle for dominance.

After the reign of Tuthmōsis I, during the reigns of Tuthmōsis II (ca. 1512–1504) and Ḥašepsowe (ca. 1503–1482), there seems to have been little Egyptian activity in Syria-Palestine. But with the beginning of the independent reign of Tuthmōsis III (ca. 1482), the apex of Egyptian power was at hand. In his first campaign Tuthmōsis III met a large Syro-Palestinian coalition led by Qadesh in the Esdraelon Valley near Megiddo. He defeated them on the field and bottled up the leaders in Megiddo itself. The city fell after a seven month siege, and Tuthmōsis took a heavy tribute and oaths of loyalty from the captured rulers.[14] An inscription of Tuthmōsis found at Jebel Barkal in Nubia claims that there were 330 princes in the coalition,[15] but this is certainly an exaggeration. The names of a total of 119 towns whose leaders were said to have been caught in Megiddo were inscribed at the temple of Amūn at Karnak in three places.[16] One of the towns listed is Damascus, the first appearance of the town's name in history. It is spelled *tỉ-ms-qȝ* in the vocalized orthography. W. F. Albright analyzed this as *ta-ms-qu*.[17]

Much research has been done on this list. The studies most helpful for understanding its structure are those of Helck and Aharoni.[18] They have proposed numerous identifications of

[14] See Breasted 1906: 2. ##408–43. For a good discussion of the Battle of Megiddo, see Faulkner 1942: 2–15.

[15] See *ANET*³: 238, for a translation of the section dealing with the campaign.

[16] The three versions of the list have some discrepancies among themselves, but these are fairly minor. List c is extended by the list of places in Naharēna that Tuthmōsis conquered in a later campaign. See Simons 1937: 28–38, 109–19.

[17] See Albright 1934: 62, #14. On the problems of reading the syllabic writing, see Simons 1937: 16–21; Edel 1966: 61–90.

[18] Helck 1971: 120–35; Aharoni 1979: 152–66.

place-names in the list, many of which are fairly certain. It is clear that the list includes towns in Palestine and southern Syria as far north as Qadesh on the Orontes, but the sources for and context of the list are much more difficult to determine. Helck believes that one part of it is composed of the itinerary of the Egyptian army on its journey to Megiddo (nos. 57–71), while the remainder is made up of another itinerary, reflecting an expedition made by the Egyptians during the course of the same campaign, perhaps during the time of the siege of Megiddo.[19]

Aharoni has a very different perspective on the list. Noting that the Amarna Letters, part of the royal archives of Amenōphis III and IV, imply that the area of southern Syria and Palestine was divided up by the Egyptians into three administrative districts, each district with its own capital (Gaza in the south, Ṣumur in the northwest, and Kumidi in the northeast), Aharoni suggests that this administrative system was probably set up by Tuthmōsis III and that the Karnak lists are actually enumerations of the towns in each of the three districts. He divides them up as follows: cities in the district of Kumidi, nos. 3–34 (and 55–56); cities in the district of Gaza, nos. 35–54, 57–71, 103–17, and 2; cities in the district of Ṣumur, nos. 72–102 and no. 1.[20] If he is correct, then a fairly clear picture of the areas controlled by each administrative capital can be constructed. The Amarna Letters indicate that the area of Upi was in the district administered from Kumidi, and Aharoni has plausibly argued that Kumidi also controlled the southern Lebanese Biqâᶜ, Bashan, and the northern Jordan Valley.[21]

Both Helck and Aharoni place the towns that are numbered 12–20 in the area of Damascus (Damascus itself is no. 13), but unfortunately none of these towns can be identified with certainty.[22]

[19] Helck 1971: 125–33. In the first edition of his book, Helck had reconstructed a number of small raids which he thought were reflected in the list. This was criticized by Aharoni in the 1969 edition of his book (p. 145; published 1969; rev. ed., Aharoni 1979), where he says, "the order of cities within the framework of these regions cannot be reconciled with logical military operations." The new edition of Aharoni's book does not take into account Helck's revision on this point.

[20] Aharoni 1979: 158–65.

[21] Aharoni 1979: 164.

[22] See Aharoni 1979: 159, and Helck 1971: 129.

Whatever the correct understanding of the list may be, the area of Damascus was under the control of Egypt at least from the reign of Tuthmōsis III. It is not necessary to imagine that Tuthmōsis directly confronted Damascus in battle, since the king of Damascus may have been captured at Megiddo and may have sworn allegiance there. There is no indication in the list that Damascus was the most important town of the land of Upi at this time—or that it was not; however, it does not seem to be considered a town of much political importance.

Following his first campaign, Tuthmōsis III kept southern Syria and Palestine under control without serious trouble. Most of his military activity took place in central and northern Syria, reaching a climax with his Eighth Campaign, in his thirty-third year, when he moved directly against Mitanni (normally called Naharēna in Egyptian texts). He met Mitannian troops west of Aleppo, defeated them, and marched on to the Euphrates, where he set up a victory stela beside the stela of his grandfather, Tuthmōsis I, near Carchemish. The Egyptians traveled down the Euphrates as far as Emar (near Meskineh) before turning back.[23] In spite of this success, Tuthmōsis was never able to place northern Syria under Egyptian control—Mitannian influence was much too strong—though again and again he returned to Syria, temporarily subjecting one area or another. Nevertheless, the reign of Tuthmōsis III represents the peak of Egyptian political power when, at least for a short time, the petty kings from the Sudan in the south to the Euphrates in the north called themselves the servants of the king of Egypt.

Tuthmōsis was succeeded by his son Amenōphis II, whose first campaign, in his third year, seems to have been quite minor, with the capture of seven princes of the land of Taḫši (near Qadesh) the only event known from it.[24] It is possible that this "campaign" was nothing more than a minor raid, and it may have occurred during the coregency of Tuthmōsis and Amenōphis.[25]

The other two known campaigns of Amenōphis II indicate that Egypt faced some serious rebellions that were probably supported by Mitanni at this time. These two campaigns are

[23] See Drower 1973: 452–59. The key texts may be found in Breasted 1906: 2. ##444–540.

[24] Breasted 1906: 2. #797.

[25] See Yeivin 1967: 120–21.

known from two identical stelae, one found at Memphis and the other at Karnak.[26] They are described as his first and second campaigns, dated to his seventh and ninth years, thus ignoring the above-mentioned military operations of his third year. The stelae do not include references to any events north of Niya (apparently located along the course of the Orontes, around the site of Apamea[27]), although it is clear that Amenōphis did go farther north, since his arrival there is described as "heading south."[28] This may suggest that the Egyptians suffered a significant defeat to the north and thus ignored that part of the campaign in the official records.[29] But on the journey homeward, in the Sharon plain, [30] the Egyptians captured a messenger of the king of Mitanni who was carrying a tablet, a letter probably intended to encourage a local ruler to anti-Egyptian actions. This incident provides an indication of the type of political intrigue present in the rivalry between Egypt and Mitanni.

In his ninth year, Amenōphis, to quash a rebellion in Palestine itself, departed from Egypt in late autumn, an unusual time to begin a campaign.[31] Little is known of the extent of the rebellion, or whether the land of Upi and other northern holdings took part, but Mitannian intrigue was likely a significant factor in the uprising. Amenōphis appears to have been successful in maintaining Egyptian domination over Palestine and southern Syria in spite of the Mitannian designs on the area, for the Amarna letters refer to Egyptian control of such places as Nuḫašše (EA 51:5), Tunip (EA 59:6–9), and Sidon (EA 85:70–71) during the following reign of Tuthmōsis IV (ca. 1425–1417).

Records mention only one campaign into Asia by Tuthmōsis IV, and there is only fragmentary information about it.[32] Tuthmōsis claims to have fought with (Mitanni) Naharēna, though the location of the battle is not given. But some time after this campaign, Tuthmōsis apparently proposed a marriage alliance between Egypt and Mitanni, which the king of Mitanni

[26] For transcription and translation of these stelae, see Edel 1953a: 113–36.

[27] See Drower 1973: 427–28.

[28] Edel 1953a: 117, line 33. See also p. 128.

[29] See Yeivin 1967: 121–22.

[30] Yeivin 1967: 125.

[31] See *ANET*[3]: 246, n 33.

[32] See Giveon 1969: 55.

agreed to, though with some reluctance, if the account of the marriage given in EA 29:16–18 is to be believed.[33] With this alliance, which led to peaceful relations between the two powers through the reigns of Amenōphis III and Amenōphis IV, Egypt maintained control of an extensive part of southern and central Syria (cf. the Amarna letters mentioned above).[34]

THE AMARNA PERIOD

The reign of Amenōphis III is considered by many to be the cultural climax of the New Kingdom.[35] The years of his reign were mostly peaceful; Egypt had firm control of the lands to the south as well as a sphere of influence in Syria-Palestine, delineated to some extent by the peace treaty between Egypt and Mitanni. Amenōphis maintained strong and friendly relations with all of the major powers of the area throughout his reign, thus allowing for extensive trade relations which brought a great deal of wealth into Egypt. The only notable military campaign was during the fifth year of his reign to suppress a revolt in Nubia.[36] The great prosperity throughout this period allowed for extensive building campaigns aimed at glorifying the pharaoh on a scale not previously attempted. The arts and crafts flourished during these years.[37]

It is from the reign of Amenōphis III and his successor, Akhenaten (Amenōphis IV), that the most important set of documents relating to Syria-Palestine during the Late Bronze Age comes. These texts are the well-known el-Amarna tablets, found in the late nineteenth century in the ruins of Akhenaten's palace at the capital city of Akhetaten. The tablets were part of the royal diplomatic archives of Akhenaten, including tablets dating from the final years of the reign of Amenōphis III. There are also a few tablets that date from the years shortly after Akhenaten. While a number of the tablets are letters from the

[33] The reluctance of the Mitannian king referred to in this letter probably only reflects the formal propriety of the father of the bride rather than any genuine doubt about forming the alliance.

[34] Giveon 1969: 58–59.

[35] See, for example, Hayes 1973b: 338–53; and Gardiner 1964: 205–10.

[36] Breasted 1906: 2. #842–45, perhaps 846–50.

[37] Hayes 1973b: 391–416.

other major political powers, such as Mitanni, Ḫatti, Babylon, etc., those that bear most directly on this study are the large number of letters from Egyptian vassals in Syria-Palestine. These letters give considerable historical information about the two or three decades which they cover,[38] while also presenting some clues, albeit often rather obscure ones, about Egyptian administrative practices in the provinces.

The letters are not explicit enough to show in detail the nature of Egyptian administration of vassal-states in Syria-Palestine, although many aspects are clearly illuminated. The work of W. Helck on this subject has been very influential over the past two decades.[39] Helck believes that the lands under Egyptian control were divided into three provinces, each under jurisdiction of a governor. The southern province was, according to Helck, probably called Canaan and generally included the area of Palestine, with its northern boundary along the coast changing from time to time (at one point reaching as far north as Byblos). The town from which the governor ruled was Gaza.[40] The second province Helck calls Amurru, with its capital at Ṣumur. This province covered the northwest part of Egypt's holdings, including the land of Amurru and the coast as far north as Ugarit.[41] The third province, according to Helck, was called Upi/Api, taking its name from the major land within its jurisdiction. The capital of the province was Kumidi.[42]

Each district was run by an official called in the Amarna letters a *rābiṣu*, 'commissioner'. There is no unambiguous evidence

[38] There is considerable controversy about the amount of time covered by the letters. The key factor in this dispute is whether there was a co-regency of Amenōphis III and Amenōphis IV. On this question, which is not of vital concern for our purposes, see Campbell 1964; and Kitchen 1962: 6–8 (see the bibliographical notes here). See also Kitchen's review of Campbell's book (1967: 178–82). For the most part, the various sides of the issue differ by no more than ten years for the length of time that the archive covers—between twenty and thirty years.

[39] See Helck 1960; and 1971: 246–55. See also Aharoni 1979: 158; and Drower 1973: 469–76, where Helck's ideas are accepted to a large extent.

[40] Helck 1960: 6–7.

[41] Helck 1960: 6.

[42] Helck 1960: 7–8.

indicating which Egyptian title this Akkadian term translates, but Helck suggests that *mr ḫ3swt mḥtt*, 'governor of the northern foreign lands', was the Egyptian designation for these officials.[43]

While Helck's reconstruction of the Egyptian administration of its Syro-Palestinian vassals is quite plausible, it is important to keep in mind that much of it is rather speculative. For example, it is not certain that the number of provinces was three. Part of the problem stems from the fact that in the Amarna letters the term *rābiṣu* seems to have a rather vague and general meaning that goes beyond designating the governors of the provinces. It often seems to designate virtually any Egyptian official. Thus, one cannot simply identify the men who are called *rābiṣu* in Amarna letters, note where they are located, and add up the number of presumed administrative capitals. Often one cannot determine which *rābiṣu* is the governor of a province and which is a lesser officer.

N. Naaman has recently suggested that there were only two Egyptian provinces, Canaan and Upi, and that only Gaza and Kumidi were administrative capitals. Ṣumur, he suggests, was merely a garrison city, like Jaffa, Ullaza, Beth-Shean, and others.[44] There are three Amarna letters which refer to the *rābiṣu*s who governed from Gaza and Kumidi together (EA 116:72–76; 117:59–63; 129:81–86), but there are none that mention the *rābiṣu* of Ṣumur in connection with the governor of either of the other two towns. He also notes that only two such commissioners, one from Upi and one apparently from Gaza (see below), are mentioned at a later time in a letter of Ramessēs II. However, none of this evidence is conclusive. The three Amarna letters that Naaman cites actually have no bearing on this question. They all come from Rib-Addi of Byblos, who asks the pharaoh to send aid to the besieged town of Ṣumur. Since a *rābiṣu* inside Ṣumur at this point would presumably be as helpless as Rib-Addi himself, a call for help by Rib-Addi would naturally only request aid from other sources, such as Kumidi and Gaza. As for the later situation under Ramessēs II, the northwest province lands that were probably controlled from

[43] Helck 1960: 8. See also Helck 1971: 251.

[44] See Naaman 1975: chaps. 7 and 8 [Hebrew] (cf. English summary, x–xi, xiii.)

Ṣumur were lost by Egypt during the Amarna period and not regained (see below). So only references to the two remaining provinces would be expected in documents from the thirteenth century. Thus, in spite of the uncertainty, it does seem likely that Egypt's west Asian territories were divided into three provinces and that the land of Upi was under the administration of the province headed by a governor whose seat was at Kumidi.

If the province governed from Kumidi, had a specific name, it is not known. The most common idea, already mentioned above, is that it was called Upi.[45] But the references to the land of Upi/Api in the Amarna letters seem to refer only to the area around Damascus, not the province as a whole. For example, Biriawaza in EA 197 refers to Api in relation to the land of Taḫši (197:19), which was surely part of the northeast province, since Biriawaza apparently hoped to take refuge from his enemies there. Aitugama, in EA 189:12 also names both Taḫši and Upi as lands under the jurisdiction of Biriawaza (in this case Aitugama is complaining that Biriawaza has given the cities of these two lands to the Ḫapiru). Akizzi of Qatna (EA 53:56–59) reports that two hostile kings, Arzauia of the town of Ruḫizi and Teuwatti of the town of Lapana, are presently in the land of Upi in an attempt to take it over, while a certain Taša is doing the same in the land of ᶜAmqi, in the Biqâᶜ Valley.[46] These are the only letters in the Amarna corpus that mention Upi, and it is clear that none of them refers to the entire northeastern province by that name. The designation Upi was only applied to the small state of that name.

The question of the extent of Upi has been studied by R. Hachmann,[47] who defines the general outline of its boundaries by identifying the lands that adjoined Upi. In his reconstruction, he locates Taḫši to the north, lying between Upi and Qadesh. To the west, Upi adjoined and perhaps included part of the southern Biqâᶜ Valley. In the northern Biqâᶜ (at least as far north as the watershed near Baalbek) was the land of ᶜAmqi. It is also possible that ᶜAmqi, rather than Upi, may have included

[45] See Helck 1960: 6; Drower 1973: 472. Note the objection to Helck's names in Aharoni 1979: 187, n 75. See also Kuschke 1981:42*.

[46] Note a fragmentary Hittite text which appears to name both Upi (KUR.URU*a-pá*) and ᶜAmqi (*am-qá*). Unfortunately, the context of this passage is not clear. See Otten 1955: Text no. 38: rs(?) 5, 7.

[47] Hachmann 1970: 84–87.

the southern Biqâᶜ,[48] but there is not enough evidence to determine this. Since Kumidi was probably located in the southern Biqâᶜ at the site now called Kāmid el-Lōz,[49] it is also possible that this area did not belong to either ᶜAmqi or Upi but was a separate political entity. To the south, Hachmann believes, there was another state that included Aštarte and several towns mentioned in EA 201–206. He suggests that this area may have been called Bašan, noting particularly EA 201, which

[48] On the location of ᶜAmqi, see also Aharoni 1953: 153–61; Kuschke 1981.

[49] On the location of Kumidi, see Hachmann 1970: 85–88, 92–93. It seems highly likely that Hachmann is correct in identifying Kāmid el-Lōz with ancient Kumidi. However, the question is a bit more complex than is usually supposed. Egyptian sources actually support two possibilities for the location of Kumidi, since two different town names may be connected with the Egyptian spelling of Kumidi. These two names are found in separate lists of Syro-Palestinian towns, one in the Tuthmōsis III list and the other in the Karnak list of Sethōs I. The former appears as *kꜣ-mỉ-tỉ* (#8 in the list; see Simons 1937: 111), while the latter is spelled *qꜣ-mᶜ-d(w)* (#55(7) in the list; see Simons 1937: 137). On the occasional spelling of the latter with a *w*, see Simons 1937: 139.

Depending on which of these names one identifies with the Amarna *ku-mi-di*, one may either accept or reject the connection with Kāmid el-Lōz. If the name from the Sethōs list is equated with Amarna *ku-mi-di*, the identity of the ancient name with the modern one (Kāmid) is lost (in this case the Amarna spelling would need to be transliterated as *qú-mi-di*). Further, the city could not be located in the Biqâᶜ Valley or anywhere in the area of inland Syria, since *qꜣ-mᶜ-d(w)* is named in a series of coastal towns, including Akko (#54) and Tyre (#57). A location along the coast is not impossible for K/Qumidi, since a coastal site would allow for a somewhat closer connection to Egypt, by sea. The difficulty with this is that such a location would have cut the capital off from the area it administered, and this is unlikely.

The other Egyptian spelling, *kꜣ-mỉ-tỉ*, also fits in well with the Amarna version of the name. The *d/t* shift is quite common in Egyptian transcriptions of Palestinian city names. See, for example, *m-k-tỉ* or *m-k-t-y* for מגדו (Tuthmōsis list, #2), *tỉ-ms-qꜣ* for דמשק (Tuthmōsis list, #13), *m-k-t-r* for מגדל (Tuthmōsis list, #71), and *ỉꜣ-t-r-ᶜꜣ* for אדרעי (Tuthmōsis list, #91). I prefer to identify the name in the Tuthmōsis list with Amarna Kumidi, since it is more likely that the capital of the northeast province would have been located inland.

See also the analysis of the Syriac and Arabic evidence by Maiberger (1970). Maiberger shows that the Syriac inscriptions mention-

mentions the town of *Zi-ri-ba-ša-ni* (= Ziri of Bašan?). In general, Hachmann's analysis provides a plausible picture of the extent of the land of Upi.

The Amarna letters give the impression that the direct administration of Syria-Palestine by the Egyptians was actually quite loose and that most of the power was left in the hands of the local city-state kings, who were permitted to administer their cities as they saw fit. The high officials within the Egyptian bureaucracy were charged with overseeing the movement of taxes and foodstuffs to Egypt, resolving disputes between the local vassals if necessary, and maintaining small garrisons of troops for emergencies.[50] A number of garrison towns were set up in Syria-Palestine in which small numbers of Egyptian troops were stationed. Several of these garrison towns have been excavated, including Beth-Shean, Jaffa, and now Apheq.[51] The garrisons apparently were under an independent administrator, since an office called "governor of the northern fortresses" is known from Egyptian documents of the Eighteenth Dynasty and later.[52] But in spite of these garrison towns, the considerable amount of inter-city fighting evident in the Amarna letters suggests that Egyptian policy was not to interfere with local feuds unless absolutely necessary.[53]

It is probable that each of the city-state rulers was required, at the beginning of his reign or at the beginning of the reign of a new pharaoh, to go before the pharaoh to swear an oath of fidelity. The account of the oath administered to the kings captured by Tuthmōsis III after the siege of Megiddo is an

---

ing a Qumiṭi that were found in a quarry near Kāmid el-Lōz do not actually mention such a town, but have been misread. He does note, however, that a town called Kāmid, located in the Biqâᶜ, is referred to in some Arabic works from the Middle Ages and that it is certainly to be identified with Kāmid el-Lōz. The Arabic *el-Lōz* appears to have become attached to the name of the town sometime after the Middle Ages.

[50] See Helck 1971: 248.

[51] For convenience, see Avi-Yonah 1975–78: 1.213–15 (Beth Shean); 2.535–38 (Jaffa). On Beth Shean, also see EA 289:20; on Jaffa, EA 294:20 and 296:33. Cf. also Helck 1960: 11. For Apheq, see now Kochavi, 1981: 77–80.

[52] Helck 1960: 11.

[53] See Helck 1960: 5; also Several 1972 and Liverani 1979: 13.

example of such a loyalty oath, and it has been suggested that the oath was binding only while both members were alive and had to be renewed whenever there was a change on either throne.[54] It reads, "We will not repeat evil against Men-ḫeper-Rēᶜ, who lives forever, our good lord, in our time of life, inasmuch as we have seen his power, and he has given us breath as he wishes."[55] Helck and others have noted that this is unlike the Hittite treaties, in which the vassal and his descendants are expected to be loyal to the king and his successors in perpetuity.

It is not entirely clear how far north the Egyptian sphere of influence extended during the Amarna period; the boundary fluctuated, usually to Egypt's detriment, particularly once the newly invigorated kingdom of Ḫatti began to expand into Syria, defeating Mitanni and taking control of its Syrian vassals. The development of the political allegiance of some of the states in Syria is fairly certain. For example, Ugarit was a long standing vassal of Egypt on the coast until the reign of Niqmaddu II, who made a vassal alliance with Šuppiluliumaš of Ḫatti.[56] To the southeast of Ugarit, Qadesh appears to have been under Egyptian control until the First Syrian War of Šuppiluliumaš (see below) in which Šutatarra of Qadesh and his son, Aitugama, were defeated in battle and were taken off to Ḫatti.[57] The land of Upi was clearly part of Egypt's domain, as was ᶜAmqi. The countries to the north of Qadesh vacillated between Mitanni and Egypt before the arrival of the Hittites. Niya, Nuḫašše, and Qatna at times seem to have been in the Egyptian sphere (see, for example, EA 53:40–44) and at other times not.[58] All of these countries in central Syria had to consider the political situation carefully to decide on the alliance which was most beneficial to them.[59]

[54] See Helck 1960: 5.

[55] John A. Wilson's translation in *ANET*³: 238.

[56] See the copies of the treaty between Niqmaddu and Šuppiluliumaš found at Ugarit in Nougayrol 1956: 40–52.

[57] Weidner 1923: 14–15, lines 40–47.

[58] Šuppiluliumaš seems to have considered them part of Mitanni when he attacked them. See Weidner 1923: 2–15, lines 1–47.

[59] For excellent discussions of other aspects of the political situation in Syria and Palestine during this period, see Liverani 1967; 1974; 1975; Ahituv 1978.

The evidence of the Amarna letters implies that, although there was considerable intrigue and violence going on in the lands under Egyptian control, this unrest was not perceived as particularly dangerous to Egyptian interests until the rise of Hittite power late in the reign of Akhenaten. During the reign of Amenōphis III, the policy seems to have been that, as long as general order prevailed, there was no reason for major direct Egyptian involvement in the area.[60]

During the reign of Amenōphis III a second reference to the city of Damascus appears. In his funerary temple in western Thebes, Amenōphis had a series of statues set up, and on their bases were inscribed the names of several cities and states that were subject to or at least friendly with Egypt. One of these statues lists a number of towns in southern Syria and northern Transjordan, including *tỉ-ms-qȝ* (Damascus) along with Taḫ̮ši, Edrei, Boṣruna, Aštarte, and others.[61]

When Amenōphis III died (ca. 1379), the two major powers in the Near East were still Egypt and Mitanni. But over the next several years the situation in the north changed dramatically. At the death (ca. 1380) of Tudḫ̮aliaš III, the king of Ḫ̮atti, his son Šuppiluliumaš came to the throne. During his reign of more than thirty years, he changed the political balance of power in the whole Near East. In his major military campaigns into Syria, especially the first great campaign described in his treaty with Kurtiwaza, his vassal king in Mitanni,[62] Šuppiluliumaš systematically took over all the Mitannian possessions in northern

[60] See Liverani 1979a: 3–13, for an extremely insightful discussion of the relations between Egypt and the vassal states. See also Schulman 1964: 61–66, and Several 1972: 123–33, who note, along with Liverani, that the Amarna letters are not to be construed as showing the dissolution of the empire through the neglect of the situation by the pharaoh, as has been so often portrayed. They point out that the letters, especially those from Palestine, indicate an effective administration of the area. Their discussion, however, particularly applies to Palestine and is not as applicable to the situation in Syria, especially after the rise of Šuppiluliumaš.

[61] Edel 1966: 9–23. Damascus is #3, right; Taḫ̮ši, #1, right; Edrei, #4, right; Buṣruna, #5, right; Aštarte, #9, left. The first five town names were published earlier (Kitchen 1965: 1–4).

[62] What I call Šuppiluliumaš' First Syrian War in this chapter is called the Second Syrian War by Goetze 1975a: 13–16. I am following

Syria and continued to the south and west, threatening Egyptian dependencies as well. By the end of his reign he had incorporated such erstwhile Egyptian vassals as Ugarit, Amurru, Qadesh, and possibly even Upi into the Hittite Empire.

The Amarna letters give some fragmentary information about the rise of Ḫatti as Egypt's major competitor in Syria, since they cover the period of the end of Mitannian importance and the rise of Ḫatti. Most of the Amarna references to Damascus and the land of Upi are found in letters from the latter part of the reign of Akhenaten[63] and deal with the Hittite challenge to this area. They are centered around a complex of events dealing with Biriawaza, an important official of Egypt in Syria-Palestine, and his conflict with a coalition of pro-Hittite forces, led by Aitugama of Qadesh.

Some background to the events referred to in the Amarna letters is described in the historical prologue of the vassal treaty between Šuppiluliumaš and Kurtiwaza, the king of Mitanni; these events took place during the latter part of the reign of Akhenaten, during the course of Šuppiluliumaš' First Syrian War.[64] This campaign began in retaliation against Tušratta of Mitanni for an attack he had made on Hittite territory, and it led to the loss of virtually all of Mitanni's possessions in Syria. After marching all the way to Waššukanni, Mitanni's capital,

---

Kitchen's terminology (1962: 2–5, 40–44). Goetze's First Syrian War is called the "Second Syrian Foray" by Kitchen (p. 41). There are numerous chronological problems related to Šuppiluliumaš and the Amarna pharaohs. See Kitchen's book (1962) for a good discussion of much of this.

[63] See Campbell 1964: 116–23. Hachmann (1970: 74) dates the letters dealing with the attack on Biriawaza more specifically to the time when Aziru was in Egypt, appearing before Akhenaten. He points out that EA 140, a letter from Ilirabiḫ, ruler of Gubla (Byblos) at a time soon after the overthrow of Rib-Addi, states that when Aziru left to go to Egypt, he sent his troops to Aitugama, where they helped him attack ᶜAmqi (140:20–27). Biriawaza mentions in 197:26–29 that "Arzawiya went to Qizza (Qadesh) and took the troops of Aziru and seized Šaddu." This appears to refer to the same period, a time when Aziru's troops were with Aitugama, but without Aziru there to lead them. This synchronism seems quite plausible.

[64] For the treaty between Šuppiluliumaš and Kurtiwaza, see Weidner 1923: 2–37. Also see Goetze 1975a: 8–16.

and neutralizing Tušratta's forces, Šuppiluliumaš turned back toward northwest Syria, took possession of Qatna, and fought with the king of Nuḫašše, whom he defeated (*KBo* I 1 37–39). He planned to attack the land of Apina, a name which is almost certainly the Hittite form of Api/Upi,[65] but on his way he was attacked by Šutatarra, the king of Qadesh, and his son, Aitugama. Šuppiluliumaš defeated them and took them prisoner to Ḫatti. He then continued his journey to Apina, where he engaged and defeated Ariwana, the king of Apina, and took him and his high officials (*rabûti*), Uambadura, Akparu, and Artaia, to Ḫatti along with much plunder (*KBo* I 1 39–45). The attack on Apina seems to have had little permanent effect on the political allegiance of the state, and, assuming that the identification of Apina with Upi is correct, there is no indication of any Egyptian retaliation for this move into previously undisputed Egyptian territory. Soon after this campaign, Šuppiluliumaš placed Šutatarra's son Aitugama on the throne of Qadesh as his vassal. It is this Aitugama who raised the anti-Egyptian coalition in southern Syria that is frequently mentioned in the Amarna letters.

The responsibility of confronting Aitugama's aggression fell to an official named Biriawaza. While Biriawaza was certainly a very high officer in the Egyptian administration, his exact position is not clear. Although he is mentioned over and over again in the Amarna corpus, he is never given a title. There have been numerous suggestions regarding his identity and function. Unger thought he was "a Mitannian prince or noble appointed by the pharaoh as his official representative in the imperial government in Upe."[66] Albright described him as "prince of the region of Damascus."[67] Both Helck and Campbell believed him to be the ruler of Damascus.[68] Goetze called him "the 'commissioner' of Kumidi."[69]

[65] This identification is not entirely certain, but seems likely. See M. F. Unger 1957: 26, 129–30, n 75; Goetze 1975a: 16; Helck 1971: 176–77, 271. Hachmann (1970: 84) is rather non-committal, but rightly disputes Klengel's argument against the identification (Klengel 1965–70: 1.138, n 7).

[66] M. F. Unger 1957: 24.

[67] Albright 1975: 101.

[68] Helck 1971: 183; Campbell 1964: 124.

[69] Goetze 1975a: 16.

The Amarna letters indicate that Biriawaza had been given a very wide area of authority by the pharaoh.[70] He is involved with the problem of Aziru in Amurru (EA 129); he has connections to the north with Akizzi of Qatna (EA 53); in the letter EA 250, ᵈIM.UR.SAG, the ruler of a town somewhere in northern Palestine, asks the pharaoh to send one of his officials to Biriawaza to have him move against the sons of Labaya of Shechem, who are threatening ᵈIM.UR.SAG's town. It is clear from the letter that ᵈIM.UR.SAG believes that Biriawaza should already have done something about the sons of Labaya, but has been ignoring his duty (250:22–27). Burraburiaš II of Babylon complains to Akhenaten that Biriawaza has plundered a caravan that was on the way to the pharaoh (EA 7:75). Even this far-off king need only give this official's name to identify him. It seems from all of this that Biriawaza's sphere of responsibility was quite extensive, covering virtually all of the northern part of the Egyptian holdings.[71]

The Amarna letters also show that Biriawaza was in Egyptian service at least as early as the beginning of Akhenaten's reign and probably somewhat earlier. EA 129, written soon after Abdi-Aširta's death, already mentions him, and Hachmann has suggested that Biriawaza's letter EA 194, the preserved portion of which speaks mostly of his loyalty to the pharaoh, belongs to the beginning of Akhenaten's reign and is in fact Biriawaza's assurance to the new king of his fidelity.[72]

The idea that Biriawaza was a prince of Damascus (Helck and Campbell) has no real support in the Amarna texts. There is no reference which explicitly connects him to that city, except for the statement in Biriawaza's letter that he had escaped from his enemies and had withdrawn to Damascus (EA 197:13–21). But this, of course, proves nothing with regard to his affiliation with the town. From Damascus he moved on to Kumidi, where he wrote EA 197. Hachmann points out that in EA 53 Akizzi of Qatna reports to the pharaoh that Aitugama has plundered Biriawaza's house (53:30–34). Hachmann believes that this must refer to the palace in Biriawaza's personal capital, thus suggest-

[70] An important study of the place of Biriawaza in the Egyptian administration may be found in Hachmann 1970: 65–76.

[71] It is of course possible that he was transferred from one province to another during the course of Akhenaten's reign.

[72] Hachmann 1970: 66–67.

ing that Aitugama had captured the capital at the time that Akizzi wrote this letter. But later in the letter Akizzi compares his faithfulness to that of Damascus, saying: *be-lí ki-i-me-e* ^{URU}*ti-ma-aš-qì i-na* KUR *ú-pì a-na* ^{UZU}GIR.MEŠ-*ka* // *qa-ti-ḫu*! *ù ki-ia-am* ^{URU}*qat-na a-na* ^{UZU}GIR.MEŠ-*ka* // *qa-ti-ḫu*, "My lord, as Damascus in the land of Upi is at your feet, just so Qatna is at your feet" (53:63–65). This suggests that Damascus had not been captured, and thus Hachmann believes that it cannot have been Biriawaza's capital.[73] While this argument is not compelling, it is suggestive when combined with the fact that no other evidence links Biriawaza with Damascus.[74]

There is not yet enough evidence to determine Biriawaza's exact position, except to say that it was very high. The extent of his responsibilities shows that he was not merely a local city-state king. It is possible that he was the governor (*rābiṣu*) of the northeast province, although this would be somewhat unusual since this position was normally held by an Egyptian. It may be that he had an even higher position than governorship of the northeast province, with responsibility over an even larger area. Despite the fact that he was not a native Egyptian (his name is Indo-European),[75] his family had been in the service of the king for at least two previous generations (194:6–10). However, Biriawaza and his family cannot be connected specifically with Damascus or the land of Upi from the evidence that is now available.

Biriawaza's connections with Upi appear to be centered around the serious revolt in that area that he was forced to oppose (EA 53, 189, 197). From the limited information available about this revolt, it can be reconstructed as follows. Soon after being placed on the throne of Qadesh by Šuppiluliumaš, Aitugama began a policy of expansion. His first step was to draw

[73] Hachmann 1970: 73.

[74] Note lines 56–62, in which Akizzi says, "My lord, behold Arzawa of Ruḫizi and Teuwatti of Lapana are dwelling in the land of Upi and Taša is dwelling in the land of ᶜAmqi. Let my lord know that the land of Upi is not my lord's. Every day they write to Aitugama and say 'Come and take all of the land of Upi." Care should be taken not to place too much weight on Hachmann's argument, since these lines suggest that Upi, and therefore Damascus, may already have been captured.

[75] See Gelb, Purves and MacRae 1943: 194, 245. Here the name is equated with the Indo-Aryan **vīrya-vāja*, "Prize of valor".

allies away from Egypt into the Hittite sphere. Akizzi of Qatna writes to Akhenaten, "And now Aitugama has written to me and said, '[Come] with me to the king of the land of Ḫatti'" (53:11–13). Although unsuccessful with Akizzi, Aitugama was able to gain allies in Teuwatti of Lapana, Arzawiya of Ruḫizzi (EA 53:35–36), and Aziru of Amurru (197:28). These allies began attacking neighboring states, including ᶜAmqi (EA 140:20–30; 53:58), Qatna (53:8–10), and the land of Upi (53:35–39, 56–62). In EA 197, Biriawaza writes urgently to the pharaoh for help against the spreading coalition. He states that as kings in the land south of Upi saw the success of the uprising, they began joining: "Biridašwa saw this deed, and he indeed set Yanuamma in motion against me. He locked the city gate against me and took the chariots in Aštarte and gave them to the Ḫapiru and did not give them to the king my lord. The king of Buṣruna saw and the king of Ḫaluna, and they made war along with Biridašwa against me" (197:7–16). The revolt was pushing in toward Upi proper from both the north and the south. Biriawaza withdrew into Damascus for a time, but he did not stay there very long before moving to Kumidi, where he wrote to the pharaoh for assistance. In the letter he states that he is guarding "Kumidi, the city of the king" (EA 197:38–39). There is no further information about this conflict and its outcome. It is possible that Aitugama and his allies were successful in overthrowing Biriawaza and temporarily taking over parts of the northeast province. If so, there is evidence from later sources that this was not a long-lasting situation.

Besides this revolt, little other evidence exists about events that occurred during the Amarna period in the land of Upi, although there are a few other fragments of information that should be noted.

One other Amarna letter mentions Damascus. At some time before the mounting of the coalition against Biriawaza, Aziru, the king of Amurru, and his brothers, who were expanding their power in the northwest province, went to Damascus. Rib-Addi of Byblos, who was a prime antagonist of Aziru, wrote to the pharaoh (EA 107:26–31) asking that he send troops to Damascus to capture them, so that they could not continue their pressure against Ṣumur. Unfortunately, there is not enough information about the reason for Aziru's visit to Damascus to understand its significance. Nor does EA 107 give any indication of the political situation in Damascus, so that the meaning of this visit for the northeast province cannot be determined.

A new piece of information has recently been recovered through archaeological work in Lebanon. In 1969, excavations in the Late Bronze Age levels of Kāmid el-Lōz in the southern Biqâ^{c} produced a small number of cuneiform tablets, only one of which is complete.[76] This intact tablet proved to be a letter from an Egyptian pharaoh to a certain Zalaia, king of Damascus (^{I}*za-la-ia* LÚ ^{URU}*ta-ma-aš-qá*).[77] After studying the script, ductus, color, and consistency of the clay of the tablet, D. O. Edzard came to the conclusion that it came out of the same scribal school as Amarna letters EA 162 and 163, which are also letters from the pharaoh.[78] Therefore, this letter may be dated to the fourteenth century.

The main message of this letter is quite interesting. It reads:

> *ša-ni-tam šu-bi-la-an-ni*
> LÚ.MEŠ SA.GAZ.ZA *a-bu-ur-ra*[79]
> *ša aš-pu-ra-ku* UGU-*šu-nu*
> *um-ma-a a-na-an-din-šu-nu-ti*
> *i-na* URU.ḪÁ *ša* ^{KUR}*ka-a-ša*
> *a-na a-ša-bi i-na* ŠÀ-*bi-šu*
> [*k*]*i-mu-ú ša aḫ-ta-bat-šu-nu-t*[*i*]

Furthermore, send me the Ḫapiru, about whom I wrote you thus: "I will place them in the cities of Kaša to dwell in their midst in place of those which I have taken away."

Here is an order to the king of Damascus to send a group of Ḫapiru to Egypt, where they will be shipped to villages in Kaša (= Nubia)[80] to live. The pharaoh was dealing with the aftermath of what was probably a rebellion in Nubia. In putting

[76] Edzard 1970. For a preliminary description of the 1969 excavations at Kāmid el-Lōz, see Kuschke and Metzger 1972.

[77] The tablet's number is KL 69:277. See Edzard 1970: 50 (photo); 52 (drawing); 55–60 (transcription, translation and commentary).

[78] See Edzard 1970: 61.

[79] On *a-bu-ur-ra*, cf. Loretz 1974.

[80] For the identification of Kaša with Nubia, see Klengel 1977. See also Edzard 1970:58–60.

down the rebellion he had some of the local population deported or made into slaves. Bringing in Ḫapiru from Syria to occupy the abandoned villages would have two functions: (1) removal of unstable, problematic Syrians, and (2) repopulation of towns that presumably had some economic importance to the Egyptians. Hachmann has suggested that this letter reflects the aftermath of the Nubian uprising which occurred during Amenōphis III's fifth year, pointing out that this is the only known revolt in that area during the reigns of Amenōphis III and Akhenaten.[81] Although this is quite possible, it is also not provable, since there may have been several minor outbreaks of violence in Nubia, about which nothing is known, which could be the background for the letter.

Damascus was not the only town involved in this deportation of Ḫapiru. A second letter found at Kāmid el-Lōz is basically a "carbon copy" of the Zalaia letter, but sent to Abdi-milki ([I]ÌR.LUGAL) of the town of Šazaena.[82] While it is fragmentary, remains of the command to send the Ḫapiru with identical wording are preserved. Presumably, letters like this were sent to several villages and towns in order to repopulate the villages of Kaša.

What was a letter to the king of Damascus doing at Kāmid el-Lōz? If the identification of Kāmid el-Lōz with ancient Kumidi is correct, then it may be that these letters belonged to the archive of the *rābiṣu* of the northeast province. Another possibility is that the letters were en route to their destinations but were stopped at this site and never delivered for some reason. Currently, it is impossible to determine why these letters were at Kāmid.[83]

THE FINAL YEARS OF THE LATE BRONZE AGE

With the end of the reign of Akhenaten (ca. 1362), a period of about forty-five years ensues in which very little information

[81] Hachmann 1970: 90–91.

[82] Tablet KL 69:279. See Edzard 1970: 50 (photo); 53 (drawing); 56–60 (transcription, translation and commentary). For the location of Šazaena, see Ephᶜal 1971. In all, seven tablets and fragments have been published from Kāmid el-Lōz. Nos. 3 and 4 are published in Edzard 1970: 60–61. No. 5 was published in Wilhelm 1973. On this letter, also see Rainey 1976. No. 6 is found in Edzard 1976. No. 7, a small fragment, was published in Edzard 1981.

[83] Hachmann 1970: 93–94.

about the Egyptian presence in Syria-Palestine has survived. It is only with the reign of Sethōs I (ca. 1318–1304) that clear records of Egyptian activity in western Asia reappear. This does not mean, as was once thought, that during the years between these two kings Egypt had lost its holdings in Syria-Palestine. In fact, the rather slim evidence that does exist suggests otherwise, that Egypt maintained an active presence throughout the second half of the fourteenth century.

Conflict between Ḫatti and Egypt in the area of Upi, ^{c}Amqi, and Qadesh continued after the death of Akhenaten. The final series of campaigns that Šuppiluliumaš waged in Syria probably took place during the last few years of Tut^{c}ankhamūn's reign and the first years of Ay's. There are two important sources of information for this period, both from Ḫatti: (1) the so-called "Deeds of Šuppiluliumaš," an account of the exploits of that king, prepared by his son, Muršiliš II; and (2) a prayer of Muršiliš II, concerning the great plague that devastated Ḫatti for decades.[84] In the Deeds of Šuppiluliumaš is recorded an attack on Qadesh by the Egyptians.[85] Presumably, this was an attempt by Tut^{c}ankhamūn to return this land to Egyptian control by defeating Aitugama, who was still on the throne.[86] No details of the attack are given, but Šuppiluliumaš retaliated by sending troops to attack ^{c}Amqi,[87] which was clearly in Egyptian hands at this time. None of this seems to have been decisive, but soon after the attack on ^{c}Amqi Tut^{c}ankhamūn died. At this point, Tut^{c}ankhamūn's widow, ^{c}Ankhesenamūn, wrote a letter to Šuppiluliumaš, asking him to send one of his sons to Egypt to become her husband and the new pharaoh.[88] After making further inquiries about the sincerity of the request, he sent one of his sons to her. The prospective groom was murdered along the way to Egypt and hostilities resumed. Šuppiluliumaš once again attacked Egyptian territory, but when

[84] See Güterbock 1956. For the prayer, see Goetze 1929a: 204–35.

[85] Güterbock 1956: 93, Fr. 28 A ii 21–25.

[86] Aitugama lived until the ninth year of Muršiliš II. See Klengel 1965–70: 2.168–69.

[87] Güterbock 1956: 94, Fr. 28 A iii 1–4; also p. 97 E3 iv 1–11. See also Goetze 1929a: 208–11.

[88] The major account of this is in the Deeds of Šuppiluliumaš. See Güterbock 1956: 94–98, 107–8. See also the brief mention of the incident in Goetze 1929a: 210–11.

the army returned from this campaign, they brought with them a plague which was to persist in Ḫatti for years.[89]

Šuppiluliumaš died of the plague ca. 1346.[90] He was succeeded by his son Arnuwandaš who was also ill and died after a short reign. He in turn was succeeded by another son of Šuppiluliumaš, Muršiliš II. Muršiliš was able to reassert control over several areas which had attempted to rebel during the previous reign.[91] During his seventh year, a revolt broke out in Nuḫašše and Qadesh, which was supported by Egyptian troops. Muršiliš sent a general, Kantuziliš, with troops to meet the Egyptian forces and defeated them, either in Nuḫašše or near Carchemish.[92] This confrontation apparently took place during the reign of Ḥaremḥab in Egypt.

Until recently there was no certain evidence of a major campaign to Syria led by Ḥaremḥab, but in 1973 a stone bowl with an inscription of Ḥaremḥab which referred directly to such an expedition surfaced briefly at a Cairo antiquities shop. It reads in part: "Regnal year sixteen, under the Majesty of the Lord of the Two Lands, Ḥaremḥab the Ruler; at the time of his first victorious campaign from Byblos as far as the land of the vile chief of Carchemish."[93] D. Redford, who published the text, suggested that this campaign to Carchemish is the same one referred to in the Annals of Muršiliš mentioned above. While this is possible, there are a number of chronological difficulties that arise in identifying the two.[94] Nevertheless, if the stone

[89] Goetze 1929a: 210–11, lines 9–10.

[90] Goetze 1975a: 19.

[91] Goetze 1975b: 120–27.

[92] Goetze 1933: 86–87. See Klengel 1965–70: 2.168–69. See also Weidner 1923: 76–79, for the text of the treaty.

[93] Redford 1973: 37.

[94] Redford 1973: 47–49; and Schulman 1978: 44, 46–47. Redford identifies Muršiliš' seventh year with Ḥaremḥab's sixteenth, and through this comes to the conclusion that the woman who wrote to Šuppiluliumaš for a husband was Nefertiti rather than ᶜAnkhesenamūn, Tutankhamūn's wife. Schulman disputes this and suggests that the stone bowl, if genuine (see p. 47, n 8), may be part of the propaganda campaign to make Ḥaremḥab the immediate successor of Amenōphis III, thus incorporating the years of Akhenaten, Smenkhkarēᶜ, Tutankhamūn, and Ay's reigns into his own. We can be fairly certain that this was being done before the end of Ḥaremḥab's reign in the light of a legal document dated to Ḥaremḥab's fifth-ninth year

bowl is taken as referring to a campaign in Ḥaremḥab's sixteenth regnal year, then the fact that the expedition began as far north as Byblos and ranged up to Carchemish shows that during his reign, Egypt continued its control of Palestine and southern Syria.

Ḥaremḥab had no heir and was succeeded by Ramessēs I, the founder of the Nineteenth Dynasty. His reign apparently lasted less than two years;[95] his son, Sethōs I, succeeded to the throne in 1318 and resumed an active interest in Syria-Palestine. Although information about his activities in Syria-Palestine is sketchy, there is little doubt that he raised a significant challenge to the Hittites. The chief source of information for the campaigns of Sethōs I is a series of reliefs in the hypostyle hall of the temple of Amen at Karnak.[96] These reliefs appear to depict four distinct military campaigns, although only one date actually appears on the reliefs ('year one'). Sethōs apparently began with a successful campaign to reestablish full control over Palestine, where some of the small kingdoms had revolted, probably during the reign of his father. This was followed by a campaign in which the Egyptians claim to have attacked and captured Qadesh,[97] bringing it into the Egyptian sphere for the first time in several decades. During the course of this campaign, Sethōs evidently regained control of Amurru. Bentešina, the king of Amurru, was forced to become a vassal of the king of Egypt, and there is an account from Hittite records of Bentešina's official withdrawal from his alliance with Ḫatti.[98]

---

which almost certainly includes the years of his four predecessors. See Gardiner 1905: 11. Thus, Ḥaremḥab's "year sixteen" could actually be year sixteen of Akhenaten, and the campaign here would then be the hypothetical campaign that has been suggested by Schulman and others, undertaken right before the death of Akhenaten. See Schulman 1964: 63–66; and Schulman 1978: 46. We also have examples of year dates, as late as year eight, which genuinely reflect Ḥaremḥab's own reign (Breasted 1906: 3. #32B), so we cannot be sure which system our inscription is using.

[95] Faulkner 1975: 217–18.

[96] See Breasted 1906: 2. ##80–156. See Simons 1937: 53–59, 137–43, for the geographical lists. See also Aharoni 1979: 176–81.

[97] Breasted 1906: 3. #141.

[98] *KUB* XXIII 1:28–39. See Goetze 1929b: 834–35. See also Klengel 1965–70:2.308–10.

Amurru (and possibly Taḫši, if it had been under Hittite control[99]) apparently remained under Egyptian control until the Battle of Qadesh between Ramessēs II and Muwatališ in 1300.

Sethōs' third campaign took place against the Libyans. This was followed by his final known campaign in which Sethōs met a Hittite army at an unknown location. Sethōs claims to have defeated the Hittites,[100] but it is possible that Qadesh was recaptured by the Hittites during this confrontation (if, in fact, if had been captured by Egypt during the second campaign), since the Hittites controlled it when Ramessēs II marched into the area in his fifth year (1300). Sometime after this last campaign a peace treaty was made between Sethōs and Muwatališ, but no details are known about it since the only reference that has survived is a mention of its existence in the great treaty between Ḫattušiliš III and Ramessēs II.[101]

When Ramessēs II came to the throne in 1304, he spent his first three years on domestic matters. In the fourth year he made his first campaign into western Asia, traveling at least as far as the Nahr el-Kelb, near Beirut, where he set up an inscription, now virtually illegible. In the next year one of the most famous campaigns of ancient Near Eastern history took place—the campaign culminating in the Battle of Qadesh. This battle, in which the pharaoh was caught in a Hittite attack without most of his troops and was saved from disaster only by his own valor and the timely arrival of fresh troops, was memorialized on the walls of several of Ramessēs' temples.[102] The battle was apparently quite vicious, with both sides sustaining heavy losses. Although the battle itself apparently resulted in a draw, the campaign was clearly a serious loss for the Egyptians. After the battle, Ramessēs felt constrained to withdraw, but the Hittite army, under King Muwatališ and his brother Ḫattušiliš, followed the Egyptians southward as they retreated through the land of Apa (= Upi) and, at least for a while, took control of Apa.[103] Furthermore, Amurru, which had

[99] Cf. Faulkner 1947: 37–38.

[100] Breasted 1906: 3. ##142–52. See also Faulkner 1947: 38.

[101] See Breasted 1906: 3. #377.

[102] For details, see Gardiner 1960. For a good bibliography relating to this battle, see *CAH* II/2: 952.

[103] *KUB* XXI 17 I 14–20. See Edel 1950: 212.

been fighting along with Egypt in this campaign, was recaptured by Ḫatti, and Bentešina was removed from the throne.[104]

For the next sixteen years there was fighting back and forth in Syria, between Ḫatti and Egypt, and, although Ramessēs was sometimes able to gain control of a significant portion of Hittite territory (Tunip and Qatna are claimed at times), these advances were only held, if at all, for very short periods.[105] Finally, in Ramessēs' twenty-first year, a peace treaty between Ḫattušiliš III and Ramessēs was negotiated, ending warfare between the two powers. Interestingly, the treaty, of which there are copies from both Egypt and Boghazköi,[106] avoids any reference to the boundaries of the two kingdoms. It has been assumed that the border probably followed the frontier that existed at the end of the reign of Šuppiluliumaš.[107] Ḫattušiliš retained control of Amurru and eventually reinstalled Bentešina as king there.[108]

The boundary situation vis-à-vis Upi is known, thanks to a letter written by Ramessēs to Ḫattušiliš which discusses the plans for transporting Ḫattušiliš' daughter, who was to marry Ramessēs, and her dowry from Ḫatti to Egypt.[109] Ḫattušiliš had written to Ramessēs that he would send his daughter and the dowry to the town of Aya where, he said, the pharaoh should arrange for someone in authority to meet them and accompany them on to Egypt. Presumably Aya was a town located at the southern boundary of Hittite territory. Ramessēs wrote back to Ḫattušiliš, notifying him: "I have written to the governor (*šākin māti*), Suta, in the town of Riamašeša-mai-amana, the town that is in the midst of the land of Upi, to take them in and lead them until the bride comes to the land of Egypt."[110] Another governor was also notified to accompany the party, although it is not known from which city he came. E. Edel has suggested that he was the governor of Canaan, at Gaza,[111] and this seems highly

[104] See Goetze 1929b: 834–35, lines 34–39; and Edel 1950: 212, lines 14–16.

[105] Goetze 1975c: 228–29.

[106] Both treaties are translated in *ANET*³: 199–203.

[107] Goetze 1975c: 259.

[108] See the treaty between Hattušiliš III and Bentešina, *KBo* I 8: 11–21, in Weidner 1923: 126–29.

[109] Edel 1953b: 29–63.

[110] Edel 1953b: 33, D 2–6.

[111] Edel 1953b: 33, D' 8–10; 50–51.

likely, since the bridal party would certainly have passed through Gaza on the way to Egypt. The fact that Ramessēs had a governor in Upi[112] shows that Upi continued to be part of Egyptian territory after the making of the peace treaty.

The peace with Ḫatti continued throughout the rest of Ramessēs' sixty-seven year reign and into the reign of his son, Merenptaḥ. There were, in fact, no more major campaigns from Egypt into Syria. Merenptaḥ's chief problems came from the Libyans to the west, who were attacking the Delta region along with a coalition of the so-called "peoples of the sea"—the Šerden, Šekleš, Turša, and Ekweš, early elements of the migrating peoples who would challenge Egypt even more severely a few decades later.[113] Merenptaḥ was able to defeat them and to make a campaign into Palestine in which he captured towns such as Gezer, Aškalon, and Yanuammu and fought the people of Israel.[114] However, nothing of the situation in Syria is revealed in the royal inscriptions.[115] It does appear that Egypt during his reign and perhaps even slightly later still maintained some official control over Upi. This information comes from Papyrus Anastasi I,[116] an Egyptian letter of the late Nineteenth Dynasty. This letter, from a scribe named Hori to another scribe, Amenemope, speaks of numerous aspects of the scribal profession in which Hori judged that Amenemope was incompetent. Among the areas that Hori criticizes is Amenemope's ignorance of the geography of Syria-Palestine. In this section,

[112] Edel believes that the city Riamašeša-mai-Amana, mentioned in this text, is to be identified with Damascus; this is entirely possible. It is also possible that the Egyptian administrative center in that area continued to be Kumidi and that this is the town referred to here. As mentioned above, Kumidi may actually have been within the territory of the land of Upi. Cf. Edel 1953b: 44–48. The fact that the town is named after Ramessēs indicates that it officially belonged to the pharaoh.

[113] Cf. Faulkner 1975: 232–34. Also Breasted 1906: 3. #572–92.

[114] Breasted 1906: 3. #602–17.

[115] Papyrus Anastasi III 1 10 gives the boundaries of Merenptah's empire in Western Asia as "from *ṯꜣrw* (Sile) to *ỉwpꜣ* (Upi)." See Caminos 1954: 69, 73. However, this phrase occurs in a series of stock epithets, and thus it cannot be used as evidence for the range of Merenptah's power. Papyrus Anastasi I seems to be a better witness (see below).

[116] The standard treatment of this text is Gardiner 1911. For a convenient translation, see *ANET*³: 475–79.

the writer mentions a fortress in the land of Upi that almost certainly was on the northern boundary of the Egyptian-controlled area. The text reads: "You do not know the name of *hꜣ-nr-ḏꜣ* in the land of Upi (*ỉwpꜣ*), the bull upon its boundary, the place where the battle array of every hero may have been seen."[117] The fact that this fortress was occupied by Egyptian troops indicates that Upi was still under Egyptian control. However, this was to last only a short time longer, for the waves of migrating peoples from the north and west were already moving into the Fertile Crescent, destroying the land of Ḫatti and its empire and eventually pushing southward into Syria. Ramessēs III (ca. 1198–1166) fought with migrating sea peoples on the very borders of Egypt and in Palestine. He was able to keep them out of his own country but could not push them out of the coastal regions of Palestine.[118] By the end of his reign Egyptian presence was gone from Syria-Palestine, and the light of history goes out on the land of Upi. When documentation returns, the culture which dominated the area of Damascus, as well as much of Syria, was Aramaean, and the Aramaeans would be in control of that land for centuries to come.

In summary, very little is known about the history of the land of Upi during the Late Bronze Age. The major sources of information come from the empires which had political and economic interests in Syria: Egypt, Mitanni, and Ḫatti, but they only mentioned Upi when events there affected them. Nothing is known about the rulers of Damascus or internal political developments within the land of Upi. Upi fit into the international political scene mostly as a vassal state to Egypt, and often at the limits of Egypt's northeastern border. Upi suffered much war during the Late Bronze Age, as did most of the states in southern and central Syria, as a result of the constant conflict between the major powers to the north and south.

As for the city of Damascus itself—about all that can be said is that it existed, it had the standard form of government,

[117] Papyrus Anastasi I 22 6. See Gardiner 1911: 24*, 66–68. Also see Helck 1971: 318. Upi is also mentioned in Papyrus Anastasi I 18 7, where it is simply stated (to Amenemope), "You have not seen the land of Upi."

[118] See Edgerton and Wilson 1936: 35–58. See also Faulkner 1975: 241–44.

i.e., a "king," and it was known for its loyalty to Egypt. It was not a politically important town during this period, though the future would prove otherwise.

DAMASCUS AND THE MONARCHS OF UNITED ISRAEL ____ FOUR

FROM THE TIME of the collapse of the empires of Ḫatti and Egypt until approximately 1000 B.C.E., when biblical reports record David's Syrian Wars, there are no texts preserved anywhere which deal with events in southern Syria. When documentation is again available for this area, a series of Aramaean states have appeared where Egypt's northeastern province once had been; but the circumstances of the rise and development of these kingdoms are shrouded in obscurity.

The origins of the Aramaeans are unknown; they are not mentioned certainly in any Near Eastern text until the end of the twelfth century. But these tribes came to have a profound effect on the Near East for, before the end of the second millennium, they were pressing into Mesopotamia where they would eventually become the dominant force in Babylonia and were setting up kingdoms throughout Syria. They would ultimately take over the Neo-Hittite states of northern and Central Syria, and their language would, by the time of the late Neo-Assyrian Empire, become the international language of Western Asia. Following is a brief discussion of these people and what is known of their early movements.

THE ORIGINS OF THE ARAMAEANS

The first Aramaeans whose existence is documented with certainty lived on the fringes of the desert in the area of the

Upper and Middle Euphrates.[1] Although they presumably had occupied this area during the Late Bronze Age, no absolutely certain reference to them has yet been found in any Hittite, north Syrian, or Mesopotamian document from the second millennium.[2] The earliest probable reference to the Aramaeans is found in one of the topographical lists on a statue base from the funerary temple of Amenōphis III at Thebes. Among the places listed on Statue D is the name *p3 ꜣirmw*. It is significant that this name does not have the "country" determinative, but rather the "man" determinative; thus it may be translated "the people Aram" or "the Aramaeans."[3]

There are a few other possible, though uncertain, references in documents of the Late Bronze Age,[4] but the first incontestable mention of the Aramaeans comes from the reign of Tiglath-Pileser I of Assyria (ca. 1116–1076). In his annals and other inscriptions Tiglath-Pileser is described as fighting a group called Aramaean Aḫlamū (gen. *aḫ-la-me-i* KUR *ar-ma-a-ia*^{MEŠ}), engaging them "from the land of Sūḫu to the city of Carchemish of the land of Ḫatti."[5] Summarizing his campaigns against this extraordinarily resilient enemy, Tiglath-Pileser in one of his later inscriptions says, "Twenty-eight times I have crossed the Euphrates after the Aramaean Aḫlamū, twice in one year. I defeated them from Tadmar, which is in the land of Amurru, Anat, which is in the land of Sūḫu, unto Rapiqu, which is in the

[1] Albright (1975b: 530) suggested that the desert fringes of eastern Syria were the original homeland of the Aramaeans, based on his analysis of the Aramaic language and its similarities to Amorite, known mainly from personal names of the Mari period. This argument is not decisive, however, because the problem of Aramaean origins is too complex to be solved merely on the basis of linguistic similarities between two Semitic dialects.

[2] See the discussion and bibliography in de Vaux 1978: 200–205. The attempt to find the Aramaeans in texts from as early as the third millennium has been justly criticized by de Vaux (1978: 203) and Albright (1975b: 529), who says, "The less said about supposed occurrences of the name Aram in cuneiform texts of the late third and early second millennium the better."

[3] The name appears as D_N, #7, right, in Edel 1966: 28–29, 93.

[4] See in particular the tablets from Ugarit mentioned in de Vaux 1978: 204. As he says, the interpretation of these occurrences is quite uncertain.

[5] Grayson 1972–76: 2. #34. See also 2. #70.

Figure 4. Syria–Palestine during the tenth century B.C.E.

land of Karanduniaš. Their booty and their property I carried to my city Aššur."[6] It is clear from the number of campaigns against the Aramaeans that the Assyrians considered them a substantial threat. This is also suggested by a fragmentary Assyrian chronicle which apparently describes a serious famine that occurred in northern Syria and Assyria; the Aramaeans pushed their way into Assyria during this crisis, perhaps even capturing Nineveh, before Tiglath-Pileser could respond to the threat.[7] The pressure of the Aramaeans on Assyria did not abate. An inscription called the "Broken Obelisk," almost certainly belonging to Aššur-bēl-kala (ca. 1073–1056), the second successor of Tiglath-Pileser I, chronicles numerous battles between Assyria and armies (?) from the land of Aram (*ḫarrāna ša* KUR *Arimi*).[8]

The considerable controversy about the meaning of the term *aḫlamū armāia* in the literature concerned with the Aramaeans turns on the question of the exact relationship between the Aḫlamū and the Aramaeans. The Aḫlamū, who were nomadic tribes along the fringes of Syrian and Mesopotamian society, are mentioned as early as the fourteenth century;[9] many scholars have identified the Aḫlamū as Aramaeans[10] or have proposed that the Aramaeans were at least part of the Aḫlamū tribes. One aspect of this problem has been whether to understand the word *aḫlamu* as a common noun, a proper name, or both. The etymology usually attributed to the word relates it to Arabic *ḫilm*, pl. *aḫlām*, which is taken to mean 'companion, confederate' and it is thus assumed that the Aḫlamū were a confederation of nomadic tribes.[11] It is suggested that the Aramaeans were one part of this confederation, which would

[6] A transcription of the cuneiform of this text may be found in Weidner 1958: 350, text 2, lines 34–36. Also see Grayson 1972–76: 2. ##97 and 83.

[7] See Grayson 1972–76: 2. #200. For a discussion of this text, see Tadmor 1979: 12–13.

[8] See Grayson 1972–76: 2. ##227–52, and p. 53, n 226. The word *ḫarrāna* here is rather obscure. It commonly refers to trade caravans, although it is also used of military contingents.

[9] Cf. de Vaux 1978: 201–2.

[10] For example, see Dupont-Sommer 1949: 16.

[11] Moscati 1959: 303–4. See especially p. 303, n 3 and 304, n 1 for bibliography about this position.

explain the references to the Aramaean Aḫlamū. This explanation has been challenged by S. Moscati,[12] who argues that the Akkadian word *aḫlamu*, pl. *aḫlamū*, is not related to Arabic *ḫilm* at all. He notes, for example, that the Arabic broken plural of *ḫilm*, which is *aḫlām*, has a long second *ā*, while this is not the case for the Akkadian plural, nor is the singular form the same, since the Akkadian singular is *aḫlamu*. The Arabic word does not mean 'confederate, companion' in the way that is normally assumed; Moscati noted that *ḫilm* in Arabic means, 'a friend of women, one who courts women". These facts create serious problems for those who accept the common etymology.

Moscati further asserts that *aḫlamu* was the proper name of a particular group and not a common noun with the meaning 'confederation' or 'bedawin'.[13] He does not believe that the Aramaeans were part of the Aḫlamū, and points out that the practice of referring to nomadic tribes by combined tribal designations, such as *aḫlamū armāia*, is paralleled several times in Mesopotamian texts, most notably in the Mari letters where such distinct groups as the Benyaminites, the Ḫaneans, the Suteans, and the Amorites sometimes appear in combinations such as Benyaminite-Ḫaneans, or Sutean-Amorites, etc. On this basis Moscati argues that there is no compelling reason to suggest that the Aramaeans were linked closely to the Aḫlamū; thus, the references to the Aḫlamū from the fourteenth to twelfth centuries do not necessarily bear on the problem of Aramaean origins.[14]

J. Brinkman has furthered the discussion by pointing out the difficulty in accepting Moscati's argument that *aḫlamu* is a proper name for a tribal group.[15] He also emphasizes the fact that there are important connections between the terms *aḫlamu* and *arumu*. Besides the above-mentioned *aḫlamē armāia*, Brinkman points to the later usage in Akkadian texts of *aḫlamu* as an appellative for "Aramaic" and "Aramaean." More information is necessary before the exact relationship between these two terms can be determined.

Biblical tradition preserves some legendary material about the origins of the Aramaeans and their relationship to the

[12] Moscati 1959: 303–7.

[13] On the translation 'bedawin', cf. Albright 1975b: 530.

[14] Moscati 1959: 304–5.

[15] Brinkman 1968: 277–78, n 1799.

ancestors of Israel. There are two references to Aram in genealogies. Gen 10:22, which is now usually attributed to the P source,[16] makes Aram a son of Shem, along with Elam, Aššur, Arpachšad, and Lud. This text clearly belongs to a period when Aram was perceived as one of the major peoples of the world. From what must be a much earlier tradition when Aramaeans were less powerful, Aram appears as the grandson of Abraham's brother Nahor in Gen 22:21.[17]

Early biblical tradition strongly insists upon a close relationship between the Israelites and the Aramaeans. Abram's family is settled in Aram-Naharaim (Gen 24:10) or Paddan-Aram (Gen 28:6–7). The wives of Isaac and Jacob, who are kinfolk of Abraham, are considered to be Aramaeans. Rebekah is called "the daughter of Bethuel the Aramaean of Paddan-Aram, the sister of Laban the Aramaean" in Gen 25:20. The confessional passage in Deut 26:5 begins with the words, "A wandering Aramaean was my father."

Several conclusions may be drawn from this biblical material. The place names, such as Aram-Naharaim and Paddan-Aram, are anachronistic; the area called Aram-Naharaim in Genesis was called Naharēna by the Egyptians and Naḫrēma in the Canaanite Amarna letters during the Late Bronze Age. It apparently was not identified as an Aramaean area until the Iron Age. It is more difficult to determine the ethnic identity of Bethuel and Laban. Perhaps the description of them as Aramaean is not precise, but the feeling of relationship between Israel and the Aramaeans must certainly have had some basis, especially since from the time of David, the Aramaean states were viewed as enemies of Israel. It would be strange for an artificial relationship to be invented at such a time. R. de Vaux has pointed out that numerous tribal groups which are lumped together as the Amorites of the early second millennium appear in documents from various centuries, sometimes connected with other groups, sometimes alone. The Aramaeans could well have been some of the tribes which took part in migrations

[16] For the attribution of v 22 to P, see Speiser 1964: 71–73, and Noth 1972: 17, 262. Albright believed that this passage reflected the situation of the tenth century, even if it belonged to P. See Albright 1975b: 531.

[17] On the genealogies, see Mazar 1962: 99–101.

through Syria during those years.[18] There is no reason why there could not have been some relation between the ancestors of Israel and ancestors of the Aramaean tribes who set up the states in Syria at the end of the second millennium.

THE ARAMAEANS AND SOUTHERN SYRIA

While there is some information about the spread of the Aramaeans into the settled areas of northern Syria and Mesopotamia,[19] there is little evidence for their spread into southern Syria. Sources for southern Syria, which are entirely from the Hebrew Bible, begin only after the Aramaean states had developed. The origin of the Aramaean population in the area cannot be determined; they may have entered through a slow migration into the area or through violent conquest, such as appears to have been the case in parts of Mesopotamia. It is also possible that the Aramaean culture of southern Syria is basically the continuing development of the local culture of the Late Bronze Age. However the Aramaean culture developed, by the time biblical sources begin speaking of southern Syria, there are Aramaean states as far south as the Biqâᶜ Valley in Lebanon and Damascus to the east. Aramaean culture apparently had not moved into northern Transjordan yet (see below), nor had Aramaeans come to control the Neo-Hittite state of Hamath.[20] The cities on the Mediterranean coast remained free of major Aramaean influence, as did Israel during the days of the Judges, as far as can be seen from the biblical account of that period.[21]

When documentation begins in 2 Samuel and its parallels in 1 Chronicles there are a number of small states to the north and east of Israelite territory, some Aramaean, some Canaanite.

[18] See de Vaux 1978: 205–9.

[19] For the Aramaean expansion into these areas, see especially Kupper 1957: 115–30; and Brinkman 1968: 267–85.

[20] Hamath during the reign of David was ruled by Toᶜi or Toᶜu, a man with a Hurrian or Anatolian name.

[21] The only reference to Aram in the book of Judges is in Judg 3:7–11, which tells the story of the oppression of Israel by Cushan-Rishathaim, king of Aram Naharaim, but this story bristles with difficulties, making it doubtful that it can be used for historical reconstruction. See de Vaux 1978: 536, for a discussion of this passage. Cf. Boling 1975: 80–81, for an interesting, but uncompelling proposal.

Because these small states are important for events during the reign of David, a brief description of them will be helpful.

Two small but significant states in northern Transjordan were Maacah and Geshur; they were situated in the Golan (cf. Josh 12:5, 13:11). Maacah's boundary was probably circumscribed by Mt. Hermon on the north, the Jordan to the west (although this boundary may have fluctuated), and Geshur to the south, with their common border to be placed about the latitude of Lake Huleh.[22] Maacah was not one of the new Aramaean states; it seems to have existed throughout the second millennium, apparently being mentioned in the Execration Texts from Saqqarah as *mᶜkȝw*. It survived the difficulties of the end of the Late Bronze Age and maintained a separate existence into the first millennium. By the end of the eleventh century, it appears to have been an ally or, more probably, a vassal of Aram Zobah (2 Sam 10:6).[23]

Geshur, the small country to the south of Maacah and extending southward probably to the Yarmuk River Valley,[24] was not originally an Aramaean state either, having also been in existence at least since the late Bronze Age. B. Mazar in his study of Geshur and Maacah has convincingly argued that the reading *ga-ri* in EA 256:23, referring to a state that, from the context, seems to be located where Geshur is found in the eleventh century, should probably be emended to *ga-<šu>-ri*.[25] Geshur seems to have maintained its independence from the Aramaean kingdoms until after the time of Solomon, since it does not appear among the members of the coalition against David during the Syrian Wars (2 Sam 8:3–8; 10:1–19).[26]

[22] See Mazar 1961: 16–17. Evidence that Maacah may have at one time included territory to the west of the Jordan comes from the town-name Abel Beth Maacah in 2 Sam 20:14–15. This town is identified with the site called Abil el-Qamḥ, west of Dan. Cf. Aharoni and Avi-Yonah 1968: map 113, also p. 174. Presumably, Abel Beth Maacah belonged at one time to Maacah and was perhaps annexed into Israel during the time of David (cf. Mazar 1961: 28).

[23] See Mazar 1961: 21–22.

[24] See M. F. Unger 1957: 45. Also note Aharoni and Avi-Yonah 1968: map 101.

[25] Mazar 1961: 20.

[26] Geshur seems to have had close relations with Israel, rather than with the Aramaeans to the north. 2 Sam 3:3 mentions that while David was still only the king of Judah, he was given the daughter of Talmai, the king of Geshur, as a wife.

A third important state was Beth-Rehob, whose location has been more difficult to pinpoint. It was common some years ago to identify Rehob with the area around the ruined site Riḥāb, some 50 km. north of ᶜAmmān.[27] However, this identification has been dropped, since archaeological surveys of Riḥāb have failed to recover any Iron Age sherds from the site.[28] The more probable location for Beth Rehob was suggested by O'Callaghan, Dupont-Sommer, Unger, and others, in the area of the southern Biqâᶜ north of Dan.[29]

A fourth state mentioned in connection with the Aramaeans of the late eleventh century is the land of Tob. Most have located it to the east-southeast of Geshur, in Gilead, but there is little certainty on the matter.[30]

The most significant state to arise in southern or central Syria was Aram Zobah (ארם צובה). By the time of David, Zobah had become the most powerful state in the region and an important rival of the new monarchy of Israel. Most scholars of recent years have placed this kingdom in the northern Biqâᶜ, with its domain extending east of the Anti-lebanon to the north of Damascus, into the plain of Ḥoms, and eastward into the desert.[31]

Finally, the land of Damascus, our focus of interest, had become an Aramaean state by the end of the eleventh century. Its exact boundaries during this period are unknown, and it was still rather insignificant politically. It is evident from 2 Sam 8:5 that Damascus had close relations with Zobah, but the type of relationship is not known; it may have been an ally, a vassal, or an occupied territory of the more powerful state. There is no information on the internal political situation in Damascus before its defeat by David.

DAMASCUS AND DAVID OF ISRAEL

About the year 1000, Damascus once again became involved in a struggle between two imperial powers, this time between

[27] See, for example, Kraeling 1918: 39–40.

[28] O'Callaghan 1948: 125.

[29] O'Callaghan 1948: 125–26; M. F. Unger 1957: 45; Dupont-Sommer 1949: 25. See also Aharoni and Avi-Yonah 1968: map 102.

[30] O'Callaghan 1948: 126; M. F. Unger 1957: 45; Aharoni and Avi-Yonah 1968: map 101.

[31] See Albright 1975b: 534; Albright 1969: 127–28; O'Callaghan 1948: 124; Malamat 1963: 3–4; Mazar 1962: 102.

the new kingdom of Israel under David and the powerful Aramaean state of Zobah under its king, Hadadezer. The sole source of information about the war between these two states is the Hebrew Bible, specifically 2 Sam 8:3–8 // 1 Chr 18:3–8 and 2 Sam 10:1–19 // 1 Chr 19:1–19.[32]

By the time David took the throne of Israel and Judah, Aram Zobah had already become the most powerful kingdom of southern and central Syria. According to the notice in 1 Sam 14:47, Zobah and Israel had begun to come into conflict with one another even during the reign of Saul, but most scholars doubt the reliability of the passage.[33]

Only one ruler of Zobah, Hadadezer (Aramaic *Hadad-ᶜiḏr*), is known. He is called *ben Rĕḥôb*, 'the son of Rehob', in 2 Sam 8:3. It has been plausibly argued that this epithet does not refer to Hadadezer's father, but rather to the land of his origin, and thus that he was a native of Beth Rehob and probably its king. If this be correct, then Hadadezer may have formed a personal union between Beth Rehob in the southern Biqâᶜ and Zobah in the north, much in the way that David had united Judah and Israel.[34] This possibility is strengthened by the fact that in 2 Sam 10:6 the armies of Beth Rehob and Zobah are counted as one unit: "The Ammonites sent and hired Aram Beth Rehob and Aram Zobah, twenty thousand foot soldiers, and the king of Maacah, one thousand men, and the men of Tob, twelve thousand men."

Hadadezer apparently had transformed Zobah into a substantial power in the Near East, with numerous vassal states as

[32] The LXX version of these passages has no variants that bear particularly on the historical aspects of the Syrian Wars. Extra sentences found in the LXX in 2 Sam 8:7, 8, deal with the fate of the booty taken from Hadadezer, not with the war itself. Nor do the few fragments of the unpublished 4QSam[a] scroll from Qumran add any information.

[33] The verse lists wars between Saul and Moab, Ammon, Edom, the kings of Zobah, and the Philistines in the MT, but there seems to be some corruption in this verse. 4QSam[a] and LXX have the singular, "the king of Zobah," which is more likely to be correct. The Lucianic text of the LXX (boc_2e_2) also adds, και εις τον βαιθροωβει, "and against Beth Rehob." But it is uncertain whether this is original or whether it entered the text due to the close association of Beth Rehob and Zobah in 2 Samuel 10. See McCarter 1980: 254–55.

[34] See Malamat 1963: 2–3. Also see Buccelati 1967: 137–45, esp. 143–45.

far north as the Euphrates, which could be called to his side for battle against Israel. 2 Sam 10:16 refers to "Aram, which is across the River" (ארם אשר מעבר הנהר), i.e., the Euphrates, as supplying forces for the battle of Helam. Maacah and Tob, which are mentioned as sending contingents to help the Ammonites in 2 Sam 10:6, may have been vassals of Zobah. In fact, Ammon itself may have had a close relationship with Zobah.

The reference in 2 Sam 10:16 to forces from the far side of the Euphrates that were under Hadadezer's control may be substantiated in an inscription of Shalmaneser III, part of the annals for his third year (856 B.C.E.). This inscription states that Shalmaneser had recovered the city of Pitru (Pethor), which had been captured previously by 'the king of Aram' (*šar*$_4$ KUR *a-ru-mu*) during the reign of Aššur-rabi II (ca. 1012–972). Since this king of Aram belongs to the same period as Hadadezer and David, it has been proposed that he was Hadadezer and that the inscription should be considered as evidence of the extent of his expansion into this area.[35] However, this proposal seems unlikely. There are no other Assyrian references to a land of Aram which might be identified with a state in southern Syria, the location of Zobah. In fact, Assyrian inscriptions from the eleventh and tenth centuries clearly refer to a land of Aram centered in Upper Mesopotamia,[36] and, since Pitru was also located in that region, it is more likely that this Aram, not Zobah, was the Aram of Shalmaneser's inscription.

It was inevitable that the two expanding, vigorous states in Syria-Palestine would eventually clash. 2 Samuel 10 and its

[35] See Rawlinson 1861–70: 3. pl. 8, col. 2, lines 36–38. For a translation of this passage, see Luckenbill 1926–27: 1. #603. See Malamat 1973: 141–43; and Albright 1975b: 533.

[36] On the "Broken Obelisk," attributed to Aššur-bēl-kala (ca. 1074–1057) from the period shortly before the time of Aššur-rabi II, the land of Aram (KUR *A-ri-mi*) is clearly located in the area of Upper Mesopotamia, probably along the Upper Ḫābūr, perhaps as far north as Mt. Kašiari, east of present-day Mardin, Turkey. See Grayson 1972–76: 2. ##235–47. An inscription of Adad-nirāri II (ca. 911–891) speaks of a land of Arumu which had captured the city of Gidara (somewhere in the area of Ḫanigalbat in Upper Mesopotamia) during the reign of Tiglath-Pileser II (ca. 966–35), some years after Zobah's power had been broken by David. In this text it is clear that the area called the land of Aram is located somewhere around Ḫanigalbat. See Seidmann 1935: 20, lines 50–54. There is no reason to look beyond this region for the

parallel 1 Chronicles 19 state that the conflict began with the outbreak of hostilities between Ammon and Israel. David had sent an embassy to Rabbath-Ammon, officially to "console" the new king, Hanun, with regard to the death of his father, Nahash. Hanun, however, regarded the embassy as a spying operation, treated the men shamefully, and sent them away. This gross insult provoked David into declaring war on Ammon, and the Ammonites were not surprised at this turn of events. 2 Sam 10:6 states that Ammon 'hired' (וישכרו) the Aramaeans of Zobah and Beth Rehob, together with the kings of Maacah and of Tob, but it is more likely that Ammon was (or was offering to become) a vassal of Hadadezer and that Hadadezer found this an appropriate time to deal with his upstart southern neighbor. For David, as for Hadadezer, control of Ammon would be an important factor toward control of the caravan trade that moved through Transjordan, up the King's Highway from Arabia.[37]

When Joab arrived at Rabbath-Ammon at the head of the Israelite army, he was surprised to discover the Aramaean army on the plain of Madeba (1 Chr 19:7), ready to attack his rear, while the Ammonite army was prepared for battle nearer the capital city. Joab divided his army, putting his best men against the Aramaeans and setting the others, under his brother Abishai, to fight against the Ammonites. The battle was indecisive; the Israelites pushed back the two armies but returned to Jerusalem (2 Sam 10:9–14).[38]

It was apparent that the Ammonite War was not over, and the Aramaeans were not ready to accept the status quo.

---

location of the Aram which captured Pitru during the reign of Aššur-rabi.

The extent of Zobah's influence in northern Syria may have been much less than is usually portrayed. 2 Sam 8:10 suggests that Hamath had remained an independent rival of its southern neighbor. If this passage is reliable, Zobah's relations with the states beyond Hamath are more likely to have been through alliance rather than domination.

[37] For a description of the King's Highway, the important trade route from Arabia through Transjordan to Damascus, see Aharoni 1979: 54–57. Rabbath-Ammon was at the key spot where the two parallel roads through the southern Transjordanian plateau merged into a single road as it headed north.

[38] Yadin (1955:343–51) has some excellent insights into the course of this battle and the succeeding one at Helam.

Hadadezer mustered a fresh army, including contingents from some of the Aramaean states in Aram Naharaim across the Euphrates. This large force began its journey southward toward Ammon but was met by the army of Israel under the direct command of David himself. The two armies fought at the site of Helam, the location of which is unknown, and the army of the Aramaeans, under the leadership of the general Shobach, was decisively defeated by David. This proved disastrous for Hadadezer—a number of his vassals immediately sued for peace with David and switched their allegiance to Israel (2 Sam 10:15–19). But it appears that Hadadezer himself managed to retain control of Zobah.

2 Sam 8:3–8 and its parallel, 1 Chr 18:3–8, give an account of a battle between David and Hadadezer which, according to 1 Chr 18:3, took place near Hamath, and in which Hadadezer was decisively defeated. Some have considered this description to be only another version of the battle described in 2 Sam 10:15–19 (the Battle of Helam).[39] Others have pointed out the many differences in the reports of the battles found in the two accounts and have noted how well the story in 2 Samuel 8 seems to fit a schema in which it follows the events of 2 Samuel 10.[40] It is likely that the latter reconstruction is correct and that the battle described in 2 Samuel 8 took place after the Battle of Helam.

In 2 Samuel 8, the decisive defeat of Hadadezer is presented as a surprise attack on his army by David, who took advantage of a march by Hadadezer's forces to the area of the Euphrates, apparently to suppress a revolt among his vassals there. If 1 Chr 18:3 is correct in locating the site of the battle near Hamath on the Orontes, then David had led his troops north, perhaps straight through Hadadezer's own land in the Biqâ^c, thus bypassing Damascus, which was still allied to Zobah. The defeat of the Aramaean force was decisive. David captured a large number of prisoners and chariotry; apparently not yet aware of the value of a chariot corps, he hamstrung most of the chariot horses. He also took booty from Hadadezer and from two of his

[39] See, for example, Eissfeldt 1965: 276; 1960: 371–72; Noth 1960: 194–96.

[40] See especially Noordtzij 1907: 16–21. Also see O'Callaghan 1948: 127–30; Kraeling 1918: 41–45; M. F. Unger 1957: 49–51, and 139, n 15; Bright 1972: 197–99.

cities, which David had apparently captured, perhaps on his journey north before the battle (2 Sam 8:7–8).

At this point Damascus first appears in the narratives of David's Syrian Wars. The Aramaeans of Damascus, according to 2 Sam 8:5, sent troops to aid Hadadezer in the conflict, but the wording of this passage implies that they fought a distinct battle, presumably after David had defeated Hadadezer. They were roundly defeated by the Israelite army, and David took control of the city of Damascus and put garrisons there.[41] So Damascus became part of the territory directly controlled by Israel, not just as a vassal state, but as an occupied territory, perhaps under an Israelite governor.

A. Malamat has suggested that Damascus was under the control of a governor appointed by Hadadezer before David took over the city. He notes that there is no mention in the text of a king of Damascus, unlike the situation for Maacah and Tob.[42] Malamat believes that this is because Damascus had the status of a conquered territory rather than a vassal state even under Hadadezer, who had removed the local king and replaced him with a governor. Thus, when David conquered the territory, he maintained the same style of administration, replacing Hadadezer's governor with his own.[43] While this suggestion is plausible, the small amount of evidence from 2 Samuel is not enough to support the conclusion drawn.

What does emerge clearly is the impression that during the reigns of Hadadezer and David Damascus was still of minor political importance. Zobah and Israel were the major powers in the area, and Damascus was merely a subject state of one or the other. But its importance was increasing, primarily because it was at one of the hubs of several trade routes leading north-

[41] The word translated 'garrisons' (נצבים) is somewhat ambiguous. In the singular, it normally means, 'governor, deputy'. In the passage under discussion, Mazar translates the word 'governors' (1962: 104). However, it is a bit awkward to refer to multiple governors in Damascus, thus 'garrisons' or 'garrison troops' fits the context better.

[42] It should be noted that there is no mention of the king of Tob, unless one were to take איש in the phrase איש טוב, translated above 'the men of Tob', to mean 'king', like *awīlum* in Akkadian. This does not appear to have been an Israelite usage; thus, Malamat's argument from silence is already seriously weakened.

[43] Malamat 1963: 5.

south from Arabia to northern Syria, as well as east-west from the Mediterranean coast in the direction of Tadmor and on to Mesopotamia.[44] In fact, control of the trade routes was probably one of the major factors in the conflict between Zobah and Israel; after the defeat of Zobah, Israel could and did establish firm control over several of the important routes. The strategic trade route from Arabia, through Edom, Moab, and Ammon, which led on to Damascus (the King's Highway) came under Israelite control as a result of David's wars (2 Sam 8:2, 6, 12, 14) and Solomon no doubt exploited this control quite extensively during his reign.[45]

Thus, Damascus became part of the empire of David, one of the most extensive empires ever put together by a Syro-Palestinian ruler. To the north, David was lord over Zobah (although the exact political status of this area within the kingdom is not known)[46] which probably extended to the plain of Ḥoms. Hamath was either a vassal state[47] or at least a friendly ally.[48] The rest of southern Syria was under Israelite sovereignty, either through vassal relationships or through direct control. Transjordan had been slowly subdued, so that Maacah, Geshur, Ammon, Moab, and Edom were subject to David (2 Sam 8:2, 12–14; 12:26–31). The Philistines and the Canaanite cities within the area of Israel proper were also now under control (2 Sam 8:1). This empire, however, was temporary, and by the end of the reign of David's successor, Solomon, much of the territory had regained its independence or fallen under other spheres of influence.

DAMASCUS DURING THE REIGN OF SOLOMON

Although the reign of Solomon was in many ways the peak of Israelite political power, it also contained the beginning of the collapse that would take place shortly after Solomon's death. During his reign, Solomon had to face some challenges to his control at the farther ends of his empire. According to 2 Chr

[44] See Aharoni 1979: 53, 54.

[45] See Albright 1969: 128–31.

[46] Malamat (1963: 2–4) offers a good discussion of the political status of Zobah, both before and after David's Syrian Wars.

[47] See Malamat 1963: 6–8, and Malamat 1958: 100–101.

[48] See Noth 1960: 196.

8:3–4, Solomon was able to maintain control in central Syria well enough, during the early part of his reign, to fortify the oasis of Tadmor, a key town on the trade route from southern Syria to Mesopotamia,[49] as well as some store cities in the land of Hamath.

But sometime during his long reign, rebellions began to occur which Solomon does not seem to have been able to suppress. 1 Kings 11 describes three of the most dangerous rebels. Hadad, a member of the Edomite royal family who had escaped from Edom when David conquered the area, was able to return home, with the support of the Egyptian pharaoh, sometime during the course of Solomon's reign (1 Kgs 11:14–22). Egypt was also involved in supporting unrest among the northern tribes of Israel when Pharaoh Shoshenq I gave asylum to Jeroboam, the son of Nebat, who seems to have been plotting against the throne during Solomon's reign (1 Kgs 11:26–40).

Unrest was not confined to the area of Palestine. 1 Kgs 11:23–24 tells of Rezon, the son of Elyada (רזון בן אלידע), a servant of Hadadezer of Zobah who broke away from him, gathered about him a band of malcontents much in the way that David had done in his early days, went to Damascus, and seized it. Rezon was declared king there[50] and withdrew Damascus from the Israelite sphere. No response to this event by Solomon and the Israelite army is recorded. If there was one, it was

[49] The reading of Tadmor is problematic, since the parallel reading in 1 Kgs 9:18 is תמר, not תדמר. Support for תדמר as the original reading in Kings comes from the Lucianic recension of the LXX. The entire passage 1 Kgs 9:15–25 is found in a different location in most manuscripts of the LXX (Ax have the section in the MT position), following 1 Kgs 10:22. The Lucianic manuscripts oc_2e_2 read θοδμορ (b has δοθδμορ) rather than a form of Tamar (manuscript B and the majority read ιεθερμαθ). This shows that the Tadmor reading belongs to an early and strong manuscript tradition and is not merely a manipulation of the Chronicler.

[50] This follows the Lucianic recension of the LXX (actually, $boc_2e_2 + gh^buv$), which reads και προκατελαβετο την δαμασκον και εκαθισεν εν αυτη και εβασιλευσεν εν δαμασκω, "And he seized Damascus and dwelt in it and became king in Damascus." The MT has plural rather than singular verbs here. This passage is not found at the same point in the text as in the MT. The LXX places it in the middle of 1 Kgs 11:14. This is one of many examples of a different ordering of episodes within the LXX of the Solomonic account.

clearly unsuccessful, since, according to 11:25, Rezon remained a problem for Israel throughout the reign of Solomon and briefly into the reign of his successor.

This turn of events in Damascus may have undermined Solomon's control of other areas in southern and central Syria; it is possible that many areas broke away as time went on. The severe shrinkage of the empire must have occurred fairly late in Solomon's reign, however, considering the reports of Solomon's power and wealth in 1 Kings 4–11.

Rezon's capture of Damascus cannot be precisely dated. Many place this event quite early in Solomon's reign and suggest that Solomon was able to maintain his northern trade connections by diverting the caravan route through the Biqâᶜ and bypassing Damascus.[51] The notice in 1 Kgs 11:23–24 also suggests that the capture took place fairly early in Solomon's reign, since v 25 says that Rezon "was an adversary of Israel all the days of Solomon." On the other hand, the language of this passage should not be pressed too far; it is more likely that the revolt of Damascus took place well along in Solomon's reign, as the entire empire began to weaken.[52]

The revolt of Damascus against Israel was the first step in the development of a new political power in Syria. Zobah, so powerful before its war with David, never recovered its political importance, and Damascus, under its rebellious chieftain, was now on the way to its era of glory and strength in Syria–Palestine. With the death of Solomon, Israel's period of dominance came to an end, and Damascus began its political ascendancy.

[51] See, for example, Aharoni 1979: 307, 319, n 54, in which Aharoni suggests that references to Solomon's fortification of towns in Zobah (he believes that the MT Hamath-Zobah should be emended, according to the LXX reading, Beth Zobah) and of Tadmor indicates that Solomon redirected the trade routes through Israelite territory so that they went through the Biqâᶜ rather than to Damascus. This seems possible. See also Noth 1960: 206, and Eissfeldt 1975: 587.

[52] Mazar (1962: 104) and M. F. Unger (1957: 54) take this view.

ARAM-DAMASCUS FROM REZON TO THE USURPATION OF HAZAEL (ca. 931–844/42 B.C.E.) —— FIVE

AFTER THE DISSOLUTION of the Israelite empire at the end of Solomon's reign and the division of the kingdom into two small rival states came a period when there was no major power in Syria-Palestine. Rezon and his successors, however, seem to have worked vigorously to make Damascus a significant presence in the area. By the mid-ninth century, Damascus was the capital of what was perhaps the most powerful state in the Levant, a state now called "Aram" by its inhabitants, a unified Aram, the name of which required no additional modifiers. Under the powerful Hadad-ᶜid̲r (namesake of the earlier king of Zobah) Damascus became the leading state in a broad coalition of western and southern Syrian states that opposed Assyrian military expansion during a period from 853 to 845 B.C.E.; but in spite of its influence, the areas under Damascus' actual political control were not extensive. To the north, Hamath maintained a considerable strength, thus limiting Damascus' northern expansion. To the south, Israel was often hard-pressed by the Aramaeans but, during the period under discussion in this chapter, maintained its independence. To the west, the Phoenician city-states also remained free of Damascene control.

The sources of information for the period from the time of Rezon to the usurpation of the throne of Damascus by Hazael ca. 844/42 B.C.E. are, especially at first glance, fuller than any sources available for previous periods. Extensive descriptions of relations between Damascus and Israel are recorded in the books of Kings and Chronicles, as well as in the inscriptions of Shalmaneser III, whose campaigns in western Syria brought him face to face with Hadad-ᶜid̲r and his coalition. Further, the one stela attributed to the royal house of Damascus, found near Aleppo and called the Melqart or Bir-Hadad Stela, may be dated to this period. However, there is less information about this century than at first appears, since much of the biblical material attributed to the period of the Omride Dynasty must actually be placed chronologically in the days of the Jehu Dynasty, and a new reading of the Bir-Hadad Stela suggests that it has no relation to Aram–Damascus.

As in the previous periods, nothing that approaches a full history for this period can be reconstructed. Again, there is virtually no information about the internal affairs of the kingdom of Aram and its capital Damascus. Again, there are no sources from the country itself—only texts from states which for some reason or other came into contact with Damascus and left brief written accounts of those contacts. These sources provide some idea of Damascus' role in international affairs without, however, giving a rounded picture of the situation. The following discussion moves in chronological order through what may be learned of Damascus during this turbulent century.

THE SUCCESSORS OF REZON

The problem of the royal succession in Damascus during the latter part of the tenth century is difficult, owing to the sparsity of sources. Data for this period come from two passages in 1 Kings: 11:23–24 (already mentioned in the previous chapter), which recounts the establishment of the independent kingdom of Damascus by Rezon during the reign of Solomon, and 15:18, which introduces the king Bir-Hadad I (the Hebraized version of the name is Ben-Hadad), who had dealings with Asa of Judah and Baasha of Israel, and who is described as בן טברמן בן חזיון מלך ארם הישב בדמשק, 'the son of Tab-Rimmon, the son of Hezion, king of Aram, who dwelt (or: was enthroned) in Damascus'.

Part of the complication about the succession has arisen because of the possibility, discussed in scholarly literature since the end of the nineteenth century,[1] that the Rezon of 1 Kings 11 and the Hezion, grandfather of Bir-Hadad I, may be the same person. This suggestion seems to have first arisen because of the reading of the name of the ruler in 11:23–25 in the LXX (11:14 in the LXX). The Lucianic (boc_2e_2) manuscripts read the name 'Εσρων (B and others have 'Εσρωμ). This could be understood as reflecting Hebrew חזרון, and it was suggested by some scholars in the nineteenth century that the names Rezon and Hezion were both merely corruptions of the original name, Hezron.[2] This particular idea has long since been discarded, but the suggestion that the two names are somehow related and that they both are connected to the same person has continued to flourish.

Kraeling thought that the original name in 1 Kings 11 was Hezion and that the form Rezon was secondary.[3] Unger followed Kraeling, suggesting that the corruption came through confusion of the name with the later Aramaean king, Rezin.[4] Mazar identified the two by suggesting that Hezion was the ruler's real name, while Rezon, a name that is related to the root *rzn*, with a derived noun *rāzôn* and participle *rōzēn*, both meaning 'ruler', was his throne name.[5] Malamat suggested that the two forms are merely phonetic variants of the same name and are thus identical.[6] Not everyone, however, has been convinced that these two names refer to the same person; Dupont-Sommer assumed that they are names of two individuals,[7] as did W. F. Albright.[8]

[1] Kraeling 1918: 48, n 2.

[2] Jepsen 1941–45: 153, n 3.

[3] Kraeling 1918: 48–49.

[4] M. F. Unger 1957: 56–57. This suggestion is hardly feasible, since in Hebrew Rezon and Rezin are not closely related at all, the former spelled רזון, the latter רצין, from two very different roots, unlikely to cause the kind of confusion Unger suggests.

[5] Mazar 1962: 104. This has been accepted by Gray (1970: 353) as most likely.

[6] Malamat 1973: 151–52, n 23. This theory will be discussed below, along with the etymology of Ḥeziôn.

[7] Dupont-Sommer 1949: 29, 33.

[8] See Albright 1975b: 534–35, where Rezon is called "an otherwise unknown Aramaean chieftain."

The best way to approach this problem is to examine the evidence that has been adduced for identifying these two names with a single person. The name in 1 Kgs 11:23 is found in the LXX as Ἐσρωμ, Lucianic Ἐσρων. However, the manuscript evidence for names in the Greek versions suggests that LXX renditions are highly variable and unreliable and therefore must be used very carefully in the case of a rare name, perhaps only as supplementary evidence.[9] In the case at hand, there is little reason to connect Greek Ἐσρων with an original Hebrew חזרון, since the latter name does not even appear among biblical Hebrew or Aramaic proper names. Nor may the Greek version's form be connected more closely with Hezion than with Rezon since, even though the Greek version may reflect the consonant order to Hezion, it also contains the three consonants of Rezon, although in a different order. The evidence here is certainly too ambiguous to base a significant hypothesis upon it, although it might be used as secondary support if other evidence warranted the suggestion.

A second piece of evidence commonly suggested as support for identifying the owners of these two names involves the assumption that the genealogy of Bir-Hadad I in 1 Kgs 15:18 is the complete list of kings from the founding of the Damascene state to Bir-Hadad, and that it should therefore name as its first member the rebel who broke away from Solomon. Unger, for instance, describes the succession in 1 Kgs 15:18 as follows:

> The biblical list, confirmed by the Benhadad inscription, thus gives us the first dynasty of Syrian kings who ruled from Damascus, and Hezion is the correct name of the first king. . . . Although the correct name of the first king of Damascus has been settled by the new extra-biblical evidence, the problem of the identity of Rezon, who seized Damascus during Solomon's administration and apparently ruled there, is still unsolved. Is Hezion identical with Rezon? If so, the form Rezon is secondary, and is to be regarded as a corruption of Hezion, probably having been confounded with Rezin, a later king of Damascus in the

---

[9] On the types of errors common in the LXX transcription of proper names, see Wutz 1933: 9–36. Note the examples of metathesis on p. 30. The name Ἐσρων appears elsewhere in the LXX for Hebrew חצרון, (son of Perez): cf. Ruth 4:18; 1 Chr 1:5, 9, 18. It is not likely that this name would be corrupted into Rezon or Hezion, since the root is different.

> time of Tiglathpileser III. If this proves to be incorrect, which seems to be unlikely, then Rezon, of course, must be considered as excluded from the dynastic list of I Kings xv, 18, which is improbable in view of the fact that he was clearly the founder of the powerful Damascene state.[10]

Kraeling comments similarly: "In 1 Kings 15:18 there appears to be preserved the succession of the kings in Damascus; the order given is Hezion—Tabrimmon—Benhadad. Apparently Hezion is identical with Rezon."[11] Mazar also assumes that the earliest name on the list, Hezion, was the founder of the dynasty.[12]

This assumption has no firm basis. The genealogy of 15:18 need not be a complete list of the kings of Damascus from the gaining of its independence, nor a complete list of the dynasty, even if the dynasty came to power after Rezon. The use of two patronyms to identify a king was common practice in first millennium Syria-Palestine, and this verse follows that practice; it was not intended to be a complete listing of the dynasty. One may note this practice, for example, in the inscription of Šipṭi-Baᶜl, the Yeḥawmilk inscription, and the Ammonite Tell Sīrān inscription.[13] There is no reason to assume that the kings mentioned in these inscriptions belonged to the third generation of their dynasties. Similarly, kings who identified themselves with only one patronym were not necessarily the second kings of their dynasties.[14] This argument must be discarded.

The chronology of the period presents no problems that would be solved by identifying Rezon and Hezion. 1 Kgs 11:25 implies that Rezon reigned during much of Solomon's era and perhaps survived Solomon's death, ca. 931, but he apparently died soon thereafter. Bir-Hadad I, the next king of Damascus for whom a synchronism (the reigns of Asa and Baasha) exists,

[10] M. F. Unger 1957: 56–57.

[11] Kraeling 1918: 48–49.

[12] Mazar 1962: 104.

[13] For the inscriptions of Šipṭi-Baᶜl and Yeḥawmilk, see *KAI* 7 and 10, respectively. On the Tell Sīrān inscription, see Thompson and Zayadine 1973: 5–11. Shalmaneser III also regularly used two patronyms in his inscriptions. Cf., for example, Michel 1947–52: 57, lines 5–6; the Monolith Inscription, I:11. Cf. Schrader 1889: 1.152, for a transliteration of this line.

[14] See, for example, the Mēšaᶜ Stela (*KAI* 181), ᵓEšmun-ᶜazor (*KAI* 14), and Kilamuwa (*KAI* 24).

need not have ascended the throne any earlier than ca. 900, and perhaps not until a decade or so beyond that (Baasha's reign may be placed at ca. 910–887).[15] This allows between thirty and forty years to be filled by rulers of Damascus. Therefore, there is sufficient time for at least two rulers to follow Rezon on the throne, namely, Hezion and Tab-Rimmon. Hezion may in fact have been the son of Rezon.[16]

No other evidence has been mustered in support of identifying Hezion and Rezon. There is neither any compelling evidence for this identification nor any compelling problem which such a hypothesis would solve. Therefore, barring new evidence, it is reasonable to assume that Rezon and Hezion were two distinct rulers of Damascus.

THE ETYMOLOGY OF ḤEZIÔN

The etymology of the name Ḥeziôn has created some controversy and cannot be determined with certainty. Two plausible etymologies have much to recommend them.

Albright was the first to point out that Hebrew/Aramaic Ḥeziôn could be cognate to the name of the father of the Aramaean king Kapara of Guzana (Tell Halaf in northern Syria), apparently a near contemporary of the Damascene Ḥeziôn, living during the late tenth century.[17] A number of cuneiform inscriptions from Tell Halaf begin with the following formula: É.GAL-*lim* [I]*Ka-pa-ra* A [I]*Ḫa-di-a-ni*, 'The palace of Kapara, the eldest son of Ḫadiānu'.[18] Albright believed that the name Ḫadiānu was cognate to Ḥeziôn and was an attempt by the

[15] This assumes the date of ca. 931 for the death of Solomon. Cf. Thiele 1965: 39–52. See also Cross 1972b: 17, n 11.

[16] Albright suggested another interpretation of the epithet, *ben-Ḥeziôn*. It is possible that the term does not refer to Bir-Hadad's grandfather, but to the tribe to which the dynasty belonged (Albright 1975b: 534–35). It was suggested above that the epithet *ben-Rĕḥōb* of Hadadezer, the king of Zobah, may have been such an epithet, in this case referring to his relationship with Beth-Rehob. Similarly, it is possible to translate 15:18: "Ben-Hadad, the son of Ṭab-Rammān, the Hezionite, king of Aram." However, it is more likely that the reference here is to the king's grandfather, like the usage noted above in the inscriptions of Yeḥawmilk, Šipṭibaᶜl, and ᶜAmminadab of Ammon.

[17] See Albright 1942: 26, n 7; 1975b: 528.

[18] See Meissner 1933.

scribe to vocalize Aramaic *ḫaḏyān*. The latter would be spelled *ḥzyn* in Old Aramaic script, just as it is in 1 Kgs 15:18. While in standard Akkadian transcription, etymological *ḏ* was normally written with *z*, there is nothing unusual for a name like *Ḫaḏyān* to be written with a *d* for *ḏ* in an area such as Guzana, where Aramaic, not Akkadian, was the primary language. Albright also noted that the name *ḫdyn* appeared at Ugarit and identified it with the two above-mentioned names. The Ugaritic form appeared to stem phonetically from an original *ḫḏyn*, since *ḏ* had virtually merged with *d* at Ugarit. Taking these three names as cognates, Albright suggested that the name comes from the root *ḫḏw* or *ḫḏy* and that the Arabic cognate *ḫaḏwāʾ* 'a person with pendulous ears' provided a probable meaning for it.[19]

Several factors cast some doubt on this proposed etymology. First, the Ugaritic *ḫdyn* may no longer be considered as a cognate. An Akkadian text from Ras Šamra, RS 11.787, lists the man who appears in alphabetic cuneiform texts as *bn ḫdyn* (cf. *CTA* 87.8; 122.1.18; 113.6.11) as DUMU *ḫu-di-ya-na*.[20] Gröndahl identifies the *ḫud-* element of the name as the Hurrian element *ḫute* 'to mark, to write', and if this is correct there can be no connection between the Ugaritic name and Ḫadiānu and Ḥeziôn.[21] Second, the name Ḫadiānu from Guzana may be related to the verb *ḫdy* 'to rejoice', the original consonants of which are *ḫdy*; if true, the name Ḫadiānu could have no connection to Ḥeziôn. With these considerations in mind, Albright's suggestion may be considered viable though clearly not certain.

The other major possibility for an etymology of Ḥeziôn is to relate it to the root *ḥzy* 'to see'. This appears to be much more likely than Albright's proposal, since *ḥzy* is a common element in West Semitic names. Ḥeziôn, then, may be understood as a hypochoristic of a name probably of the form *ḥazā*-DN, '(The god) saw'. In fact, a name of this type is attested among Aramaic names from Damascus, *viz.*, the name of the ninth century king, Ḥazā-ʾēl.

A third proposal was made recently by Malamat in the course of an argument for identifying Hezion and Rezon. He

[19] Albright 1942: 26, n 7.

[20] Virolleaud 1941: 10–11.

[21] See Gröndahl 1967: 233. In any case, the *u*-vowel in the name creates serious difficulties for maintaining a connection with the other two names.

related Ḥeziôn to the Akkadian noun *ḫazan(n)u* 'mayor' and suggested that the two names Hezion and Rezon are variants of the same name. He referred to B. Landsberger's proposal that there was a phonetic change (in Hebrew?) of *ḥet* to *reš* in some cases, and that Akkadian *ḫazan(n)u* 'mayor, city official' and Hebrew *rāzôn, rōzēn* 'ruler' are cognates. "Thus," says Malamat, "Hezion—like Rezon—could simply mean 'potentate' or the like."[22] He also points out that a personal name, *ḫaziānu*, appears in Neo-Assyrian texts, and he relates it to the noun for 'mayor'. However, this proposed phonetic shift is of dubious validity, and it is not necessary to relate the personal name *ḫaziānu* (or *ḫazânu*), which appears in texts from the Ur III to the Neo-Babylonian period,[23] to the word for 'mayor'. It is likely that both forms are hypochoristics, like Ḥeziôn, related to the root *ḥzy* and not specifically related to *ḫazan(n)u* 'mayor'.[24]

It seems probable that the name Ḥeziôn is a hypochoristic (with the *-a̱nu* > -ōn in the Hebraized version of 1 Kgs 15:18), most likely from the root *ḥzy*, and probably pronounced something like *Ḥazyān* in Aramaic. However, Albright's suggestion of relating it to *ḫḏw/y* cannot be entirely discarded, particularly in view of a recently discovered but as yet unpublished Neo-Assyrian stela found at Pazarcik, Turkey, dating to the reign of Shalmaneser IV; it mentions a Ḫadiānu as ruler of Aram Damascus in 773 B.C.E. Since royal names often were repeated, this eighth century ruler's name may have been the same as that of the tenth century king called Hezion in 1 Kings; the stela would then support Albright's etymology. Of course, the same ambiguities about the etymology of Ḫadiānu mentioned above still apply to this new evidence—it cannot be determined whether the name is related to *ḫḏw/y* or *ḫdy* and therefore

[22] Malamat 1973: 151–52, n 23.

[23] Cf. *CAD* Ḫ: 165. Albright, in considering this etymology, also connected a name from Egyptian sources, *ḥṯyn* (*ḥa-ṯi-ya-na*), with the Akkadian names (1942: 26, n 7).

[24] It appears that the word for 'mayor' was originally of unknown etymology, written *ḫazannu* in the Ur III period. Later, it seems to have been reinterpreted as coming from the Semitic root *ḥzy* and understood in the sense of 'overseer'. But the re-etymologization from the same root as the name *ḫaziānu* does not mean that the two had the same meaning. See Gelb 1968: 101; and *CAD* H: 165.

whether it is in fact the same name as biblical Hezion. The question remains open.[25]

ṬAB-RAMMĀN

The only information available about the successor of Hezion is his name, though its etymology is more straightforward. He is mentioned only in 1 Kgs 15:18, where he is called *Ṭab-Rimmōn*. The vocalization of the second element is certainly wrong: *rimmōn* is the Hebrew word for 'pomegranate'. *Rammān*, on the other hand, is a well-known epithet of the storm god Hadad, and it is clear from 2 Kgs 5:18 that it was the characteristic epithet of Hadad of Damascus, who was the patron deity of the city.[26] It is derived from the verb *ramāmu* (as it appears in Akkadian) meaning 'to thunder'. It is a natural epithet for Hadad ('the thundering one') and the root occurs in Akkadian texts as well as in this name.[27] Thus, the name of this king of Damascus means 'Rammān is good'.

BIR–HADAD I

The first concrete historical information about the kingdom of Damascus after Rezon comes from the early ninth century, when Bir-Hadad I, son of Ṭab-Rammān, king of Damascus, becomes involved in a boundary war between Israel and Judah. The only source of information about this incident is 1 Kgs 15:16–22 and its parallel, 2 Chr 16:1–6.

Sometime during his reign, Baasha of Israel attempted to fortify Ramah, a site on the southern boundary of Israel now identified with the Arab village of er-Ram, ca. 5.5 miles north of Jerusalem,[28] in order to stop or at least control travel on the main north–south route to and from Jerusalem. This threat,

[25] The Pazarcik stela is to be published by Kemal Balkan. Preliminarily, see Hawkins 1982: 401, 404–5. The proper name Ḫaziānu, Ḫazânu, in the Akkadian texts could reflect the first etymology (i.e., from *ḫḏw/y*), as well as the second one. Etymological *ḏ* was normally transcribed with a *z* in Akkadian. Thus *ḫaḏyan* would come into standard Akkadian as *ḫaziānu*.

[26] Cf. 2 Kgs 5:17–18. On the god Rammān, see Greenfield 1976.

[27] Cf. *AHw* 949; and Greenfield 1976: 196–97.

[28] Cf. Aharoni and Avi-Yonah 1968: map 123 and p. 182.

which King Asa of Judah appears to have been powerless to oppose, created considerable consternation in Jerusalem, so that Asa gathered together what wealth was still in the temple and palace treasuries[29] and sent it to Bir-Hadad in Damascus. Asa's message to Bir-Hadad, as preserved, begins somewhat ambiguously, ברית ביני ובינך בין אבי ובין אביך (1 Kgs 15:19). This may be translated, "There is a covenant between me and you, as between my father and your father," although it is possible that the first phrase should be taken as optative, "Let there be a covenant between me and you."[30] The translation ambiguity leads directly to a problem in interpretation. Was Asa attempting to prompt Bir-Hadad to live up to a covenant that already existed, or was he trying to reinstate a relationship that had ceased to exist? The message clearly indicates that there was some sort of treaty relationship between Damascus and Judah during the previous generation of kings, although it is not certain what kind of covenant it was. Perhaps it was a mutual aid treaty against Israel. The fact that Asa sent an expensive gift to Bir-Hadad does not settle the argument, since a gift like this could certainly be sent in both situations—if there were no active treaty between the two, in order to encourage Bir-Hadad to make one, or, if there were a treaty, to ensure that Bir-Hadad would honor it.

According to v 19, Bir-Hadad also had a treaty with Baasha; unfortunately, it is not clear what kind of treaty this was nor whether it would have allowed a continuing treaty between Damascus and Judah. Thus, the meaning of the opening phrase of 15:19 remains ambiguous.

At any rate, Bir-Hadad did not hesitate to break his treaty with Israel. He attacked most of Israel's land north of the Sea of Galilee, destroying a number of important towns, "Iyon, Dan, Abel-beth-Maacah, and all of Kinneroth, over all the land of Naphtali" (15:20). Significant destruction layers have been found at both Dan and Hazor (one of the major cities within the borders of Naphtali) which may be attributed to the campaign of Bir-Hadad. At Dan the destruction of the sacred area attributed to the building activity of Jeroboam I, Bamah A, fits into

[29] Judah's wealth had been severely deplenished in the fifth year of Rehoboam, due to Shoshenq's plundering of Judah. See 1 Kgs 14:25–28.

[30] Cf. *GK* 141f.

this time-frame.[31] At Hazor, it was the destruction of Stratum IX, intermediate between Solomonic Stratum X and Omride Stratum VIII, that appears to be evidence for this campaign.[32] This ploy by Asa worked—Baasha withdrew immediately from Ramah, but what terms Baasha reached with Bir-Hadad are not known.[33]

The land thus captured by Bir-Hadad was quite valuable, since through it went important trade routes to the coastal cities of Sidon, Tyre, Achzib, and Akko.[34] How much of this land remained in Bir-Hadad's hands after the campaign is uncertain, since no information is available on this point. However, control of this area by Aram did not last long; archaeological evidence from Hazor and Dan suggests that these two towns were back in Israelite hands by the time of Ahab, perhaps as early as fifteen years later. At both of these sites, public buildings with the architectural styles and building techniques similar to those of Ahab's building projects at Samaria and Megiddo have been uncovered.[35] However long the land was held, it is certain that the entire affair greatly profited Bir-Hadad, since he had gained territory (however temporarily) from one state with minimal military hardship (after all, Baasha had been concentrating on affairs at the southern end of his kingdom when Bir-Hadad attacked), while at the same time he had received a handsome gift from another state, as well as possibly other concessions for his actions.

There has been considerable controversy about the date of this incident, stemming from the incongruities which arise from

[31] Biran 1980: 175.

[32] See Yadin 1972: 142–46.

[33] The account of Baasha's response to the attack (1 Kgs 15:21 and 2 Chr 16:5) is ambiguous in the extreme. Baasha abandoned Ramah and, according to Kings, returned to Tirzah. No more is said. The Chronicles version of this verse is even more ambiguous. Instead of וישב בתרצה, it reads וישבת את־מלאכתו, 'and he ceased his work'.

[34] Cf. Aharoni and Avi-Yonah 1968: map 10. Cf. also Gray 1970: 354; and Kraeling 1918: 49–50.

[35] For Hazor, see Yadin 1972: 165 (city wall), 167 (postern gate), 169–72 (the citadel). For Dan, see Biran 1980: 175–77, where the excavator attributes the impressive fortification system of Iron II to the time of Ahab, as well as the second phase of the Israelite "High Place" (Bamah B).

the date that appears in the Chronicles account (2 Chr 16:1). There, Baasha's aggression is dated to the thirty-sixth year of the reign of Asa. This, however, contradicts the system of synchronisms found in the books of Kings, where Elah, the son of Baasha, is said to have succeeded to the throne after Baasha's death in the twenty-sixth year of Asa's reign (1 Kgs 16:8). Albright was skeptical about the synchronisms in the books of Kings and was convinced that the Chronicler had a reliable document before him when he dated this incident.[36] By accepting this date, Albright faced an alternate problem, explaining how Asa's thirty-sixth year could be the same as Baasha's twenty-fourth and final regnal year. His solution was to suggest that Rehoboam's reign was exaggerated and should be shortened by nine years.[37] Albright was required, then, to assume that the incident occurred in the last year of Baasha's reign; an earlier date would require a further reduction in the length of Rehoboam's reign. But there is no evidence that the incident occurred so late.[38]

Albright supported the accuracy of the date in 2 Chr 16:1 by his reading of the Bir-Hadad Inscription. Albright believed that this inscription, on a stela found north of Aleppo, was set up by Bir-Hadad I, and he read the second line of the inscrip-

[36] Albright 1945: 18–19.

[37] Albright 1945: 20, n 14.

[38] Thiele (1965: 59–60) dates this incident to the sixteenth year of Asa's reign, i.e., the thirteenth year of Baasha. He suggests that Baasha's fortification at Ramah was in response to the great festival that Asa celebrated in his fifteenth year, according to 2 Chr 15:9–15. V 9 in fact mentions the presence of numerous persons from the northern kingdom at this ceremony.

Thiele explains the reference to the thirty-fifth and thirty-sixth years in 2 Chr 15:19 and 16:1, respectively, as referring to the thirty-fifth and -sixth years after the disruption of the monarchy, rather than the years of Asa's reign. Since Rehoboam ruled seventeen years and Abijam three, the thirty-sixth year after the disruption would be Asa's sixteenth, the year following the great festival in Jerusalem. Pavlovsky and Vogt (1964: 329–30) also place the incident in Asa's sixteenth year. Thiele, Pavlovsky, and Vogt all point out that the great festival provides a logical background for the actions of Baasha, and this proposal should be kept in mind by those considering Albright's assumption that the incident took place at the end of Baasha's reign. However, it is also important to recognize that the suggestion of Thiele and Pavlovsky

tion, which gives the ancestry of Bir-Hadad, "the son of Ṭab-Rammān, the son of Ḥeziōn." Because the epigraphy of the inscription placed it in the middle of the ninth century, during the Omride Dynasty in Israel, Albright concluded that the Bir-Hadad who fought with Ahab and Joram (1 Kings 20–2 Kings 8) must be the same as the Bir-Hadad who was the son of Ṭab-Rammān of the time of Baasha. Following the chronology implied by the books of Kings, Bir-Hadad would have been ruler of Damascus for some fifty years, a rather doubtful circumstance considering the vigorous activities he carried on at the end of his reign. If the Chronicles date is accepted, his reign could be reduced to about forty years, not such an extraordinary length of time.[39] The identification of the Bir-Hadad of Asa's time with the one of Ahab and Joram's days relied entirely on Albright's interpretation of the Bir-Hadad inscription. But, as noted below, his reading of line two must now be discarded and, with it, the need to propose a single ruler in Damascus for the first half of the ninth century. Thus, Albright's use of the inscription to support his preference for the Chronicler's date is no longer viable.

The relative merits of the chronological systems of the Deuteronomistic History and the Chronicles account must be weighed if any conclusions about this problem are to be reached. If the synchronisms of Chronicles are trustworthy, then the synchronistic entries in Kings were artificially created by a historian working with faulty lists of the regnal lengths, producing an inaccurate picture. If the Kings chronology is accepted as reflecting in general the correct synchronistic history of the rulers, then some explanation of the incorrect dating system in

---

and Vogt is not conclusive. Another interpretation of the Chronicler's account of Asa's reign suggests that all of the dates in these chapters are artificial, and that the date of the festival is not certain (see below).

A date late in Baasha's reign does in part fit some aspects of the account found in 1 Kings 15 better. V 16 says that there was war between Asa and Baasha all their days. The story of Bir-Hadad's attack on Baasha, especially since it ends with defeat for Baasha, suggests that this event climaxed and brought to an end the struggles between the two kings, and thus that it occurred late in Baasha's reign. Unfortunately, these possibilities remain speculative.

[39] See Albright 1942: 27–28.

the story of Asa in 2 Chronicles must be found.[40] This is not an appropriate place to go into a full-scale analysis of the problem of the chronology of the kings of Israel and Judah, but a few points should be noted.

Albright's support of the Chronicler's dates was based in large part on his belief in the reliability of the non-Deuteronomistic elements in the books of Chronicles. As he says:

> In view of the fact that Chronicles contains a considerable amount of original material dealing with the history of Judah which is not found in Kings and that the historical value of this original material is being established by archaeological discoveries, we have no right to disregard the datings by regnal years of the kings of Judah which we find there, especially when they are as consistent and reasonable as, e.g., in the case of Asa.[41]

Others, however, have pointed out that the Chronicler has not in fact always been found to be reliable, and they have been much more reluctant to reject the basic validity of the chronological system found in Kings.[42] There are virtually no other independent synchronisms in Chronicles outside the story of Asa, and most have been reluctant to discard the system found in Kings on the basis of the one set of conflicting dates in 2 Chr 15:19 and 16:1, a position with which I agree.[43]

[40] Some have supported the Chronicles date. Cf. M. F. Unger 1957: 59; Richardson 1958: 10–11. Most, however, have preferred the Kings chronology. See, for example, Schedl 1962: 112; Pavlovsky and Vogt 1964: 329–30; Miller 1967a: 278–79; Thiele 1965: 59–62.

[41] Albright 1945: 18–19.

[42] Cf. Miller 1967a: 278–79.

[43] A few comments about the Kings chronology for the period from the disruption of the monarchy to the time of Baasha are appropriate. Two of the best studies of this period are Shenkel, 1968: 31–35; and Miller 1967a: 280–81. The problems in the chronology before the time of Baasha are rather minor (mainly connected with a difference in the length of the reign of Abijam between the MT and the LXX). But there is a divergence between the MT and the Greek texts about the reign of Baasha itself. With the exception of bic_2, the Greek texts agree with MT that Baasha became king in the third year of Asa (bic_2: fifth year) in 1 Kgs 15:33. They all agree with MT that he reigned for twenty-four years, although the OG and Lucianic recensions go on

If the Kings chronology is preferable, how then can the dates found in Chronicles be explained? It is doubtful that the Chronicles dates are simply errors that have crept into the text. Another possibility (discussed above, n 38) is that the dates refer not to Asa's thirty-fifth and thirty-sixth years, but to the thirty-fifth and thirty-sixth years from the disruption of the monarchy, and thus to Asa's fifteenth and sixteenth years and Baasha's twelfth and thirteenth years. Perhaps the most interesting suggestion has been made by W. Rudolph, who proposed that the Chronicler gave the dates recorded in the story of Asa for theological reasons.[44] According to Rudolph, there were two aspects of Asa's reign, unanswered in the Kings account, that the Chronicler had to explain according to his theology. (1) Since severe illness is a punishment for sin in the Chronicler's work, when and how did Asa, a pious king, sin such that Yahweh would punish him with a fatal disease? (2) Since piety guarantees peace in the Chronicler's theology, what is the explanation for the long war described in 1 Kgs 15:16?

In 1 Kgs 15:23, the illness is said to have occurred in Asa's old age. The Chronicler puts it in his thirty-ninth year. The grounds for the illness in Chronicles is the mistreatment of the prophet Hanani after the latter criticized the king for relying on the king of Damascus for aid, rather than on Yahweh. Thus, for the Chronicler, the war with Baasha became the theological explanation of the king's punishment with disease at the end of his life, and this event therefore must have occurred late in Asa's reign. The answer to the second problem is that the Chronicler has simply dropped out the notice of the long,

---

to contradict this by stating that Baasha died in the twentieth year of Asa (1 Kgs 16:6), thus giving him a reign of about eighteen years. Although Miller accepts the eighteen year reign suggested by these texts, it is more likely that the twenty-four year total is correct, since all the texts, including those which give the twentieth year death date, have the twenty-four year total for his reign.

None of this material supports the Chronicles date. If anything, the discrepancies suggest a shorter reign for Baasha, which would require supporters of the Chronicles date to abridge further the reigns of Rehoboam and Abijam, which could hardly be done.

[44] Rudolph 1952.

drawn-out war between Asa and Baasha. As a reward for his piety, Asa was given thirty-five years of peace (with one exception, 14:9–15). It is possible, then, that the presentation of Asa's reign in 2 Chronicles 14–16 has been influenced by the author's theology and that the placement of events, and therefore the dates of those events, are also influenced by his theology.

AHAB AND THE KINGS OF DAMASCUS

After the account of Bir-Hadad's attack on Israel during Baasha's reign, Damascus is not mentioned in 1 Kings until chap. 20, which gives an account of two battles between Israel and Aram–Damascus. The text of chap. 20, as it now exists, identifies the king of Israel in these stories as Ahab, son of Omri; the battles are presented as taking place late in Ahab's reign, four and three years, respectively, before the battle at Ramoth-Gilead (1 Kings 22) in which Ahab lost his life (cf. 22:1). At the same time the royal inscriptions of Shalmaneser III of Assyria provide another source of information about Damascus and Israel during the reign of Ahab. Shalmaneser faced a strong coalition including Damascus and Israel during his campaigns in western Syria.

For some time there has been considerable doubt that the picture of the relations between Damascus and Israel in the biblical accounts and that in the inscriptions of Shalmaneser can be reconciled. The famous Monolith Inscription, which describes Shalmaneser's battle with the Syrian coalition at Qarqar in his sixth year, describes Hadad-ᶜiḏr of Damascus, Irḫulena of Hamath, and Ahab of Israel as the three major allies who opposed him in the battle. Ahab, according to the monolith, supplied the allied army with 2,000 chariots, by far the largest contingent of this type, and 10,000 foot soldiers.[45] This indicates that Ahab was very powerful and on an equal footing with the major powers of the day. But in 1 Kings 20, Ahab is portrayed at first under the complete domination of the king of Damascus. He then rebels against his master and defeats him with a significantly inferior force (20:15, 27).

A number of suggestions have been made to harmonize these two different pictures of Ahab. J. Morgenstern suggested

[45] For convenience, see Oppenheim's translation in *ANET*[3]: 278–79.

that the battles in 1 Kings 20 took place early in Ahab's reign, not near the time of his death.[46] This allows as much as twenty years between the period when Ahab was a weak vassal of Damascus and the time when he appeared as a major ally. Others, such as Unger, believe that the difficulties have been overemphasized and that the events described in 1 Kings 20 could easily have taken place in the final years of Ahab's reign.[47] A third proposal, which has gained considerable acceptance in recent years, is that the stories in 1 Kings 20 and 22:1–38 (the battle at Ramoth-Gilead) were not originally about Ahab at all, but concerned a king of the dynasty of Jehu, either Joahaz or Joash.[48] This is a very important issue for understanding the status of Damascus during the mid-ninth century and thus will be explored in detail below.

The Problem of the Identity of the King of Israel

Scholars have long noted a series of apparent discrepancies between the portraits of Ahab in chap. 20, in chaps. 16–19 and 21, and in the Monolith Inscription of Shalmaneser III. Already mentioned above is the obvious discrepancy between the apparent military might noted in Shalmaneser's inscription (where the number of chariots attributed to Ahab, 2,000, is almost equal to the number of chariots used by the Assyrians[49]) and the obvious weakness of the king in chap. 20, dominated by the king of Aram and able to muster only 7,000 men to fight (20:15). Furthermore, within the story of chap. 20, the Aramaeans show very little concern about the existence of a chariot force in Israel; when Israel defeated the Aramaeans, apparently in a battle in the hills (20:23),[50] the servants of the king of Aram are quoted as assuring him that in the plain the Aramaean forces could easily defeat Israel. 1 Kgs 20:23–25 implies that the Aramaeans were defeated because they could not deploy their

[46] Morgenstern 1940: 385–92. Cf. also Gray 1970: 414–15; and Kraeling 1918: 76–77.

[47] M. F. Unger 1957: 70–74.

[48] See Jepsen 1941–45: 154–59; Whitley 1952: 144–49; Miller 1966; Lipinski 1969: 159–63; Gray 1970: 416–18; Donner 1977: 399–400. See also Miller 1964: esp. 78–86.

[49] See Elat 1975: 26–29.

[50] For an excellent analysis of the battle strategy, see Yadin 1955: 333–41.

chariotry and that they expected to win had they been able to do so. But Ahab, according to Shalmaneser's inscription, had a formidable chariot force, 800 stronger than that fielded by the king of Damascus, although the numbers are probably exaggerated (see below).

Furthermore, in v 34, after Bir-Hadad was defeated at Apheq, he offered the following concessions to Ahab: "And he said to him, 'The cities which my father took from your father I will return, and you may set up bazaars in Damascus, as my father set up in Samaria.'" It is highly doubtful, from what is known about Omri, that he could have been under Aramaean domination to the extent assumed by this passage. Omri had successfully concluded an important treaty with Tyre, sealed with the marriage between his son and the daughter of the king of Tyre. In his fairly short reign he was able to build and fortify a very impressive new capital city, Samaria. He expanded Israel's control east of the Jordan to include a significant part of Moab (as noted in the Mēšaᶜ Stela) and created enough stability to establish the first successful multigenerational dynasty in the northern kingdom. All of this conflicts with the idea that Damascus had seized territory from Omri and forced major commercial concessions in the new capital of Samaria, as is presupposed in 1 Kgs 20:34.[51]

The obvious weakness of the king described in chap. 20 further does not correlate with what is known of Ahab's reign from archaeological remains. Several sites in northern Israel, including Samaria, Megiddo, Hazor, and Dan,[52] have revealed extensive public building projects which date to Ahab's reign. These clearly indicate his wealth and power. Nor should so weak a king have been able to maintain control over Moab at the same time.[53]

[51] M. F. Unger (1957: 60–64) downplays most of the problems in this chapter, but agrees that this passage cannot refer to Omri. He explains the passage by following Albright's rather weak proposal that the reference to 'father' should be understood as 'predecessor' and that 'Samaria' simply means 'Israelite capital'. Thus, according to Unger, Bir-Hadad here refers to towns seized by Hezion or Ṭab-Rammān during the reign of Jeroboam I or Nadab, and bazaars set up in Tirzah or Shechem. See Albright 1942: 27.

[52] See, for example, Kenyon 1971a: 71–110. For Dan, see, provisionally, 1980: 176–77.

[53] See 2 Kgs 1:1 and 3:5. An argument can be made from the Mēšaᶜ Stela, however, that Moab broke away during Ahab's reign. Lines 7–8

Certain other details of chaps. 20 and 22:1–38 are significant for this discussion. The distinctive style of these two passages, in contrast to the other chapters dealing with Ahab (17–19, 21), has long been noted. One of the major characteristics of these two chapters is the very common use of the title מלך ישראל when referring to the king, instead of using the king's name. In the Masoretic Text of chap. 20, the name Ahab appears three times (vv 2, 13, 14). In two of the three cases, it is modified with מלך ישראל (vv 2, 13). מלך ישראל appears eleven other times in the chapter (vv 4, 7, 11, 21, 22, 28, 31, 32, 40, 41, 43), while המלך appears with reference to the king of Israel twice (vv 38, 39). In the Old Greek translation, represented by Codex Vaticanus (B), the name Ahab (᾿Αχααβ) appears four times in chap. 20 (vv 2, 14 [twice], 15), but only two of these occurrences are in places where the name is found in the MT (v 2 and the first appearance in v 14; the OG has only βασιλει ᾿Ισραηλ in v 13). The Lucianic manuscripts boc_2e_2 have Ahab's name five times, the first four in the same locations as in the OG, but a fifth at the beginning of v 34, where the OG and MT have "And he said to him." The Lucianic manuscripts have και ειπεν βασιλευς συριας προς ᾿Αχααβ. Again, only two of the five occurrences overlap with the MT. The small number of appearances of the name of Ahab and the wide variation in the locations of its appearance in the MT and LXX suggest that the

read, "Omri possessed all the land of Mehdebah and dwelt in it all his days and half the days of his son, forty years." A couple of difficulties arise from an analysis of these lines. First, should the reference to forty years be taken literally or as a general and non-specific number of years? If it is taken literally, then the end of Israelite control of the area must be placed several years after the death of Ahab. Second, what exactly is the turning point that is referred to in these lines? Miller (1974: 15–16) places the Mēšaᶜ Stela in the genre of Memorial Stela and plausibly suggests that the turning point referred to in lines 7–8, the event which took place halfway through Ahab's reign, was not the rebellion against Israel, but the accession of Mēšaᶜ to the throne. He then accepts the biblical notices of the time of the actual rebellion.

Another plausible suggestion was made by Cross and Freedman (1952: 39–40, n 13), who argue that the word *bnh*, 'his son', should be understood as 'his descendent', and that the king referred to here is Joram, the grandson of Omri. This would be in harmony with the reference to the forty years of oppression, as well as the biblical account of the revolt.

proper name of the king has been added at a later time and that the story originally only identified the king as מלך ישראל.

The identification of the king simply with the title מלך ישראל is also a characteristic of chap. 22, where Ahab is only named once in the MT and OG (v 20; however, boc_2e_2 has the name five times—vv 2, 5, 10, 20, 37!), and also of the Elisha stories which include a king of Israel as a character (2 Kgs 5:1–27; 6:8–23; 6:24–7:20). In these latter cases, no name has been secondarily attached to the king. In addition, the style of 1 Kings 20 and 22:1–38 is quite similar to these stories from the Elisha cycle, and it has been argued that they belong to the same source.[54] It is interesting to note that the stories in 1 Kings 20 and 22 make no mention at all of Elijah, Ahab's main antagonist in the rest of the Ahab material (1 Kings 17–19, 21). This is perhaps most surprising in chap. 22, where Micaiah ben-Imlah plays a role very similar to what might be expected of Elijah.

One other aspect of the text itself should be noted. In the OG and Lucianic versions of 1 Kings, chaps. 20 and 21 are reversed, with chap. 20 immediately followed by chap. 22. Shenkel, in his study of the LXX text of Kings, asserts that the LXX order is superior to the MT because it keeps all of the Elijah stories together.[55] It is clear that the story of Naboth's vineyard is not connected, in a strict chronological sense, to the war stories of chaps. 20 and 22.[56] The first verse of chap. 22 seems to pick up the story where chap. 20 left off. It is therefore probable that the LXX order is correct in uniting these two chapters into a single, uninterrupted narrative of the Aramaean wars.

In summary, there is evidence to suggest that these stories do not belong to the time of Ahab, neither early nor late in his reign. The accounts of the three battles found in 1 Kings 20 and

[54] See Miller 1966: 447–54.

[55] Shenkel 1968: 88.

[56] Note that the story of Naboth's vineyard is a complete story in itself and that the narrative ends with Ahab repenting of the sin he has committed, so that he is forgiven by Yahweh. It is unlikely that the story was written with the account of Ahab's death in battle in mind. Note also that the prophecy of Ahab's blood being licked by dogs at the same spot where Naboth's blood was licked is not fulfilled precisely in the story (22:38), whereas the details of the death of Joram follow the curse closely (2 Kgs 9:21–26). See Miller 1967b: 309–17, for a discussion of the story of Naboth.

22 seem to have been written about an unidentified king of Israel. It is, after all, the prophets in these stories who were the characters of greatest interest to those who preserved them.[57] The anonymous king was eventually identified as Ahab, the most famous king of the Omride Dynasty, and the narratives were inserted into the history of his times, although several aspects of the stories simply did not fit the period or personage of Ahab. If this proposal is correct, then these stories need to be fitted into their proper place.

In an important article in the early 1940s, Alfred Jepsen argued that 1 Kings 20 did not belong to the time of Ahab, but rather to the period of the Jehu Dynasty.[58] A similar viewpoint was put forward by C. F. Whitley, and then in greater detail by J. M. Miller, first in his dissertation and later in a series of articles which appeared between 1966 and 1968 in various journals.[59] The arguments for adopting this view deserve elaboration.

While the portrayal of a dominated Israel in 1 Kings 20 clashes with the conditions existing during the period of Omri and Ahab, it fits perfectly into the time of Joahaz, the son of Jehu, and Joash, the son of Joahaz. 2 Kings 13 vividly describes the era of oppression under Hazael and Bir-Hadad, his son, during the reigns of these two Israelite kings. The army of Joahaz is described in terms very similar to those used of the army in 1 Kings 20: "For there only remained to Joahaz an army of fifty horsemen, ten chariots and ten thousand footsoldiers, for the king of Aram had destroyed them and had made them like dust for threshing" (13:7).

In 2 Kgs 13:14–19, the dying Elisha predicts that Joash will overthrow the Aramaeans, but only in three battles. The fulfillment of this prediction is mentioned in 13:25, but with no details. Jepsen, followed by the others, suggested that the battles described in 1 Kings 20 are the accounts of the first two battles predicted in 13:19 and that they were originally the accounts of how Israel recovered from Aramaean oppression. Note the following similarities. First, the king of Israel in these stories was originally anonymous, but the king of Aram is

[57] See Shenkel 1968: 98–99.

[58] Jepsen 1941–45: 153–59.

[59] Whitley 1952; Miller 1964; 1966; 1967b; 1968.

referred to by name over and over again—Ben-Hadad, the king who according to 2 Kgs 13:25 was defeated by the weak but reviving Joash. Second, Elisha, in the story in 2 Kings 13, predicts that Joash will decisively defeat the Aramaeans at a place called Apheq (v 17). In 1 Kings 20, the second and decisive battle does in fact take place at Apheq (vv 26–30). Third, Bir-Hadad's suggested terms for peace in v 34, are significantly incongruent with the situation during the reigns of Omri and Ahab, but fit perfectly with what is said in 2 Kings about the period of the Jehu Dynasty. Hazael, king of Aram, captured virtually all of Israel's territory east of the Jordan, beginning in the reign of Jehu (2 Kgs 10:32–33), and continued his oppression into the reign of Joahaz (13:3, 22). It was Hazael's son, Bir-Hadad, who, according to 13:25, was defeated by Joash and was forced to return the cities which his father had taken from Joahaz. Thus, the terms—"The cities which my father took from your father I will restore; and you may establish bazaars for yourself in Damascus, as my father did in Samaria"—fit extraordinarily well in the context of Joash's reign.[60]

Excavations at Hazor illustrate dramatically the great difference in the power of the Israelite state between the time of Ahab and the period of Joahaz and Joash. According to the excavator, the citadel in Area B of the tell was apparently built during the reign of Ahab and has the characteristic building style of Ahab, i.e., field-stone walls with corners built from carefully carved ashlars, doorjambs of ashlars, the proto-Aeolic capitals, among other things.[61] This indicates that Hazor was firmly in the hands of Ahab, but in the succeeding period (Stratum VII), the official use of the citadel seems to have ended and the building was used as living quarters, probably for squatters or laborers.[62] Again the story in chap. 20 fits the later period much better than the earlier one.

The situation regarding the account of Ahab's death in 1 Kings 22 is more complex. Again, it is difficult to imagine a war between Aram and Israel soon after the battle of Qarqar against Assyria in 853 B.C.E.; according to the chronological

[60] The reference to 'your father' in Bir-Hadad's speech (20:34) could, of course, refer to Joahaz or to Jehu.

[61] See Yadin 1972: 169–72.

[62] See Yadin 1975: 168.

data, Ahab must have died very soon after that battle.[63] There is no evidence of the disruption of the Anti-Assyrian alliance, which might be expected if Israel had declared war on Damascus. The fact that Shalmaneser III fought with the same coalition in 849, 848, and 845 suggests that the alliance remained active until the usurpation of Hazael, after 845. Although Israel is not mentioned in the preserved accounts of the campaigns in those years, it probably remained a significant partner in the coalition.

Other problems surrounding the account of Ahab's battle at Ramoth-Gilead, while not decisive, do provide additional support for redating the passage. For example, while 22:3 indicates that Ramoth-Gilead was under Aramaean control during the events recounted in the story, 2 Kgs 10:32–33 implies that Gilead in general, and therefore Ramoth-Gilead, did not fall into Aramaean hands until the reign of Hazael. Certainly, at the end of the reign of Joram (2 Kgs 9:14), Ramoth-Gilead was in Israelite hands.

Details in the account of Ahab's death in 1 Kings 22 are reminiscent of events during the reign of Joram:[64] Joram was wounded in battle against Aram at Ramoth-Gilead, and Joram is also connected in his death with the story of Naboth the Jezreelite (2 Kgs 9:21–26). Miller has suggested that since Ramoth-Gilead was in Israelite hands at the time of the battle in which Joram was wounded, the account in 1 Kings 22 has included elements of another story about a battle to restore Ramoth-Gilead to Israel, perhaps a story of its recapture during the Jehu Dynasty.[65]

[63] Inscriptions of Shalmaneser III confirm that Jehu was on the throne by 841. See, for example, the inscription dealing with Shalmaneser's eighteenth year, which describes Shalmaneser's first battle with Hazael and mentions the tribute brought by Jehu ¹*ia-ú-a* DUMU *ḫu-um-ri-i*): Michel 1947–52: 265–67. The reading of the name *ia-ú-a* will be discussed in the next chapter. If Ahab's sons Ahaziah and Joram are to be credited with anything approaching the two and twelve years assigned to them, respectively, in 1 Kgs 22:51 and 2 Kgs 3:1, Ahab must have died about 853. If war broke out between Israel and Aram, it had to occur very shortly after the battle of Qarqar. On this, see Pavlovsky and Vogt 1964: 327; Miller 1967a: 284–86.

[64] This is pointed out very well by Miller (1966: 444–46 and 1967b: 307–17).

[65] What has apparently happened is that the story, now related to Ahab, is used to illustrate Yahweh's punishment of the king who was

Another reason to suspect the account of Ahab's violent death is found in 1 Kgs 22:40, a passage from the Deuteronomistic framework for Kings. Here the account of Ahab's reign is concluded with the formula, "And Ahab slept with his fathers," a formula which elsewhere in Kings is used only of kings who died a natural death.[66] This suggests that the original author of Kings did not include the account of Ahab's death at Ramoth-Gilead in his work and in fact had no knowledge of a violent death for Ahab.

So it is probable that the accounts of war between Aram and Israel during the reign of Ahab in 1 Kings 20 and 22 do not belong to his reign, but rather to a king of the Jehu Dynasty. There has not, however, been unanimity concerning the identity of the king who took part in these battles. Jepsen and Whitley both assumed that the king in question was Joash, because 2 Kgs 13:14–19 identifies Joash as the king Elisha said would defeat the Aramaeans three times in battle, and because 13:25 states that Joash did in fact recover the cities from Aram in three battles.[67] But Miller has questioned the accuracy of these passages. He notes that, according to 13:5, Yahweh sent Israel a savior in response to the prayer of Joahaz, and Israel escaped from Aram at that time. He believes that the king of Israel in 13:14–19 was originally anonymous, similar to the situation noted above in 1 Kings 20 and 22, and only later was he identified with Joash. This identification led to a revision of the information about Joash in order to identify him as the one who freed Israel from the oppression of Aram. According to Miller, the writer of v 25 has changed the facts in order to suggest that Hazael had taken the land east of the Jordan from Joahaz instead of from Jehu, as is stated in 2 Kgs 10:32–33. He also notes that 13:22, which says that Hazael oppressed Israel all the days of Joahaz, contradicts 13:3, which states that Ben-Hadad, the son of Hazael, was the oppressor of Israel during the reign of Joahaz. Therefore, Miller believes that the king who fought the battles of 1 Kings 20 and 22 and who was the original subject of 2 Kgs 13:14–19 was Joahaz, not his son, Joash.[68]

---

so hated by the prophetic school which preserved these stories. See Miller 1966: 446–53.

[66] Cf. Jepsen 1941–45: 155; and Miller 1966: 445, esp. n 20.

[67] Jepsen 1941–45: 157; and Whitley 1952: 144–45.

[68] Miller 1966: 442–43.

There are reasons to be cautious about Miller's arguments on this point. His key passage, 2 Kgs 13:3–7, presents some ambiguities. Who, for example, is the savior whom Yahweh sent? It was not Joahaz himself, or the writer would probably have indicated so. Two suggestions which have received some critical support are (1) that the deliverer was Elisha, who in 13:14–19 inspires the king to fight the Aramaeans,[69] or (2) that it was Adad-nirari III, the king of Assyria, who attacked Damascus sometime around 800 B.C.E., weakening it so that Israel was able to "escape" from its control.[70] However, if it is correct to see in 1 Kings 20 and (a kernel of) 22 the accounts of the three battles for liberation from Aram referred to in 13:14–19, and since the king is viewed as a leading force (cf. 20:21), especially in the two battles in chap. 20, then the deliverer referred to here may be Joahaz's son, Joash. The rise of a successful son could have been viewed as the answer to the prayer of Joahaz.

A study of the form of 2 Kgs 13:3–6 also throws doubt on Miller's interpretation of this passage, for these verses are general and formulaic in tone. In v 3 the names of the two Damascene kings who oppressed Israel because of Yahweh's anger against his people are given. Vv 4–5, in Deuteronomistic style reminiscent of the framework of Judges, tells of the repentance of the king and his supplication to Yahweh that resulted in Yahweh's sending of a savior who delivered the land from Aram, allowing the people to live in peace. According to v 6, the people of Israel unfortunately did not learn from their experience but continued to walk in the sins of the house of Jeroboam. This is not a discussion of the reign of Joahaz in particular, but a capsulized version of the entire history of the Aramaean oppression and deliverance (from a theological point of view). In v 6 this capsulized history is carried beyond the period of oppression and salvation to the time when Israel continued in its sinful ways. This generalized history need not be restricted to the reign of Joahaz but may easily be understood to cover the period of both Joahaz and Joash.

Similarly, Miller takes the context of 2 Kgs 10:32–33 too literally; he suggests that Hazael captured all of Israel's Transjordanian territory during Jehu's reign, which makes it impossible

[69] Cf. Gray 1970: 595; Miller 1966: 442–43.

[70] See Gray 1970: 594–95; Lipinski 1969: 166.

for Bir-Hadad to have returned towns that his father had captured from Joahaz. The form of these verses, especially the general nature of the opening clause, "In those days Yahweh began to cut off parts of Israel," indicates that the description of Hazael's conquests in Transjordan was intended as a summary of the Aramaean king's activities, not specifically a description of his deeds only during Jehu's reign.

It is preferable (in agreement with 2 Kgs 13:25) to propose that Joash was the king who defeated Bir-Hadad and restored Israel's possessions east of the Jordan in three battles, two of which are described in 1 Kings 20 and one of which may have been used in part to build the story of Ahab's death in 1 Kings 22.[71]

The several accounts of Elisha and the Aramaeans, insofar as they may be regarded as historical, should also be placed in the period of the Jehu Dynasty. In these stories, found in 2 Kgs 5:1–27, 6:8–23, and 6:24–7:20, the king of Israel is always anonymous, and they are put together without any chronological framework.[72] It is clear that in the story of Naaman, which has little political import, the king of Israel is a vassal to the king of Aram (cf. 5:6–7). The story in 6:8–23 gives no data which would permit precise dating, even assuming a historical background to the story. In the third major tale of Elisha and the Aramaeans, the siege of Samaria (6:24–7:20), the name of the king of Aram is given as Ben-Hadad.[73] If this identification is correct, it most likely refers to Bir-Hadad, the son of Hazael, since the story takes place at a low point in the fortunes of Israel and thus falls naturally into the period of Joahaz and Joash, before the liberation.

If it is correct to attribute the accounts of the Aramaean Wars in 1 Kings 20–2 Kings 8 to a later period, then it becomes clear that there is virtually no information in the biblical sources about Damascus during the time of the Omride Dynasty. This view of the biblical material represents a considerable departure

[71] On the question of why the king of Judah is identified with Jehoshaphat in 1 Kings 22, cf. Shenkel 1968: 104–8; and Miller 1966: 447–48.

[72] None of the Elisha material from 2 Kings 4:1 to 8:8 is in a chronological framework. Each story is basically complete in itself.

[73] The name appears only once, in 6:24, and may be secondary, since it is followed by the standard epithet, 'king of Aram'.

from the standard interpretation of Damascene history during the mid-ninth century. No longer is Damascus seen as dominating Israel during the reigns of Omri and Ahab, nor must scenarios be devised which explain the change in the military status of Israel from the situation in 1 Kings 20 to its position evident in the inscriptions of Shalmaneser III. Furthermore, the king called Ben-Hadad in 1 Kings 20 and 2 Kgs 6:24 no longer needs to be identified with Hadad-^{c}iḏr of the Shalmaneser inscriptions,[74] as has so often been done (Hadad-^{c}iḏr is usually called Ben-Hadad II in the literature, and various proposals have been made to explain why the king is called by two different names[75]). The Ben-Hadad of 1 Kings 20 may now be identified with Bir-Hadad, the son of Hazael, and the Damascene king of the period of Ahab may simply be known as Hadad-^{c}iḏr. Thus, while Damascus was a very powerful state during the second quarter of the ninth century, it was not strong enough to subdue its vigorous southern neighbor under the Omride Dynasty. Damascus' period of imperial expansion to the south did not begin until the reign of Hazael, well after the days of Ahab.

THE ASSYRIAN SOURCES FOR THE REIGN OF HADAD–^{C}IḎR

A number of Assyrian inscriptions provide vital information about Aram–Damascus' role in international affairs during

[74] See, for example, Dupont-Sommer 1949: 34–35; Mazar 1962: 106–9; Malamat 1973: 144.

[75] See Mazar 1962: 106; M. F. Unger 1957: 67, 71, and 152, n 33, 153–54, n 49. Kraeling 1918: 75–76; and Shea 1978–79: 169–71.

Dropping the identification of Hadad-^{c}iḏr with the Ben-Hadad of Kings also allows us to dispose of the idea that the name Bir-Hadad was a royal title of the kings of Damascus. This suggestion arose to explain the apparent occurrence of two Bir-Hadads in succession, when Hadad-^{c}iḏr was identified as having that name, as well as Bir-Hadad I. There is no parallel for a father and son having the same name in the royalty of Western Asia, so the best explanation of this occurrence was that Bir-Hadad, 'the son of Hadad', was a title used by all of the kings of Damascus. This of course is no longer necessary, if our reconstruction is correct. See on this, Shea 1978–79: 171–72, who recognizes the problem of the two Bir-Hadads, but ends up compounding it by suggesting that Bir-Hadad I also had the same personal name as Hadad-^{c}iḏr, like the proposed Bir-Hadad II!

the period from 853–841 B.C.E. The first reference to Aram-Damascus is found in the inscriptions of Shalmaneser III, in the account of the campaign of Shalmaneser's sixth year, 853 B.C.E.[76] Following the lead of his father, Aššur-nāṣir-apli II, who began the policy of expansion that was to bring Assyria to the heights of imperial power, Shalmaneser III (858–824) moved toward gaining greater control of the trade routes that traversed northern Syria. In a series of campaigns in his first years, Shalmaneser was able to defeat Bit-Adini, one of the most powerful of the north Syrian states, and annex it to the Assyrian empire.[77]

In his sixth year, according to the Monolith Inscription, which provides the most detailed account of this campaign,[78] Shalmaneser again turned westward with his army. After forcing the resubmission of a state on the Baliḫ River and receiving tribute from most of the other countries of northern Syria, Shalmaneser determined to bring the important kingdom of Hamath under Assyrian suzerainty, the first direct move by the Assyrians into central Syria. He captured three towns of Irḫulena, king of Hamath, and plundered and burned the palaces in those towns. He then continued on to the royal city of Qarqar, which is probably to be located in the northern end of the Ǵāb, the river valley of the Orontes, to the northwest of the city of Hamath.[79]

[76] For recent discussion on the exact date of this battle, see Shea 1977; and Brinkman 1978b.

[77] For good discussions of the economic reasons for Assyria's expansion to the west, see Tadmor 1975 and Grayson 1976: 134–38.

[78] The cuneiform text of the Monolith Inscription was published in Rawlinson 1861–1909: 3, pls. VII and VIII. A transliteration of the text may be found in Rasmussen 1897: 2–30; and Schrader 1889: 1.150–74. English translations may be found in Luckenbill 1926: #594–611; and *ANET*³: 277, 278 (first and sixth years).

Shorter accounts of the battle of Qarqar are found in several inscriptions. See Michel 1947–52: 464 (= Bull Inscription); Michel 1954–59: 32, 148 (= Black Obelisk); Michel 1964: 152, 154; Laessoe 1959: 150–52; Hulin 1963: 53–54. For a description of all the known inscriptions of Shalmaneser III, see Schramm 1973: 70–105.

[79] There is a tell seven km. south of Jisr eš-Šuġūr, which has the name Tell Qarqūr and has been identified with the town of Qarqar by several. See, for examp̌le, Courtois 1973: 88; Klengel 1965–1970: 3. 53, 65, n 14; Noth 1955: 39; 1956: 81. Although excavations at Qarqūr have uncovered Iron II remains (Lundquist 1984), there are some

Figure 5. Probable extent of Aram–Damascus during the reign of Hadad-ᶜid̲r, mid-ninth century B.C.E.

After attacking and destroying Qarqar, Shalmaneser met a formidable army mustered by a coalition of central and southern Syrian states. The army was led by Adad-idri (^{d}IM-ʾ*i-id-ri*), an Akkadian version of the Aramaic name Hadad-ᶜidr (= Hebrew Hadad-ᶜēzer), the king of Imērišu, i.e., the land whose capital was Damascus.[80] The coalition included Irḫulena of Hamath and Ahab, the Israelite (^{I}*a-ḫa-ab-bu* KUR *sir-ʾi-la-a-a*, col. II, lines 91–92), as its other two major members. The numbers of troops provided by the allies against Shalmaneser are quite significant. Hadad-ᶜidr brought 1,200 chariots, 1,200 horsemen, and 20,000 footsoldiers. Irḫulena provided 700 chariots, 700 horsemen, and 10,000 footsoldiers, while Ahab furnished 2,000 chariots[81] and 10,000 footsoldiers. Smaller contingents are listed in the Monolith Inscription from the states of *Qù-a-a* (Que), ^{KUR}*Mu-uṣ-ra-a-a*, ^{KUR}*Ir-qa-na-ta-a-a*, ^{URU}*Ar-ma-da-a-a* (Arvad), ^{KUR}*Ú-sa-na-ta-a-a*, ^{KUR}*Ši-a-na-a-a*, ^{KUR}*Ar-ba-a-a* (Arabia), and ^{KUR}*A-ma-na-a-a* (all of these names are in gentilic form). Few details of the battle are recorded; Shalmaneser claims that he defeated the coalition, but the claim is questionable. If he did defeat them, his own losses must have been serious enough to dissuade his advance into Hamath, for his accounts of the sixth year end with the battle of Qarqar, with the exception of the

reasons to doubt the identification. First, the tell appears to be some distance from the most important part of the trade route going through the area. Second, there is a large tell beside the Orontes at the modern town of Jisr eš-Šuġūr, located at the best location to ford the river and directly on the east–west route from Aleppo to Latakia. This site is the largest tell in the entire northern Ġab and is so strategically located that it appears to be the most likely candidate for the site of Qarqar. The site is merely called et-Tell by the locals. Only a very preliminary survey of it was done in 1979, and a few possible Iron II sherds were found.

[80] For a discussion of the Assyrian name of Aram–Damascus, Imērišu or Ša-imērišu, see chap. 1.

[81] If this number is approximately correct (it is probably inflated), then Ahab had virtually as many chariots as Shalmaneser. See Elat 1975: 26–29. Naaman 1976: 97–102, challenges the number 2,000 on the grounds that Israel could not have afforded to maintain so many chariots. Though this is probably true, and though the scribe probably exaggerated all of the numbers in this passage, I am reluctant to accept Naaman's emendation of the text to 200 chariots.

Bull Inscription and its parallel,[82] which mention a journey to the Mediterranean at the end of the campaign. Even this indicates an abandonment of the campaign to the south. The Assyrians did not return to western Syria for at least four years. The accounts of the succeeding confrontations between Shalmaneser and the Syrian coalition are considerably shorter than the version of the battle of Qarqar on the Monolith Inscription (and the latter is by no means a detailed account!). The references to these other battles occur in late summaries of Shalmaneser's campaigns and thus give only the barest of details.[83]

In his tenth year (849), after again pacifying Carchemish and Bīt-Agūsi, Shalmaneser pushed southwest but was again met by the coalition headed by Hadad-ᶜiḏr and Irḫulena. For a second time he claims to have defeated the coalition, but again the battle ends the account of the tenth year, with no indication of a continuation of the campaign southward. The short description of the battle is written in formulistic language: "At that time, Adad-idri of the land of Imērišu, Irḫulena the Hamathite, together with the twelve kings of the seacoast trusted in their combined forces. To wage war and battle against me, they assaulted me. I fought with them. I accomplished their defeat. Chariots, their cavalry-horses, their battle equipment, I took away. They went into hiding to save their lives."[84]

[82] Michel 1947–52: 464 has the parallel. For other accounts of the battle, see n 78, above.

[83] The most famous version of Shalmaneser's annals is the Black Obelisk Inscription, which summarizes the events of thirty-one years. See Michel 1954–59: 137–57, 221–33 for a transliteration of the text from the Black Obelisk. See also Luckenbill 1926: #553–93 for a translation, noting especially, for our purposes, the accounts of the years ten, eleven, and fourteen. Other accounts of the campaigns of these years may be found in Michel 1947–52: 466–69; Michel 1954–59: 34–37.

[84] For the Akkadian text, see Michel 1947–52: 466. There is some uncertainty about whether there actually was a battle between Shalmaneser and the coalition in the tenth year. The Black Obelisk and the account of the tenth year in Michel 1954–59: 34 make no mention of this battle. However, it is present in the accounts of Michel 1947–52: 67, and 466, and at this point the assumption that it did take place must stand.

In his eleventh and fourteenth years (848 and 845), Shalmaneser again met the coalition headed by Hadad-ᶜiḏr, and the descriptions of these battles are as vague as those of the tenth year. Never is there any follow-up to the battle, never is there any mention of taking the cities of the coalition members or of their submission to Shalmaneser; the alliance was strong enough during these years to keep the Assyrians from gaining any significant ground in central and southern Syria.

Although this is all the explicit information about the reign of Hadad-ᶜiḏr of Damascus, some inferences may be made from the Assyrian inscriptions. The extent of Damascus' power during the reign of Bir-Hadad I, the son of Ṭab-Rammān, early in the ninth century, is not clearly established; however, under Hadad-ᶜiḏr Damascus was among the leading states of Syria, and may have been the most powerful. The fact that Hadad-ᶜiḏr is named as the leader of the south Syrian coalition in every campaign in which he participated (the sixth, tenth, eleventh, and fourteenth years of Shalmaneser) indicates that he led the strongest force in the alliance. This is borne out by the numbers recorded on the Monolith Inscription, which lists Hadad-ᶜiḏr as contributing the largest number of horsemen and footsoldiers and the second largest number of chariots.

The list of members of the coalition may provide some clues as to the area under the control of Hadad-ᶜiḏr. The chief states in the alliance were Aram, Hamath, and Israel, who together contributed over half of the combined forces. A number of the other allies were states from the northern Phoenician coast (Irqanata, Arvad, Usanata, Šian, Byblos,[85] and possibly Amana[86]) and Egypt (Muṣri). To the south, troops came from Arabia (one thousand camels) and perhaps from Beth-Rehob.[87]

[85] On emending *Gu-a-a* to *Gu-<bal>-a-a* ('the Byblian'), and on identifying KUR *Mu-uṣ-ra-a-a* with Egypt, see Tadmor 1961b. In general, see Aharoni and Avi-Yonah 1968: map 127.

[86] It has often been assumed that ^{KUR}*A-ma-na-a-a* is the land of Ammon in Transjordan. See, for example, Aharoni 1979: 336. However, Ammon was normally written, ^{KUR}*bit am-ma-na*, in Neo-Assyrian documents. See Parpola 1970: 76. It is more likely that ^{KUR}*A-ma-na* was a small country, ᶜAmmana, located somewhere in northern Syria. See Cross 1973: 27–28. But also see Naaman 1976: 98, n 20.

[87] Malamat 1973: 144. Baasha, the son of Rehob, may have been king of Beth-Rehob, similar to the case of Hadadezer, the son of Rehob (2 Sam 8:3).

Mazar has noted that no other Aramaean state is listed in the coalition (unless Beth-Rehob is a part of the list). He takes this as evidence that Hadad-ᶜiḏr had conquered all of the Aramaean states and had reorganized them into provinces, forming a genuine Aramaean empire ruled from Damascus. This theory will be explored in more detail in the next chapter; but Mazar carries the evidence of the list of coalition members to conclusions which it cannot support. Doubtless a number of small states, such as Geshur, Maacah, and perhaps Rehob and Zobah, had come under the domination of Damascus;[88] but whether they were controlled by local dynasts or by Damascene governors is not now known and cannot be determined on the basis of the list in the Monolith Inscription (Mazar's use of biblical material will be discussed below). The evidence from the period of David's empire indicates that the suzerain chose the form of rule in each subject state, depending on individual circumstances. The forces ascribed to Hadad-ᶜiḏr on the inscription certainly include levies from his vassal states, whether those states were governed by local kings or Damascene governors. A similar case may be found in the listing of Israel, which probably included levies from Judah (which had an alliance with Ahab) and Moab (which was subject to Israel), while both of these states retained their own kings.

Besides the fact that the kingdom of Aram–Damascus was located between Israel on the south and Hamath on the north, there is little other indication of its geographical extent. Presumably it included a number of the small states to the south and southwest of Damascus that were formerly independent, such as Geshur and Maacah,[89] and perhaps Beth-Rehob and Bashan. It seems, from the scanty information on the extent of Israelite territory during the mid-ninth century, that Israelite extraterritorial expansion tended to be toward the southeast, toward Moab and the associated areas. There is no mention of expansion to the north. As stated earlier, the conquest of northern Israel by Bir-Hadad I was not permanent, since evidence from the excavations there (especially Hazor and Dan) indicates continued Israelite occupation and fortification of the

[88] If it is true that Baasha, son of Rehob (of the list on the Monolith Inscription), was king of Beth-Rehob, then it is probable that Beth-Rehob maintained an independent existence.

[89] On these two states, see Mazar 1961: 16–28.

towns,[90] at least as early as the reign of Ahab. It is likely, then, that the land of Naphtali and Dan had returned to Israelite control during the time of Hadad-ᶜiḏr. Furthermore, if the explanation of 1 Kings 22 provided above is correct (i.e., that it does not reflect events during Ahab's reign and that Ramoth-Gilead did not fall into the hands of Aram until the days of Hazael), then Aram's boundary with Israel east of the Jordan Valley was in the area of the land of Bashan.

With the limited information available, the boundaries between Aram-Damascus and its western and northern neighbors cannot be ascertained, but the former land of Zobah probably formed part of these boundaries. The northern border must have abutted the limits of the state of Hamath, but the precise location is not known.[91]

THE DEATH OF HADAD-ᶜIḎR AND THE RISE OF HAZAEL

The next event which presents significant problems is the death of Hadad-ᶜiḏr and the rise of the usurper Hazael to the throne of Damascus. Among those who have accepted the identity of Hadad-ᶜiḏr and the Ben-Hadad of 1 Kings 20–2 Kings 8, these events present no particular difficulty: 2 Kgs 8:7–15 gives the account of how Hazael, an official in the court of Ben-Hadad, murdered the king and seized the throne. Although the story concentrates on the prophet Elisha and contains major legendary elements (Elisha as the instigator of the revolution in Aram), most commentators have assumed the general historicity of the account of the assassination itself and refer to a text of Shalmaneser III which appears to verify the biblical version.[92] This text reads in part: ^{Id}IM-*id-ri* KUR-*šu e-mi-id*

[90] Of course, this archaeological evidence is not conclusive, since it is not certain that the building techniques attributed to Ahab were not used by the Aramaeans as well. Only excavations in the Damascene will advance our knowledge of the architectural styles of the Aramaeans of Damascus and substantiate or negate the archaeological argument.

[91] It is of course possible that the territory of Zobah had been incorporated into the land of Hamath.

[92] See, for example, M. F. Unger 1957: 75; Kraeling 1918: 78–79; Dupont-Sommer 1949: 38; Bright 1972: 250.

^{I}*ḫa-za-*ᵓ- DINGIR DUMU *la ma-ma-na* ^{GIŠ}GU.ZA *iṣ-bat*,[93] 'Adad-idri died.[94] Hazael, the son of a nobody, seized the throne.'

However, as argued above, the stories in 1 Kings 20–2 Kings 7 which include Ben-Hadad as a character probably belong to the period of Bir-Hadad, the son of Hazael, rather than a Bir-Hadad contemporary with the Omride Dynasty of Israel. Thus, 2 Kgs 8:7–15 presents a problem for this hypothesis, since the king murdered by Hazael in this pericope is called Ben-Hadad, and this story cannot be dated with the others to a later time.

Two plausible solutions to this problem should be considered. The first and perhaps simplest solution is to suggest that the king of Aram in the story was originally anonymous and that the name Ben-Hadad was added to the text later, when the other Ben-Hadad stories were inserted into the account of the Omride dynasty. If so, then the name would simply be a mistake; the king actually assassinated by Hazael would have been Hadad-ᶜiḏr.[95]

A second proposal was made in the early 1940s by A. Jepsen.[96] Aware that 2 Kgs 8:7–15 is the only story concerning a Ben-Hadad which must be related to the period of the Omride dynasty, he suggested that the name of the king may be correct and that Hazael did not murder Hadad-ᶜiḏr, but rather a son of Hadad-ᶜiḏr named Bir-Hadad. Jepsen pointed out that there is sufficient time between the last dated reference to Hadad-ᶜiḏr in Shalmaneser's inscriptions (845 B.C.E.) and the first reference to Hazael (841) for a short reign of this Bir-Hadad. He assumed, then, that the Assyrian account of Hadad-ᶜiḏr's death and the seizure of the throne by Hazael was simply mistaken in naming Hadad-ᶜiḏr as the victim of the assassination.

93 The cuneiform text of this inscription is published in Messerschmidt 1911: 1. #30. The lines transliterated here are obv. 25–27. A transliteration of the entire text may be found in Michel 1947–52: 57–63.

94 Most who use this passage as confirmation of the biblical account have understood the idiom *šadā*(KUR)-*šu ēmid* to mean, "to die of unnatural causes." See Michel 1947–52: 16, n 14. On this translation, see n 98 below.

95 This proposal is supported by Lipinski 1969: 172–73; also see Kraeling 1918: 79; and Jepsen 1941–45: 158.

96 Jepsen 1941–45: 158–59.

While the first solution may be more likely, Jepsen's proposal cannot be ignored. The evidence for the first solution is not as strong as might first appear. An alternative interpretation of the relation between the appearance of the name Ben-Hadad in 2 Kings 8 and the other Ben-Hadad stories may be given. It is possible that the name Ben-Hadad originally appeared in this story and that this was partially responsible for the confusion that led to the insertion of the later Ben-Hadad stories in their present context.

Furthermore, the Shalmaneser inscription which commonly is understood as referring to the murder of Hadad-ᶜiḏr by Hazael cannot be used as evidence for the first solution. A close examination of that text exposes several weaknesses in the standard interpretation.

The text, *KAH* 30, was inscribed on a statue of Shalmaneser found at Aššur. The inscription begins on the front of the statue, continues on the left hip (which is damaged), and then proceeds onto the back.[97] The front part of the inscription reads as follows:

^{Id}SILIM.MA-*nu* MAŠ *šárru* GAL-*ú šárru dan-nu*
šar$_4$ *kúl-lat kib-rat 4-i ik-du*
li-ᵓi-ú ša-nin mal-ki^{MEŠ}
ša kiš-ša-ti GAL.MEŠ *šárru*^{MEŠ}*-ni*
DUMU *aš-šur*-PAP-A *šar*$_4$ ŠÚ *šar*$_4$ KUR *aš-šur*
A TUKUL.MAŠ *šar*$_4$ ŠÚ *šar*$_4$ KUR *aš-šur-ma ka-šid*
KUR *en-zi* KUR *gíl-za-a-nu* KUR *ḫu-bu-uš-[ki-a]*
KUR *u-ra-[ ] na-aš-pan-t[a-šu-nu]*
aš-ku[n-m]a ki-ma ^{d}BIL.[GI]
UGU-*šú-nu a-ba-ᵓ* ^{I}*a-ḫu-ni*
DUMU *a-di-ni a-di* DINGIR.MEŠ-*ni-[šú]*
ÉRIN.ḪÁ(!)-*šú* KUR-*šú* NÌ.GA É.[GAL-*šú a]-su-ḫ[a]*
a-na UN.MEŠ KUR-ia a[*m*]*-nu-šu*
^{Id}IM-id-ri ša KUR ANŠE-[*šú*]
a-di 12 mal-ki^{MEŠ} *ri-ṣi-šu*
BAD$_5$.BAD$_5$-*šú-nu aš-kun-ma* 20 LIM 9 LI[M]
a-li-li mun-daḫ-ḫi-iṣ-šú
ú-ni-li ki-ma šu-bi
si-ta-at ÉRIN.ḪÁ-*šú-nu a-na*

[97] See Messerschmidt 1911: 1. #30. Also see Michel 1947–52: 57, for a description of the statue. See also n 93 above.

[17]*a-ra-an-te* [21]*at-bu-uk*
[22]*a-na* [23]*šu-zu-ub* [24]ZI.MEŠ-*šú-nu e-li-ú*
^{Id}IM-*id-ri* KUR-*šú e-mi-id*
^{I}*ḫa-za-ʾi*-DINGIR DUMU *la ma-ma-na*
^{GIŠ}GU.ZA *iṣ-bat* ÉRIN.ḪÁ-*šú ma-ʾ-du*
id-ka-a a-na e-peš
MURUB *ú* MÈ *a-na* GAB-*a it-ba-[a]*
it-ti-šú am-taḫ-ḫi-iṣ BAD$_5$.BAD$_5$-*šú*
aš-kun BÀD *uš-ma-ni-šu e-kim-šú*
a-na šu-zu-ub ZI.MEŠ-*šú*
e-li a-di
^{URU}*di-ma-aš-qi*
URU *šárru-ti-šú ar-di*

Shalmaneser, the great king, the mighty king, king of all of the four corners, the fierce one, the strong one, who competes with kings of all the great kings, [5]son of Aššur-nāṣir-apli, the king of all, the king of Aššur, son of Tukulti-Ninurta, king of all, the king of Aššur, conqueror of Enzi, Gilzanu, Ḫubuškia, and Ura[ ]. I accomplished their defeat. Like fire [10]I swept over them. Aḫuni of Bīt Adini, together with his gods, his army, his land, the possessions of his palace, to the people of my land I delivered him.

Adad-idri of the land of Imērišu, [15]together with twelve kings who aided him, I accomplished their defeat. 29,000 of his mighty warriors I struck down like sheep. The remainder of their army I cast into [20] the Orontes. They went up to save their lives. [25]Adad-idri died (or: disappeared[98]). Hazael, the son of a nobody, seized the throne. He summoned his numerous army. He marched against me to wage battle and combat. [30]I fought with him. His defeat I accomplished. I took away the wall of his encampment. He went up to save his life. As far as Damascus, [35]his royal city, I pursued.

[98] On the meaning of *šadāšu ēmid*, see *CAD* E 140, and Lambert 1967: 283. Although it seems clear that this phrase is a euphemism for 'to die', it is no longer to be understood as always implying a death from unnatural causes, as had been previously thought (see Michel 1947–52: 60, n 14). Apparently, the general idea of the idiom is "to disappear without a trace and forever," and it need not necessarily refer to death. Cf. the Akkadian poem, *ludlul bēl nēmeqi* I:43, in Lambert 1967: 32.

What becomes clear when this inscription is read carefully is that it gives only a brief summary of the achievements of Shalmaneser. More precisely, it summarizes all of his dealings with one geographical area, as if all the events in that area occurred at one time, before it goes on to describe activities in the next location. Thus, it briefly describes Shalmaneser's dealings with Bīt-Adini, then his dealings with Damascus. On the back of the statue, the inscription summarizes events in the lands of Namri, Que, and Tabalu. Examination of the description of Shalmaneser's battles with each state shows that numerous confrontations, which recurred year after year, have been telescoped into highly reduced accounts and portrayed as if they were parts of a single campaign. We know from the Black Obelisk and the Monolith Inscription (among others) that Shalmaneser's struggle with Aḫuni took place over a four year period, during Shalmaneser's first four years, before he finally captured Aḫuni.[99] This has been summarized in a single sentence in *KAH* 30, which merely reports Aḫuni's capture.

The telescoping of events is much clearer in the account of the interactions between Shalmaneser and Damascus. This section begins with a description of Shalmaneser's defeat of Hadad-ᶜiḏr and the twelve allies. Few details of the battle are given here, but there is one indication that the battle being described is the battle of Qarqar: "The remainder of their army I cast into the Orontes."[100] The battle of 853 is the only one that is known to have taken place along the Orontes. After mentioning this conflict, all subsequent fighting between Shalmaneser and the Syrian coalition is ignored by the account. The defeated Syrian soldiers are described as fleeing to save their lives. The next statement is that Hadad-ᶜiḏr died. If this were the only extant inscription of Shalmaneser, the natural conclusion would be that there was a single battle between Shalmaneser and the Syrian coalition and that Hadad-ᶜiḏr either was killed in the battle or died very shortly thereafter. Other evidence proves that this was not the case at all and that the inscription has severely distorted events by ignoring three subsequent battles over a period of eight years. The inscription then continues, "Hazael, the son of a nobody, seized the throne. He summoned his numerous army. He marched against me to

[99] For convenience, see Luckenbill 1924: #559–61, 599–609.
[100] See the Monolith Inscription II: 100–101.

wage battle and combat. I fought with him." Again there is no hint of the fact that four years elapsed between the last battle with Hadad-ᶜiḏr and the first with Hazael. The telescoping of events is evident. The account of Shalmaneser's dealings with Damascus in *KAH* 30 is so distorted, due to its particular literary form, that its historical value is extremely limited, even with regard to the change of dynasty in Damascus. There is no necessary cause and effect relationship between any two clauses within this part of the inscription. If the connection made between the battle of Qarqar and the death of Hadad-ᶜiḏr cannot be trusted (and, of course, it cannot), then there is no certainty about the connection between the death of Hadad-ᶜiḏr and the rise of Hazael, as presented in the inscription. If Hadad-ᶜiḏr was succeeded by a son Bir-Hadad II, there would be no reason for that information to be preserved in this inscription, since Shalmaneser had no confrontation with this Bir-Hadad. The important facts for the author of *KAH* 30 were the death of Hadad-ᶜiḏr and the rise of Hazael, which are reported in rapid succession in order to continue the telescoped version of Shalmaneser's triumph over his enemies in Imērišu.[101] This does not prove that Hazael did not murder Hadad-ᶜiḏr and thus seize the throne; however, the literary form of the inscription is such that it cannot be used as a substantial piece of evidence in support of the conclusion that Hadad-ᶜiḏr was killed by Hazael.

The problem of the death of Hadad-ᶜiḏr may be summarized as follows. 2 Kgs 8:7–15 states that a Ben-Hadad, king of Aram was murdered by Hazael, who then seized the throne. It is possible that the biblical text is incorrect and that Hazael actually murdered Hadad-ᶜiḏr. But it is also possible that Hadad-ᶜiḏr was succeeded after 845 by a Bir-Hadad who was then

[101] This kind of distortion continues in the accounts of the battles with "Que and Tabala" (rev. line 5). Shalmaneser attacked Que in his twentieth and twenty-fifth years, while he marched against Tabala and into the silver mountain in year twenty-two. All of this is mixed together on rev. lines 2–8. See the Black Obelisk for the descriptions of the campaigns mentioned here (Michel 1954–59: 154–57, 221–23.

There are other examples of this form of inscription from other Neo-Assyrian kings. See, for example, the Sabaʾa Stele and the Kalaḫ Slab of Adad-nirari III, discussed below in chap. 6. On these, and the "summary inscription" form (as it is called by Tadmor), see Tadmor 1973.

murdered by Hazael. The evidence available for the critical period of 845–841 B.C.E. is insufficient to settle the matter, and both possibilities must be taken seriously.

THE BIR-HADAD STELA

The Bir-Hadad or Melqart Stela, a basalt monument found in the late 1930s at the village of Bureij, 7 km. north of Aleppo, has played a significant part in the attempt to reconstruct the history of Aram–Damascus during the ninth century. The stela, slightly more than a meter in height, is carved with a relief representation of the god Melqart, surmounting a four-line Aramaic inscription (one letter on a fifth), which identifies the donor of the monument as a certain Bir-Hadad. It was found, out of its original context, incorporated into the remains of some Roman Period walls at Bureij. Since there is no evidence of Iron Age occupation around Bureij, the stone was probably brought in from someplace nearby during the Roman period, when the settlement there was built. It is possible that the original location of the stela was Aleppo.[102]

Although the inscription is short and stereotypical in form, it has been the center of enormous controversy since its discovery. The significance of the inscription is related to the problem of the identity of the Bir-Hadad who erected the stela. Unfortunately, the one part of the inscription which has been badly effaced is the left half of line 2, which gives the patronymic of Bir-Hadad. The other lines are quite simply read:

> *nṣb*ᵓ*.zy.śm brh*
> *dd.br* [ ]
> *mlk* ᵓ*rm lmr*ᵓ*h lmlqr*
> *t. zy nzr lh wšm*ᶜ *lql*
> *h*

> The stela which Bir-Hadad, the son of [ ], the king of Aram, set up for his lord, Melqart, to whom he made a vow and who heard his voice.

The occurrence of the name Bir-Hadad and the title "king of Aram" immediately suggested that the donor of the stela belonged to the royal house of Damascus. M. Dunand, who first

102 See Dunand 1939: 65–66.

published the stela in 1939, was reluctant to propose a reading for most of line two, although he made suggestions concerning the identification of the letters there. He felt inclined, however, to identify Bir-Hadad with the Ben-Hadad of 1 Kings 20–2 Kings 8, i.e., a Ben-Hadad contemporary with Ahab and his sons.[103]

In 1942 Albright proposed the following reading, based on his examination of the photo published by Dunand: *br.Ṭ⸢br⸣[m]n [b]⸢r⸣.* *⸢Ḥzy⸣[n]*, 'son of Ṭab-Rammān son of Ḥaḏyān'.[104] This restoration makes the patronymic identical to that of Ben-Hadad I in 1 Kgs 15:18, and Albright proposed that it was this king who set up the stela. However, because he dated the script of the stela to the mid-ninth century, during the period of the Omride Dynasty, Albright identified the Ben-Hadad of 1 Kings 20–2 Kings 8 with the Ben-Hadad of 1 Kings 15, thus proposing that there was only one Damascene king from the time of Baasha (early 9th century) to the usurpation of the throne by Hazael. Albright's reading of line 2 has been accepted by many,[105] but from the beginning it has been disputed. Both Dunand and de Vaux studied the stela itself in the Aleppo Museum and argued emphatically that Albright's reading was impossible.[106]

A new phase in the discussion of the stela began in the 1970s, when a number of studies appeared which were based on the examination of more recently published photographs of the inscription.[107] The first of these, F. M. Cross's article which appeared in 1972, has been very influential.[108] Cross read the name and epithets of the donor as follows: *br.h*^{2}*dd br ᶜzr[.] mś⸢q⸣y⸢ᵓ⸣b[r]*^{3}*mlk ᵓrm*, 'Bir-Hadad, the son of ᶜEzer (ᶜI̱dr), the Damascene, son of the king of Aram'.[109] Cross identified Bir-Hadad as the son of Ben-Hadad II (=Hadad-ᶜiḏr), the crown

[103] Dunand 1939: 70, 72–73.

[104] Albright 1942: 25–26.

[105] Cf. M. F. Unger 1957: 56–60; Gibson 1975: 1–4; M. Black in Thomas 1961: 239–41; Rosenthal in *ANET*^{3}: 655.

[106] Dunand 1942–43: 41–42; de Vaux 1967b: 486–87, n 7.

[107] Dunand's photo is in 1939: pl. XIII. The new photos appear in Pritchard 1954: 170, #499; and Birnbaum 1954–57: 2. #010. See also Thomas 1961: pl. 15.

[108] Cross 1972a.

[109] Cross 1972a: 37–39.

prince of Aram-Damascus. He suggested that the young Bir-Hadad had perhaps taken his aging father's place as leader of the army of the Syro-Palestinian coalition fighting Shalmaneser III during one of Shalmaneser's conflicts with that coalition in 849–845. The stela might have been erected in commemoration of a victory over Shalmaneser in northern Syria. In any case, the Bir-Hadad of the stela became Bir-Hadad III in Cross's reconstruction of the period, a crown prince who may never have come to the throne.[110]

Lipinski dated the inscription to the early eighth century and connected it to the family of Hazael, in part agreeing with Cross's readings. He differed, however, on three letters and on his interpretation of the second line. He read: *br.h[2]dd.br ᶜzr⌜š⌝mš z⌜y⌝.ᵓb [3]mlk ᵓrm*, 'Bar-Hadad, son of ᶜId̲rī-Šamš, who (was) the father of the king of Aram.'[111] He believed that the donor of the stela was the brother of the king of Aram, not the king himself. He proposed that ᶜId̲rī-Šamš, identified as the father of the king of Aram, was the father of Hazael. He would have been given the title "father of the king" because he was the father of a usurper and not a king himself. Thus the Bir-Hadad of the inscription according to Lipinski was a brother of Hazael, otherwise unknown.

Shea, also accepting most of Cross's readings, proposed the following: *br.h[2]dd.br ᶜzr dmśq brmn [3]mlk ᵓrm*, 'Bar-Hadad, son of ᶜId̲r of Damascus, son of Rimmon, king of Aram'.[112] For Shea, Bir-Hadad of the inscription is to be identified with Ben-Hadad II (= Hadad-ᶜid̲r). Shea then identifies ᶜId̲r, the son of Rimmon, with Bir-Hadad I, the son of Ṭab-Rammān. In so doing, he must assume that both Bir-Hadad I and II had the alternate name, Hadad-ᶜid̲r, an unlikely prospect.

Discussion has continued into the 1980s. J. M. Miller, without venturing a reading of the line, suggested that Bir-Hadad be identified as the son of Hazael,[113] while A. Lemaire, using new photographs, proposed yet another new reading: *br.h̊[2]dd.br ḥ̊z̊ẙn̊ b̊r̊.[ḥzᵓl]*, 'Bir-Hadad the son of Ḥazyân son of Ḥazaël'. Lemaire suggested that Bir-Hadad III was actually the

[110] Cross 1972a: 42.

[111] Lipinski 1975: 15–19. Lipinski's earlier reading of this text (1971a: 101–4)—actually much closer to my own reading—is abandoned in his newer study (1975: pp. 15–16, n 3).

[112] Shea 1978–79: 159–76, esp. 166.

[113] Dearman and Miller 1983: 100–101.

grandson of Hazael and that his father was a previously unattested king named Ḥazyān.[114]

In 1983 the first study based on a direct examination of the stela since that of Dunand appeared.[115] In their article, Bordreuil and Teixidor presented the following reading: *brh²dd.br ᶜzr³ mlk. br rḥb ³mlk ³rm*, 'Bir-Hadad, son of Ezra³, king, the Rehobite, king of Aram'. Bordreuil and Teixidor connect Bir-Hadad not with Aram–Damascus, but rather with the kingdom of Zobah, by noting the dynastic title 'son of Rehob', found in 2 Sam 8:3 and here in their reading.

In summary, the Bir-Hadad of the Melqart Stela has been identified with each Ben-Hadad (I, "II," and III) of the books of Kings, as well as with a brother of Hazael and a son of Ben-Hadad "II", and he has also been linked to the dynasty of Zobah. This wide divergence in readings of line 2 hardly inspires confidence in the possibility of reaching certainty about the identity of Bir-Hadad.

One important aspect of all of these proposed readings is that, with the exception of the proposal of Bordreuil and Teixidor, all of them have been made on the basis of photographs rather than personal examination of the stela itself. During the summer of 1985, I had the opportunity to spend several hours examining the Bir-Hadad stela in the Aleppo Museum.[116] As a result, I reluctantly came to the conclusion that I must present a new and different reading of line 2. I found that the photographs that have been published to date do not accurately depict the traces of the letters that are on the stone. In the near future, I plan to publish my findings in detail, with closeup photographs of each disputed letter in line 2. However, a summary of what I have found will be given here.

The name and epithets of the donor of this stela are the following: *brh²dd.br ᶜtrhmk. ³mlk ³rm*. The name of Bir-Hadad's father is ᶜAttar-hamek or ᶜAttar-hamak. The first element of the name is well known from such names as ᶜAttar-samak, the king of Arpad in the late ninth century, ᶜAttar-idri, ᶜAttar-bi³di,

[114] Lemaire 1984: 347–49.

[115] Bordreuil and Teixidor 1983.

[116] I would like to thank Dr. Afif Bahnassi, Director General of Antiquities and Museums; Dr. Adnan Bounni, Director General of Archaeological Excavations; and Mr. Wahed Hayatta, Director of Antiquities and Museums for the Aleppo region, for their help and support during my stay in Damascus and Aleppo.

ᶜAttar-nuri, etc. This is the divine name ᶜAṯtar, here pronounced ᶜAttar.[117] The second element is certainly verbal, but the root is ambiguous. The form may be a *haphel* perfect from *mkk*, a root known in Hebrew and later Aramaic. In the *qal*, the Hebrew means 'to be low, humble, humiliated', and it occurs once in the *hophal* with the meaning, 'to be brought low'. In Targumic Aramaic it basically means the same thing, although it is not attested in the causitive. If this is the root, then the name probably means something like 'ᶜAttar has humbled'. However, the element may also be the *hiphil* of *mwk*, also known from Targumic Aramaic and from Hebrew. In this case the name could be interpreted as 'ᶜAttar has crushed', or 'ᶜAttar has brought down'. Or the element may come from a root *hmk* not attested in Hebrew or Aramaic to my knowledge, but which in Arabic means 'to urge, press'.

A few comments on the readings are in order, although evaluation of the arguments must await the publication of the photographs. The *ᶜayin* and the *reš* of *ᶜtr* may be considered certain. What appeared to be a clear *zayin* between them in the photographs published by Pritchard and Birnbaum proves to have been a trick of the lighting. The vertical stroke continues below the presumed bottom line of the *zayin*. It is also clear that the proposed upper horizontal stroke was actually the result of the lighting on irregularities in the stone. The letter is certainly a *taw*.

The *heh* is badly damaged, but still quite discernible (particularly to the touch). The right-hand vertical stroke is well preserved, and two of the three horizontals can be made out. The horizontals do not meet to form a triangle and cannot be traced to the right of the vertical. Thus, the letter cannot be an *ᵓalep* as proposed by Bordreuil and Teixidor.[118]

The *mem* is clear, although the head has been slightly damaged. Bordreuil and Teixidor have mistaken the left downstroke of the head of the *mem* for a *lamed*.[119] The small size of this stroke when compared to the other *lamed*s in the inscription shows clearly that it belongs to the *mem*.

Cross's proposed *śin* following the *mem* also proved to be a lighting effect in the photographs. Examination showed that the left-hand downstroke of the "*śin*" was not connected to the

[117] See Fitzmyer 1967: 26.
[118] Bordreuil and Teixidor 1983: 273.
[119] Bordreuil and Teixidor 1983: 273.

rest of the letter and that it was actually a word divider. The letter to the right of the word divider proved to be a *kap*, the "horizontal *v*" quite clear, and the downstroke, while damaged, still discernible.

To the left of the word divider I could see no traces of any letters at all. Because there seems to be no appreciable difference in the level of wear between the stone above and below line 2, where the letters of lines 1 and 3 are still discernible, I would propose that for reasons unknown the scribe left this section blank. The epithet style, 'PN, son of PN, king of GN', which we thus find here is very common in Old Aramaic inscriptions.[120]

This new reading has a significant bearing on the interpretation of the stela. With the exception of Bordreuil and Teixidor, the stela has always been attributed to a member of the royal family of Aram–Damascus. But the name of Bir-Hadad's father now seems to have no relation to any known king of Damascus. Is it possible that the land of Aram ruled by this Bir-Hadad and his father ᶜAttar-hamak was an area in northern Syria rather than Aram–Damascus? Evidence that the name Aram was used as a general term for the Aramaean-dominated lands to the north of Hamath is found in the eighth century Sefîreh treaties. These inscriptions will be discussed in chap. 6, but a few comments may be made here. The stelae preserve the texts of a treaty that was made between a certain Bir-Gaᵓyah, king of *Ktk*, and Matiᶜᵓil, king of Arpad.[121] Stela I, face A, opens with a list of all the parties to the treaty: on Matiᶜᵓil's side this includes Matiᶜᵓil, his sons, his offspring, Arpad itself, the lords of Arpad, all Aram and Muṣr, as well as all upper and lower Aram. Although there is some difficulty in the interpretation of the lines dealing with the references to Muṣr and upper and lower Aram,[122] it is clear that the treaty has been made specifically with Matiᶜᵓil. Therefore, it should be assumed that the geographical references in this prologue are to the lands which Matiᶜᵓil controlled. It is likely, then, that the references to Aram

[120] See *KAI* 214 (Pannamuwa); 216 and 217 (Bir-Rakib); and 222 (Sefîreh). The style almost never occurs in Phoenician inscriptions, which usually read, "PN, king of GN, son of PN, King of GN." But see *KAI* 1 (Ittobaal).

[121] For the text of this inscription, see Fitzmyer 1967.

[122] See Fitzmyer 1967: 29–31 and Naaman 1978: 225–27. On this, see the discussion in chap. 6, below.

in these inscriptions are to the Aramaean states north of Hamath which were under the domination of Arpad.

Since the Bir-Hadad Stela was found in the region of Arpad, a preliminary suggestion that Bir-Hadad was a king of Arpad may be appropriate. However, this proposal must remain speculative at this time. With regard to Aram–Damascus, however, the new reading of line 2 strongly indicates that the stela is not related to any of the known kings of that southern Syrian state and cannot be used to reconstruct the royal succession of Damascus.

CONCLUSION

A list of the kings of Aram–Damascus until the mid-ninth century, according to the reconstruction suggested here, is:

Rezon	mid-tenth century
Ḥazyān (Hezion)	late-tenth century
Ṭab-Rammān	late-tenth/early-ninth century
Bir-Hadad I	early-ninth
Hadad-ᶜiḏr	mid-ninth century–ca. 844
(Bir-Hadad II)?	ca. 844/842
Hazael	ca. 844/842–

The century from ca. 931 to ca. 844/42 was a period of extraordinary vitality for Damascus. From the obscurity of being an occupied territory in the days of David's empire, the city had embarked upon a course of development that led from the rebellion against Israel under Rezon to the rise of a powerful political entity. By the beginning of the ninth century, Aram–Damascus under Bir-Hadad I was strong enough to interfere in Israelite and Judean affairs, and by the mid-ninth century its king had become the leader of a significant Anti-Assyrian coalition of states from Syria–Palestine. Although its territory was not particularly large, Aram had become one of the major political and military forces in the Levant, one that the Assyrians had to take very seriously. When Hazael seized the throne, Damascus was still rising in power and prestige, and Hazael brought the state to even greater heights.

ARAM-DAMASCUS FROM THE RISE OF HAZAEL TO THE FALL OF THE CITY IN 732 B.C.E. — SIX

When Hazael rose to power in Damascus, the political situation in central and southern Syria changed significantly. The anti-Assyrian coalition, which had successfully fought with Shalmaneser four times between 853 and 845, dissolved. It is impossible to know whether this was due to the change of dynasty in Damascus, but it may have been a factor. By 841, when Shalmaneser once again returned to Syria, only Damascus among the former allies was prepared to wage war.

THE REIGN OF HAZAEL

2 Kings provides a little information about the period between Hazael's usurpation and the battle with Shalmaneser in 841, incidental data embedded in the narrative describing the background to the revolution of Jehu and his assassination of Joram in 2 Kgs 8:28–29 and 9:14–15a. These texts imply that relations between Aram and Israel deteriorated dramatically during the reign of the new king in Damascus. A battle between the two states took place near Ramoth-Gilead, resulting in the wounding of Joram of Israel. The reasons for this battle are obscure, and it is not even clear which state was the aggressor. Perhaps Israel seized the opportunity presented by the dynastic change in Damascus to attempt to expand its control northward into Bashan. On the other hand, Hazael may have decided to

push into Israelite territory in response to breaking of relations at his assumption of power. It is more likely that Hazael initiated the hostilities, in view of the statement in 2 Kgs 9:14b: "Now Joram had been guarding Ramoth-Gilead, he and all Israel, against Hazael, king of Aram." This appears to indicate that the Israelites were defending against an attack. In any case, it was during this period of tensions that the revolution of Jehu took place, and Ramoth-Gilead was the place where Jehu was proclaimed king by his soldiers and from which he departed to seize the throne.[1]

The change of dynasty in Israel, with Jehu now on the throne, did not reduce hostilities between the two states, as events soon revealed. Jehu's revolt must have occurred in 842 or 841, and Hazael very soon thereafter was no longer able to fight his southern neighbor, for Shalmaneser III once again turned west in 841.[2]

The inscriptions recounting this campaign in Shalmaneser's eighteenth year provide considerable information. The most notable item of interest is that for the first time Shalmaneser fought Aram-Damascus alone; there is no supporting coalition. Hamath, which had been next to Damascus in importance in the alliance, had made peace with Assyria; the inscriptions do not

[1] Kraeling (1918: 79), followed by M. F. Unger (1957: 74), suggested that the background to the battle of Ramoth-Gilead was that the town had remained in Aramaean hands from the time of Ahab, who had been killed trying to recover it for Israel (1 Kings 22). Joram, then, had taken advantage of the uncertain situation in Damascus to attack and seize Ramoth, thus creating the hostile situation depicted in 2 Kgs 8:28–29 and 9:14–15. This idea, of course, relies on the traditional understanding of 1 Kings 22, which was disputed above. No explanation of how Ramoth-Gilead got back into the hands of the Israelites is required, since Ramoth did not leave Israelite control until the reign of Jehu (2 Kgs 10:32–33). Even if Kraeling were correct in taking 1 Kings 22 at face value, there is no evidence to support his theory of Joram's capture of Ramoth.

[2] There are several preserved accounts of this campaign. The most detailed ones are found in Rawlinson 1861–1909: 3, pl. 5, no. 6; transliteration and translation in Michel 1947–52: 265–67; also see the text in Michel 1947–52: 265–67; also see the text in Michel 1954–59: 38–39; and Kinnier-Wilson 1962: 94, lines 21–30. A shorter version is found on the Black Obelisk: see Michel 1954–59: 154–55.

Figure 6. Syria–Palestine from the mid-ninth century through the mid-eighth century B.C.E.

mention Hamath, through which Shalmaneser presumably would have passed in order to reach Damascus. Israel, Tyre, and Sidon are listed in the inscriptions, but they brought tribute to Shalmaneser, thus isolating Damascus as the only major state actively opposing Assyria.

Hazael organized his forces for battle near a fortress at Mount Senir (KUR *sa-ni-ru*)[3] and was defeated. He retreated into the city of Damascus, which Shalmaneser besieged temporarily. However, the Assyrians did not maintain the siege long enough to capture the city. Shalmaneser had the orchards in the oasis round about Damascus destroyed, and then turned southward and devastated a number of villages in the Hauran area, before moving westward to the coast. It was beside the Mediterranean, at a place called *Baᶜli-raᵓši*, 'by the seaside, opposite Tyre',[4] that Jehu of Israel (*ia-ú-a* DUMU *ḫu-um-ri*)[5] brought tribute, along with the kings of Tyre and Sidon.[6]

Damascus had survived—barely—but had to face the Assyrians again three years later, when Shalmaneser returned to Syria in his twenty-first year and once again fought Damas-

[3] The Mt. Hermon area. See M. F. Unger 1957: 160, n 16.

[4] See Michel 1954–59: 38, col. IV: lines 8–9.Three identifications for Baᶜli-raᵓši have had widespread support: (1) the headlands of Mt. Carmel (cf. Aharoni 1979: 341); (2) Nahr el-Kelb, near Beirut (cf. Smith 1929: 24); and (3) Rās en-Nāqūra, which seems to me to be the most likely (see especially Lipinski 1971c: 84–92).

[5] Until quite recently the identification of Jehu and *Ia-ú-a* has had virtually universal scholarly approval. In 1974, however, McCarter (1974: 5–7) suggested that *ia-ú-a* or *ia-a-ú* (as the name appears in Michel 1954–59: 38, col. IV, line 11) may simply represent the divine name Yaw and thus be a hypocoristic form of either Joram (ninth century form—Yawrām) or Jehu (ninth century form—Yaw-hūᵓ). Because of the epithet "son of Omri" and because of the slight chronological difficulties involved in the lengths of the reigns of Ahab's two sons, McCarter came to the conclusion that *ia-ú-a* was probably Joram.

Weippert (1978) has responded to McCarter's argument and suggested that *ia-ú-a* represents *Yah-hūᵓa, i.e., the ninth century version of Jehu's name. He points out convincingly that there is no need to abandon the identification of Jehu and *ia-ú-a*.

[6] Astour has developed a unique interpretation of this period (1971: 383–89). He proposes that the battle between Aram and Israel at Ramoth-Gilead that lead to Joram's wounding was not a battle between Israel and Aram at all, but rather one between Israel and Assyria, during the course of the campaign of Shalmaneser's eighteenth year. He suggests that Shalmaneser, as he was ravaging towns in the Hauran, attacked Israelite towns as well. Joram was then wounded when he counterattacked the Assyrians. At this point, Jehu assassinated Joram and immediately brought tribute to Shalmaneser at Baᶜli-raᵓši, which Astour identifies with Mt. Carmel (see pp. 384–86),

cus alone.[7] The details of this conflict are uncertain because of two circumstances. First, the preserved accounts are either very short or are fragmentary. More important, there is evidence that these accounts conflate two campaigns to the area of Damascus by Shalmaneser during his twenty-first and twenty-second years.[8] The fragmentary eponym chronicle for the latter part of Shalmaneser's reign provides an interesting bit of evidence. The eponym texts $C^{b}4$ and *STT* I:46 both begin at Shalmaneser's nineteenth year (840 B.C.E.)[9] and at first are corroborated by the annals text of the Black Obelisk. But at year twenty-two the eponym chronicles list a campaign which has no parallel in the annals to Danabu, a town located near Damascus. The following years in the chronicles then resume the pattern found in the annals, but displaced one year from the annals:

---

to prevent any further retaliation against Israel. The story of Joram's wounding only later became confused.

While it does seem clear that Jehu's action in bringing tribute to Shalmaneser was to avoid Assyrian attack and possibly to secure Assyrian support for his revolution, much of Astour's argument is weak. Astour states: "There are good reasons to assume that Joram continued his father's policy of alliance with Aram and resistance to Assyria, and that the change on the throne of Damascus in 842 did not affect it." While the first part of this key assertion is true, the second part decidedly is not. The only evidence for relations between Joram and Hazael is the biblical description of the hostility between them in 2 Kgs 8:28–29 and 9:14–15. Note also that the entire anti-Assyrian coalition had abandoned Damascus by the time of the attack in Shalmaneser's eighteenth year. This suggests widespread discontent with Hazael, and there is no reason to assume that Joram continued good relations when none of the other allies did. Thus, the only way Astour can make his hypothesis work (since Israel must still be allied to Aram as long as Joram was alive, in his scheme) is to disregard all the evidence currently available on the period of Hazael and Joram.

[7] There are two preserved accounts of this campaign. Unfortunately the more detailed one, from Nimrud, is badly damaged. It is found in Laessoe 1959: 154: Fragment E, lines 9–19, esp. 11–16, which apparently deal specifically with Hazael and Aram. The less detailed version is on the Black Obelisk: see Michel 1954–59: 154–55, lines 102–4.

[8] Reade 1978.

[9] See *RLA* 2: 433; and Gurney and Finkelstein 1957: 1. #46: obv. lines 1–5. See also Reade 1978: 251–52, 254.

Regnal Year	Eponym Chronicles	Annals
19	to the Cedar Mountian	to Mt. Amanus
20	*a-na* URU*qu-u-e*	to Que
21	*a-na* KUR*ma-la-ḫi*	Damascus
22	*a-na* KUR*da-na-bi*	Tabala
23	*a-na* KUR*ta-ba-li*	Melid
24	*a-na* KUR*me-li-di*	Namri
25	*a-na* KUR*nam-ri*	Que
26	*a-na* KUR*qu-e*	Que

This suggests that the annals may have combined the campaigns to Malaḫu and Danabu into one. Both Malaḫu and Danabu are towns located in the Damascus area. A cylinder seal found at Assur refers to booty taken from a temple of the god Šēru from the town of Malaḫu, URU *šárru-ti-šú šá Ḫa-za*-DINGIR *šá* KURANŠE-*šú*, 'a royal city of Hazael of the land of Imērišu'.[10] This booty presumably came from the campaign of the twenty-first year. In the fragmentary description of the twenty-first year in the Nimrud statue, there is an apparent reference to the attack on the city of Danabu (URU*da-na*[ ]URU.MEŠ-*ni dan-nu-te*, 'the city of Dana[ ] the fortified cities', line 14), shortly after the reference to Hazael in line twelve. Danabu was apparently located at the site of the modern town of Ṣeidnāyā, some 20 km. north of Damascus.[11] It is difficult to determine whether the eponym canon has accidentally used the names of two towns from a single campaign to the Damascus region in forming the list, or whether the author of the annals has conflated two campaigns to the same area into one.

In any case, after this conflict with Hazael, Shalmaneser turned his attention northward and never returned to central

[10] Michel 1947–52: 269.

[11] In the mid-1850s, J. L. Porter (1855: 1. 346) wrote the following: "In an Arabic manuscript in my possession, entitled 'A History of the Seven Holy General Councils,' written near the beginning of the seventeenth century, by Macarius, who was first bishop of Aleppo and afterwards patriarch of Antioch, are given the names of the ancient episcopal cities; and attached to most of them are their *modern appellations*, which a careful investigator could then, no doubt, easily obtain from the old documents in the various convents and churches. In this book I have found the name of Saidnâya recorded as one of the episcopal cities under Damascus, its ancient name being *Danaba*."

or southern Syria. More than thirty years passed before an Assyrian army came into this area again.

The breakup of the anti-Assyrian coalition, combined with widespread acquiescence to the expansion of Assyrian power among Aram's former allies and the subsequent vicious attacks on Damascus by Shalmaneser, might have spelled the end of the political dominance of Aram; but this was not the case. Once pressure from Assyria abated, Hazael began to take military action against Israel and Jehu. Israel, seriously weakened by the bloody purge that followed Jehu's seizure of the throne (2 Kings 10), fell victim to Hazael's expansionist policy, particularly in the areas east of the Jordan. 2 Kgs 10:32–33 reports: "In those days, Yahweh began to cut off parts of Israel, and Hazael smote them in all the territory of Israel from the Jordan eastward, all the land of Gilead, the Gadites, the Reubenites, the Manassites, from Aroer, which is on the Arnon Valley, Gilead and Bashan." Not all of this area was necessarily captured during the reign of Jehu; some of it probably fell during the time of his son, Joahaz (cf. 2 Kgs 13:25). This summary indicates that Damascus's army remained strong in spite of the earlier challenges it faced, and the result was a very grim period for the state of Israel.[12]

When Jehu died ca. 814, he was succeeded by his son Joahaz. Hazael continued his expansion at Israel's expense during the reign of Joahaz to such an extent that Israel must have been virtually, if not in actuality, a vassal to Aram. Hazael was able to reduce Israel's army, which had been so powerful a few decades before, to a pitiful condition—10 chariots, 50 horsemen, and 10,000 troops (2 Kgs 13:7).[13] Israel was no longer a threat to Hazael.

During the reign of Joahaz, Hazael extended his conquests well into the area west of the Jordan. The Lucianic manuscripts of the LXX contain an addition following 2 Kgs 13:22 and

[12] This period may also be reflected in a short passage, 1 Chr 2:23a, which reads, "Geshur and Aram took Havvoth-Yair from them and Qenath and its villages, sixty towns." This notice appears within the genealogical tables of Hezron, the grandson of Judah, and there is no indication of the date of the capture of these towns, so that this piece of information cannot be set into a chronological framework. See Mazar 1962: 105, and Miller 1969: 60–61, for two different proposals.

[13] It is likely that the number of footsoldiers has been secondarily expanded, since ten thousand men seems to be a very respectable force in the Shalmaneser account of the forces of the anti-Assyrian coalition.

preceding v 24 (v 23, a late addition, appears after v 7 in boc_2e_2) which reads, και ελαβεν αζαηλ τον αλλοφυλον εκ χειρος αυτου απο θαλασσης της καθ εσπεραν εως αφεκ, 'And Hazael seized Philistia from his hand from the Western Sea unto Apheq'. This presumably indicates that Israel retained control of the northern Mediterranean coast of Palestine, Apheq probably being the southernmost city in Israelite hands at the time. Hazael did not stop with this conquest, however, but pushed into Philistia proper, where he attacked and captured Gath (2 Kgs 12:17). He then turned toward Judah, planning to attack Jerusalem. But King Jehoash of Judah gathered up the treasures of the temple and his palace and sent them to Hazael, a move which resulted in Hazael's withdrawal from Jerusalem (2 Kgs 12:17–18). In so doing, Jehoash probably became a vassal to Hazael. Whatever the exact situation, it is clear that Hazael had become the dominant force in southern Syria and Palestine.

Did Hazael also expand his influence north of Damascus? This question raises the larger question of whether Damascus became the capital of a great Aramaean empire covering most of Syria during the second half of the ninth century. The proposal that there was such an empire was put forward by Jepsen and has been elaborated upon most significantly by Mazar.[14] Jepsen believed that this empire was essentially founded by Hazael and lasted until the early part of the reign of Bir-Hadad III, his son. Mazar, who assumed that 1 Kings 20 and 22 describe events of Ahab's reign, placed the founding of the empire under Hadad-ᶜiḏr. Since there are no texts which specifically refer to any conquests by Damascene kings in central and northern Syria during the ninth century, the evidence adduced for an Aramaean "empire" is circumstantial and should be examined carefully.

Mazar's arguments are more elaborate and will therefore be examined first. According to Mazar's proposal, 1 Kgs 20:1–21 describes a battle between Aram and Israel in which Ben-Hadad (= Hadad-ᶜiḏr) was supported (20:1) by 32 vassal kings. When Aram was defeated, Ben-Hadad, after conferring with his advisors, decided to change the form of government in the lands he controlled, removing the vassal kings from their positions and placing his own governors over the vassal kingdoms (20:24–25). This unified all of the satellite states into one consolidated empire, with Damascus as its capital. Areas that were formerly

[14] See Jepsen 1941–45: 168; and Mazar 1962: 108–16.

states now became administrative districts. Mazar then pointed out that names which he identified as belonging to administrative districts of Aram begin to appear in Assyrian texts (names such as Manṣuate, Hauran, Qarnaim), while the names of the southern Aramaean kingdoms and small countries around Damascus disappear from the texts of the next two centuries.[15] Mazar also thought there was evidence that the lands which Ben-Hadad controlled extended into northern Syria. He attributed the Bir-Hadad Stela (discussed in the previous chapter) to Hadad-ᶜiḏr/Ben-Hadad, and believed that its findspot near Aleppo is evidence that Ben-Hadad's empire extended to this area. He also suggested that Hazael was able to maintain and even expand the empire in the north, since an ivory plaque discovered at ᵓArslān Ṭāš (ancient Ḫadattu) on the Euphrates, inscribed in Aramaic, reads in part, למראן חזאל, 'belonging to/for our lord, Hazael'.[16] According to Mazar, this is sufficient evidence to prove that Hazael controlled northern Syria as far east as the Euphrates.[17] He summarizes his conception of the Aramaean empire thus:

> Aram-Israel relations from the end of Ahab's rule down to Jehoash's time become clear if we bear in mind that Ben-Hadad II consolidated the Aramean kingdoms in Syria into one state, officially named Aram, with its capital at Damascus. This was a vast empire occupying a central position in the political and economic life of the Near East. Aram achieved this position by its successful consolidation of civil and military administration, and the spread of Aramaic as the official language of business and administration. Hazael, the founder of the new dynasty in Damascus, not only managed to preserve the stability of the empire, but also to broaden and strengthen it internally and externally. The turning point in the fate of the Aramean empire came during the reign of Ben-Hadad III, his successor. The expeditions of Adad-nirari III, king of Assyria, brought about the dissolution of the empire.[18]

There are several problems with this interpretation of the position of Aram in the last half of the ninth century. To begin

[15] For this, see esp. Mazar 1962: 108–9.

[16] On this inscription, see Thureau-Dangin, *et al.* 1931: 135–38; *Atlas*: pl. XLVII: #112a. A convenient reproduction of the photograph may be found in Mazar 1962: 112.

[17] See Mazar 1962: 112, 114.

[18] Mazar 1962: 116.

with, as shown in the previous chapter, the battles described in 1 Kings 20 and 22 probably do not belong to the period of the Omride Dynasty. But even if they did, Mazar's interpretation of the events of this period relies very heavily on his understanding of 1 Kgs 20:24. Mazar translates v 24, "'And do this: remove the kings, each from his post, and put governors (פחות) in their places.'" The key to this verse is determining who these *paḥôt* who are to replace the kings are and the functional nature of the replacement. The context of these verses indicates that the reform being recommended is strictly military, not organizational. Note the following: (1) 1 Kgs 20:1 states that the vassal kings took part in the first battle, which was lost. (2) Vv 24–25 give the advisors' recommendations on how to win the next confrontation with Israel: replace the kings, refit, and remuster the army. To understand v 24 as a recommendation to restructure the entire administrative system of the Aramaean state, as Mazar does, simply does not fit the context. Rather, the recommendation is to replace the kings within the military hierarchy, presumably by seasoned and competent soldiers. The word that Mazar translates 'governors', (*paḥôt*) is the key to his understanding of the passage. An examination of the contexts within which this word occurs in the Hebrew Bible shows that while it most often means 'governor of a province',[19] there are places in which it refers to a military office. This is the meaning in 2 Kgs 18:24 // Isa 36:9, in the course of the Rabshakeh's speech to the officials of Judah during Sennacherib's siege of Jerusalem. In vv 23–24 he emphasizes the utter weakness of Judah's army: [23]"And now make a deal with my lord, the king of Assyria: I will give you two thousand horses if you can put riders on them. [24]How can you turn back even one captain (פחה) among the minor servants of my lord, when you rely on Egypt for chariots and horsemen?" It is clear that the *peḥāh* referred to here is a

[19] With five exceptions, the word פחה appears in Babylonian and Persian period contexts only. The first exception is the passage under discussion. The other four are actually two pairs of parallel texts (2 Kgs 18:24 // Isa 36:9; and 1 Kgs 10:15 // 2 Chr 9:14). Thus there are in fact only three appearances of the word in texts dealing with pre-Babylonian periods. The meaning 'governor of a province' is parallel to the Akkadian *bēl pīḫāti*. The word *pīḫātu* in Akkadian has a more general meaning of 'area of responsibility, obligation, duty', as well as the meaning of 'province'.

military officer of minor rank. It is quite probable, in view of the military context of 1 Kgs 20:24, that the word *paḥôt* here also means 'military officers, captains'. If this is correct, then a key piece of Mazar's evidence for the reform of the Aramaean state is considerably weakened.

The second line of argumentation, that place names which Mazar believes are administrative district names only begin to appear in the second half of the ninth century, does not bear much weight: it was not until this period that Assyria began to invade the area of southern Syria. Place names in this area would not begin to appear in Assyrian records until the Assyrians came into contact with those areas. That some of the names attested earlier no longer are attested at this time is an argument from silence and may be due to several factors, among them, the scarcity of texts.

The findspot of the Bir-Hadad Stela and the Hazael ivory from ʾArslān Ṭāš, both of which Mazar thought indicated the extent of control held by Damascus, do not provide conclusive evidence. As shown in chap. 5, the Bir-Hadad stela probably had no relation to Aram–Damascus at all. But even if it did, its discovery near Aleppo would prove nothing about the political situation in the region. The practice of erecting monuments in areas where important events occurred was common in the ancient Near East and did not necessarily indicate that the land where the monument is found was under the domination of the one named on the stela. This would be especially true of the Bir-Hadad Stela, since the inscription makes no reference to military conquests or the subjugation of other lands, which would be expected if the stela were intended to portray a conqueror. The other piece of evidence Mazar relied on, the ivory of Hazael from ʾArslān Ṭāš, certainly cannot be used as evidence for his control of that area. Mazar has ignored the fact that ʾArslān Ṭāš was the location of an official royal residence of Tiglath-Pileser III in the eighth century B.C.E. Excavators there uncovered the royal palace itself, constructed in typical Neo-Assyrian style, as well as an Assyrian temple of Ištar. The Hazael ivory was discovered, along with numerous other pieces, in a building next to the royal palace; this building's construction style was also characteristically Assyrian.[20] It is virtually

[20] On the excavations at ʾArslān Ṭāš, see Thureau-Dangin, *et al.* 1931. On the palace, see pp. 16–61; on the temple of Ištar: pp. 54–68;

certain, since the ivory was found in this building, that it was part of the booty taken from Damascus either during the reign of Adad-nirari III[21] or of Tiglath-Pileser III himself. Thus, the ivory has no more value in determining the extent of the empire of Hazael than does a second ivory, which also reads [מר]אן חזאל and which was found at Nimrud during the British excavations under M. E. L. Mallowan.[22] No one would suppose from the latter discovery that Kalaḫ had been annexed into Hazael's empire.

Jepsen conceived the empire under Hazael from a quite different viewpoint. He emphasized the importance of the Zakkūr inscription from ʾAfiz (see below). Zakkūr was the king of Hamath and Lu^{c}aš who according to the stela was attacked by Bir-Hadad III and a coalition of north Syrian and Anatolian states.[23] Jepsen believed that Bir-Hadad was the suzerain over all the states which joined him in this battle. He also thought that the inscriptions of Adad-nirari III imply that this Assyrian king had to go as far as Damascus during his western campaign because Damascus was the center of the rebellion. Since he places the events of 1 Kings 20 in the time of Bir-Hadad, son of Hazael, he connects the reference to 32 vassal kings in 1 Kgs 20:1 with the Zakkūr inscription, which places Bir-Hadad at the head of a similar group of kings. Jepsen doubted that all of this political expansion could have occurred under Bir-Hadad, and he believed that much of it was due to Hazael's expansionist policy. He saw Hazael as the greatest king of Aram, a ruler who molded a unified state from southern Palestine to the Taurus Mountains.[24]

---

on the building where the ivories were discovered: pp. 41–51. On the construction techniques used in the latter building, see pp. 49–51. See also the historical sketch on pp. 5–9. Also see Turner 1968.

[21] See the Kalaḫ Slab, line 20. Cuneiform text in Rawlinson 1861–1909: 1, pl. 35, #1. Transliteration in Tadmor 1973: 148.

[22] Mallowan 1966: 1. 598–99. Cf. also p. 472. This fragment was found in Fort Shalmaneser, in a room that included booty from Hamath and other western locations. The various finds in this room could be dated from the mid-ninth to the mid-seventh century, so it is impossible to say in whose reign this particular ivory fragment was brought to Kalaḫ. See pp. 472–73.

[23] For his discussion of Hazael's empire, see Jepsen 1941–45: 168.

[24] It should be noted that Jepsen does not see the empire of Hazael in the strict sense that Mazar does. He believes that the kings of the

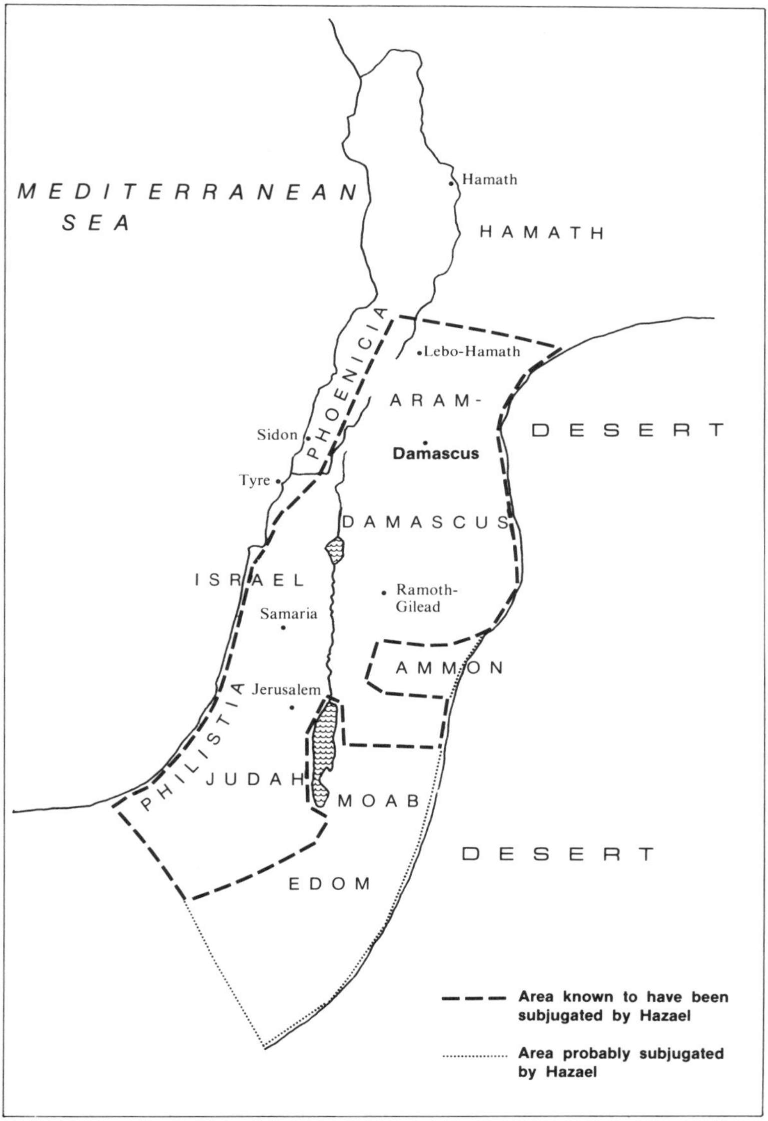

Figure 7. The area under the control of Aram–Damascus during the reign of Hazael.

But none of the evidence adduced actually points to an Aramaean empire of such proportions. The reference to Bir-Hadad as the leader of the coalition against Zakkūr need not indicate a suzerain–vassal relationship (cf. the similar case of the list of states in the coalition headed by Hadad-ᶜidr in 853 B.C.E.). Unfortunately, the reasons behind the coalition's attack on Zakkūr are not clear, although it is probable that it was connected with Hamath's pro-Assyrian stance. But it cannot be assumed that because a state participated in the battle, it must have been a vassal of the commander-in-chief. Furthermore, Hamath (and presumably Luᶜaš) stood directly between Aram–Damascus and the northern states of the coalition. A major geographical gap of this sort in an empire is hardly likely. Therefore, the Zakkūr inscription provides no evidence for Damascene domination of northern Syria during the reign of Bir-Hadad, much less for the reign of Hazael.

This leaves the last of Jepsen's evidence, the campaign of Adad-nirari III which reached southern Syria. However, even if Hazael or Bir-Hadad III had no more of an empire than southern Syria and Palestine, this would still have been one of the most significant states in the west and would obviously be an important target for the Assyrians. Finally, the reference to 32 vassal kings under Ben-Hadad in 1 Kgs 20:1 does not prove the existence of a pan-Syrian empire, since it is difficult to be certain of the reliability of the number and since there is no indication of where these vassals ruled.

In conclusion, then, there is evidence that Hazael's expansionist policy led to the subjugation of the area south of Damascus, including Israel, Philistia, and Judah, and perhaps extending southward east of the Jordan Valley as well. But there is no evidence that he was able to extend his influence farther north than his border with the kingdom of Hamath, Aram's ally under Hadad-ᶜidr, but now a powerful enemy. The size of Hazael's empire was significant enough to make Damascus the capital of one of the most powerful states of Syria, one that Assyria would have to deal with as it began to stir once again at the end of the ninth century.

---

various states were vassals of Hazael, and he makes no suggestion of a consolidated empire like Mazar. See Jepsen 1941–45: 168.

The exact date of the death of Hazael is uncertain. The best evidence that is available is the biblical notice in 2 Kgs 13:22, which reads, "Now Hazael the king of Aram oppressed Israel all the days of Joahaz." This passage implies that Joahaz and Hazael died about the same time. 2 Kgs 13:24–25 also seems to suggest this, since it refers to the accession of Bir-Hadad and then immediately states that Joash, the son of Joahaz, recovered the cities lost to Aram during Hazael's reign. This might be taken to mean that Joash attacked Bir-Hadad as soon as the latter came to the throne; however, this passage must be interpreted with caution. The account in 13:22–25 is an extremely condensed description, and it is by no means certain that Joash's military successes occurred immediately after he and Bir-Hadad rose to the throne. The summary form of this account does not provide sufficient evidence to reach such a conclusion.

Miller, in his analysis of these events, placed Hazael's death considerably before the death of Joahaz, based on his interpretation of 2 Kgs 13:3–5.[25] But it has been demonstrated here that this passage is a generalized summary of the entire period of oppression by and salvation from Aram. Therefore, the reference in v 3 to the reigns of Hazael and Bir-Hadad actually covers the periods of Joahaz and Joash and is thus of little chronological help. Instead, 13:22 provides the best evidence for the time of the end of Hazael's reign.

The problem remains that the statement in 13:22 is so general that it is not clear whether Hazael died before or after Joahaz. But it is apparent that the two died within a few years of one another. Joahaz' death is usually assigned to sometime between 801 and 798 B.C.E.[26] If Hazael died approximately 800 B.C.E., then he had ruled Aram for more than forty years, an impressive achievement for a usurper who had begun his reign in a period of great crisis and disintegration. Hazael had brought Damascus through this unstable period and, when he left it to his son, it was the capital of a state which encompassed a sizeable area including most of southern Syria and Palestine. The reign of Hazael was the period of Aram's greatest power.

[25] See Miller 1966: 442. This was with regard to his argument that Joahaz was the king who defeated Bir-Hadad. See chap. 5.

[26] See, for example, the chronological systems of Albright (1945: 21), Thiele (1965: 75), Campbell (1965: 292), Begrich (1929: Table IIc).

But it was not to last long, for during the reign of his son, Bir-Hadad III, Aram–Damascus entered an era of decline, as the Palestinian states subject to Aram revived in strength and Assyria once again returned to central and southern Syria.

THE REIGN OF BIR–HADAD III, SON OF HAZAEL

Three major sources of information exist for Bir-Hadad III's reign. First, there are the references in 2 Kgs 13:3–7, 22–25, as well as the accounts of the battles in 1 Kings 20 and 22, and the siege of Samaria in 2 Kgs 6:24–7:20. Another important source is the inscription of Zakkūr, king of Hamath and Luᶜaš, which describes a military campaign against Zakkūr led by Bir-Hadad. The final source is a group of inscriptions of Adad-nirari III of Assyria, who attacked Damascus and received considerable tribute from its king, who is called Marᵓī in the Assyrian inscriptions.

Unfortunately, it is impossible to place the events described in these sources in chronological order. The events known include Adad-nirari's attack on Damascus, Bir-Hadad's military losses in Palestine, and his defeat at Ḥazrak in northern Syria, but the order of these events is unknown. The Adad-nirari inscriptions are the most problematic of the sources for this period and will be discussed first.

After Shalmaneser III's final campaign to Syria, ca. 837 B.C.E., the Assyrians were forced to turn their attention to other areas north and east. Shalmaneser was succeeded by his son Šamši-Adad V, who was faced with the task of consolidating his grasp on the throne against the opposition of his older brother, who had revolted against Shalmaneser late in the latter's reign. Most of Šamši-Adad's reign was occupied with reestablishing order and again subduing Babylonia and some of the areas to the north and east which had naturally enough broken away from Assyrian control during the period of the rebellion. Šamši-Adad V was succeeded by Adad-nirari III (810–783 B.C.E.), who found things secure enough to attempt to resubdue the lands to the west.[27]

[27] For a summary of events from the end of the reign of Shalmaneser III to the rise of Adad-nirari III, see Grayson 1982: 269–71.

Unfortunately, there are no extant annals from the reign of Adad-nirari. The two primary lines of evidence are: first, three "summary inscriptions,"[28] which summarize Adad-nirari's activities in the west in the same style as *KAH* 30 (which summarizes activities of the reign of Shalmaneser III; see chap. 5), and second, the eponym lists, which give some indication of the locations of the campaigns of the king year by year.[29]

The three major inscriptions, like *KAH* 30, lack a strict chronological framework, thus making the dating of the events described very difficult or impossible. The one stela that provides a date for a campaign into the west is the Saba᾿a Stela, which refers to a mobilization of the Assyrian army for battle in the west[30] in the fifth year. The stela then describes Adad-nirari's reconquest of the kings who had rebelled against Šamši-Adad, his father. A description follows of his march to the land of Ša-imērišu, where he subdued its king, who is called ᴵ*ma-ri-*᾿*i*, in Damascus and received a large tribute (lines 18–20). The second inscription, known as the Kalaḫ (or Nimrud) Slab, opens with a series of royal titles and then lists a number of lands under the king's control, both to the east and to the west (the western lands include Ḫatti, Amurru "in its totality," Tyre, Sidon, Ḫumri (= Israel), Edom, and Philistia). The slab goes on to describe the encounter with Damascus (lines 14–21), the only place in the west discussed in detail. Adad-nirari tells of shutting Mar᾿ī up in Damascus, of Mar᾿ī's surrender, and of the

[28] Tadmor (1973: 141) describes "display or summary inscriptions" as follows: "A distinctive feature of this type . . . is the condensation of early with later events into one geographically but not chronologically coherent narrative. Usually an inscription of this category is much shorter than any edition of the royal annals."

[29] Transliterations of the Saba᾿a Stela and the Kalaḫ Slab, two of the three inscriptions which refer to the campaign against Damascus, may be found in Tadmor 1973: 144–46 and 148–49, respectively. The Saba᾿a Stela was originally published by Unger (1916). For the Kalaḫ Slab, see above, n 21. The third stela, that from Tell el-Rimah, was published by Page (1968: 141–43). See pl. XXXIX.

[30] The early reading of the goal of the campaign was *ana* ᴷᵁᴿ*pa-(erasure)-la-ás-*[*tú*]. This was challenged by Tadmor (1969), who suggested, more plausibly, *ana* KUR *ḫat-*(erasure)*-te* GAL*-te*. In Tadmor 1973: 145, the end of line 12 is read *ana* KUR *ḫat-te-*⸢*e*⸣.

Assyrian king's receipt of tribute at Marʾī's palace in Damascus.[31] The inscription then turns its attention to the area of Babylonia before breaking off.

The third inscription, the el-Rimah Stela, describes the conquest of the west as an event which took place "in a single year" (line 4). All of Ḫatti and Amurru were subdued in one campaign, according to the stela. A short list of the tribute received from several kings is given in the course of the description of the campaign, although this list was originally not planned as part of the inscription; while the rest of the account of the campaign is recorded in the first person, the two sentences which describe the tribute refer to Adad-nirari in the third person. This suggests that the account of the tribute from Damascus, Israel, Tyre, and Sidon came from a source separate from the rest of the account.[32]

The inscriptions present the submission of Damascus as the chief accomplishment of Adad-nirari's campaigns in the west. Unfortunately, this event cannot be dated with any certainty because the one date that is mentioned in the texts, the 'fifth year' in the Sabaʾa Stela, apparently does not correspond to the year of the campaign when Damascus was conquered. The problem becomes evident when the eponym list for the reign of Adad-nirari is considered: the eponym for the fifth regnal year (806 B.C.E.) refers to a campaign to *Man-na-a-a*, a country located in the east.[33] Because of this, those who have tried to date the Damascus campaign have been guided in their attempts to find a solution by the evidence of the eponym lists for campaigns in the west. The years 805–802 and 796 are those in which the eponym canon provides evidence of campaigns in the west. The destinations found in the list for these years are:

[31] The amounts of the tribute received from Marʾī vary in each of the three accounts of the campaign. Sabaʾa: 100 talents of gold, 1000 talents of silver, and one other item, the text unfortunately broken; Kalaḫ: 2300 talents of silver, 20 talents of gold, 3000 talents of copper, 5000 talents of iron, unnumbered garments, an ivory bed and couch, and other property; Rimah: 2000 talents of silver, 1000 talents of copper, 2000 talents of iron, 3000 garments. Accuracy in numbers seems to have meant very little to those who wrote these inscriptions.

[32] Cf. Tadmor's analysis of this inscription (1973: 141–44).

[33] See *RLA* 2: 428–29. See also Shea 1978: 105–6; and Tadmor 1973: 146–47.

805—to Arpad; 804—to Ḫazazi; 803—to the city of Baᶜli; 802—to the sea; 796—to Manṣuate.[34]

Several have assigned the campaign which included the taking of Damascus to the years 803-802.[35] Most who have chosen this date have assumed that the campaign of 802 was to the Mediterranean Sea, and some have identified the town of Baᶜli with Baalbek in Lebanon or Baᶜli-raʾši of the Shalmaneser inscriptions. Both of these campaigns are in fact very difficult to link with specific known geographic locations. Brinkman has pointed out that if the eponym 'to the sea' refers to the Mediterranean (or to any body of water, for that matter), it would be unique in the eponym canon; no other eponym designates a body of water as a destination. He suggests quite plausibly that 'to the sea' instead refers to the Sealand of southern Mesopotamia as the direction of the campaign for that year.[36] Millard has pointed out the difficulty of identifying the location of Baᶜli, since the name is such a common one. The best that can be said is that it probably does refer to a location in Syria, since the name is West Semitic.[37]

The cities mentioned in the eponym canon for the years 805 and 804 are both located in northern Syria. A battle with a coalition of states under the leadership of Atar-šumki, the king of Arpad, is described on two fragmentary stelae published by Millard and Tadmor.[38] The final campaign with a destination that can definitely be located in Syria is that of 796, to Manṣuate. This country has not been precisely located, but may confidently be placed in central or southern Syria.[39] This is thus the only campaign which definitely took the Assyrians into the general area of Aram-Damascus, and is thus the most likely candidate for the campaign that led to the confrontation between Adad-nirari and Marʾī. Millard and Tadmor have argued persuasively for a reconstruction of Adad-nirari's activity in the west in which the campaigns of 805-803 are Adad-nirari's attempt to reestablish control over northern Syria, so that it was not until

[34] *RLA* 2: 429.

[35] See, for example, Jepsen, 1970; Cazelles 1969: 110; Soggin 1970: 367-68; Donner 1970: 57.

[36] Brinkman 1968: 217, n 1359.

[37] Millard 1973: 161-62.

[38] Millard and Tadmor 1973.

[39] See Lipinski 1971a.

796 that he was able to move into southern Syria and defeat Aram.[40]

One of the factors that has added to the chronological controversy has been the fact that the Rimah stela mentions Joash of Israel. Most chronologies place Joash's accession to the throne between 801 and 798. If the fifth year of the Sabaʾa Stela is the year in which the entire campaign described in the text, including the capture of Damascus, took place, this event would have occurred 806–805, a date which creates a chronological problem for most reconstructions of Israelite history. Shea, who believes that the Sabaʾa Stela should be taken at face value and that the campaign that reached Damascus should be dated to 805, has proposed a solution to the problem, arguing that the reigns of Jehu and Joahaz both have been inflated by seven years because the seven-year usurpation of Athaliah has been counted twice, once for Athaliah (although this was never the case in official documents) and once for Jehoash of Judah, who was viewed as the legitimate successor of his father.[41] While this is possible, it is also unprovable. The date of Adad-nirari's attack on Damascus (taking the 'fifth year' of the Sabaʾa Stela at face value is to ignore the form of the inscription) cannot be determined, so there is no way to know if the Israelite chronology has been skewed as Shea suggests.

Several reasons, none of which are compelling, make the dating of this campaign to 796 more likely: (1) If the campaign that included the taking of tribute from Damascus had also been the one in which Adad-nirari had fought and defeated the coalition led by Atar-šumki of Arpad, a reference to this latter battle would be expected in the Sabaʾa, Kalaḫ, and Rimah inscriptions, since a double victory of this sort would have been quite significant. In these stelae, however, the later attack on Aram overshadowed the reestablishing of control over northern Syria, the latter apparently being the main event described in the two fragmentary, and presumably much earlier, stelae that mention Atar-šumki. (2) The non-chronological character of these inscriptions is quite evident and has parallels in other Assyrian texts; on the other hand, taking the Sabaʾa inscription's 'fifth year' as the date of the campaign conflicts with the eponym canon. Once it is accepted that the reference to the fifth

[40] See Millard and Tadmor 1973: 61–64; and Millard 1973: 161–63.
[41] Shea 1978: 111–13.

year has little or no chronological value, there is nothing *a priori* to prevent assigning the campaign to any year in which a western campaign occurred. However, the eponym chronicle's references for 805–803 appear to refer to campaigns in the northern part of Syria (802 is uncertain), while that for 796, to Manṣuate, certainly came close to Damascus, which fits the requirements of the details of the campaign better than any other year. (3) The year 796 as a date for the campaign creates no chronological problems for the presence of Joash in the Rimah Inscription as king of Israel.

A further problem needs to be resolved: the identity of Marʾī, king of Aram, mentioned in the Assyrian inscriptions. There are three possibilities, all of which have been proposed at one time or another. In the late nineteenth and early twentieth centuries, some included Marʾī in the succession of kings of Damascus, succeeding Bir-Hadad III.[42] But more often it has been assumed that the name refers either to Hazael or to Bir-Hadad III. The form of the name indicates that the Assyrian scribe was transcribing the Aramaic word/name מראי 'my lord'. It has been suggested that the Assyrians mistook one of the titles of the Aramaean king for his name, or that Marʾī was the personal name of Hazael or Bir-Hadad, perhaps a hypocoristic of a name such as Marʾī-Hadad.[43]

It is very difficult to find room for another king, Marʾī, in the succession, along with Hazael and Bir-Hadad, given the evidence from the Hebrew Bible and the Zakkūr Stela. Adad-nirari's campaign to Damascus was dated (above) no later than 796, some two to five years after Joash took the throne of Israel, and there is hardly enough time to fit Bir-hadad in and allow for a succession to the otherwise unknown Marʾī before 796.

Both de Vaux and Unger preferred to identify Marʾī with Hazael,[44] mainly for chronological considerations. Both scholars

[42] Cf. Meyer 1931: 345; Olmstead 1931: 414; Zimmern 1909: 300; Pognon 1907: 177; Dhorme 1910: 185.

[43] See de Vaux 1967a: 77–79. See also Albright 1942: 28, n 16; Millard and Tadmor 1973: 63, n 22.

[44] See de Vaux 1967a: 80–82; and M. F. Unger 1957: 83, 164, n 2. Lipinski (1969: 1. 168, esp. n 40) also identifies Marʾī with Hazael and constructs a strange scenario in which Adad-nirari III attacked Damascus in 803 B.C.E., when the old king was in the city, but his son Bir-Hadad was in Israel besieging Samaria (1 Kgs 20:2–4 and 2 Kgs 6:24–7:20).

assumed that the campaign to Damascus occurred between 805 and 802, during the time when Joahaz was still on the throne of Israel. They also assumed that the notice in 2 Kgs 13:22, stating that Hazael lived as long as Joahaz, is accurate, and thus that Hazael died about 800 B.C.E. However, as shown above, it is not necessary to date the Assyrian campaign so early, nor can the campaign be dated to the period of Joahaz, since Joash is mentioned within the context of the Damascene campaign on the Rimah stela. Thus, much of the force of the arguments of de Vaux and Unger is gone.

Most of those who have studied the problem now identify the Marʾī of the Adad-nirari inscriptions with Bir-Hadad III.[45] While absolute certainty cannot yet be reached, this is the most likely possibility, particularly since Joash is mentioned in the Rimah Stela. The name Marʾī in the Assyrian inscriptions may indeed be a mistake by the Assyrian scribe, who confused an Aramaic title with the king's name. Several have pointed out that the Hazael ivory from ʾArslān Ṭāš, with its reading למראן חזאל 'to our lord Hazael', implies that מרא was a royal title of the kings of Damascus.[46] However, the conclusion that מרא qualifies as a title of the kings of Aram seems a bit strained. The parallel biblical Hebrew term, אדני 'My lord' is a term of address to the king in Israel, not what could be called a title.[47] The possibility that a scribe derived the name from the Aramaic phrase מראי מלך דמשק 'my lord, the king of Damascus' cannot be ruled out. On the other hand, it would not be surprising to discover that Bir-Hadad had more than one name, a situation well known in Syria-Palestine during the first millennium B.C.E.

To summarize: the inscriptions of Adad-nirari III refer to a campaign during which tribute was taken in person from Damascus by the Assyrian king. The inscriptions are not annalistic and, in spite of the year notation in the Sabaʾa Stela, do not date this campaign. Evidence from the eponym canon suggests two periods when the campaign may have occurred, 805–803 (802) and 796. There is evidence for campaigning in northern Syria during the earlier series of dates, especially in

[45] See, for example, Millard and Tadmor 1973: 63, n 22; Jirku 1918: 279; Vattioni 1969: 367; Albright 1942: 28 n 16; Cross 1972a: 41, n 22.

[46] See Page 1968: 149; Vattioni 169: 368–69; Lipinski 1975: 19.

[47] Millard and Tadmor (1973: 63, n 22) point out the same thing.

805 and 804. The geographical references in the inscriptions dated to 803 and 802 are too vague to locate the direction of the campaigns with certainty. Only the campaign of 796 was clearly aimed at central and southern Syria, and therefore it is the most likely candidate for the date of the campaign in question. Tadmor has shown that the Sabaʾa and Rimah Stelae must both be dated later than 797 B.C.E.[48] The reference to Joash of Israel in the Rimah Stela also accords best with the date of 796, in conjunction with most chronologies of Israelite kingship. Of course, none of this evidence is conclusive and it remains open to other interpretations.

The second source of information about Bir-Hadad is the Hebrew Bible. All of the data in the Bible deals with the revival of Israelite power under Joash. The key passage is the oft-mentioned 2 Kgs 13:22–25. These verses form a conclusion, to some extent, to the story of the death of Elisha and include his final interview with Joash, in which Joash is told to perform two symbolic acts. First, he is to shoot an arrow out the window, toward the east. Elisha interprets this as signifying Yahweh's arrow of salvation, a sign of victory over the Aramaeans at Apheq (vv 16–17). Elisha then instructs Joash to take his arrows and strike the ground with them. Joash does so three times, but Elisha is furious with him because he only struck the ground three times, rather than five or six, for each stroke signified a victory over Aram, and three victories would not be enough to make an end of Israel's enemy. In vv 25–26 there is a terse description of the battles waged by Joash: "And Joash the son of Joahaz recaptured the cities from the hand of Ben-Hadad the son of Hazael, which he had taken from the hand of Joahaz his father in war. Three times Joash smote him and he recovered the cities of Israel."

In the previous chapter it was demonstrated that the battles recorded in 1 Kings 20 (and 22) probably belong to this period. Furthermore, the account of the siege of Samaria in 2 Kgs 6:24–7:20 may perhaps be dated to the early part of Bir-Hadad's reign, before the victories of Joash. It is unclear, due to the legendary nature of the story of the siege of Samaria, what the exact nature of the siege was, nor is it certain who the Israelite

[48] Tadmor 1973: 147–48. Some of the areas said to be under the governorship of Nergal-ereš on these stelae did not come under his control until after 797.

king was, since it is possible (see above) that Bir-Hadad came to the throne sometime shortly before the death of Joahaz. Thus, Joahaz may have been the king of this story. About all that can be said with some assurance is that Bir-Hadad besieged Samaria and was on the point of succeeding in capturing the city when, for reasons that are not clear, he was forced to withdraw (the deserted camp, with its horses, booty, and food, are probably part of the storyteller's elaboration of the tale).

The author of the battle stories in 1 Kings 20, while primarily interested in the prophetic role in the events, has preserved convincing accounts of these two battles. The first battle (vv 1–21) has been interpreted very plausibly by Yadin,[49] and one of the chief contributions of his study of this passage is the recognition that Bir-Hadad's headquarters during the course of events was at the town of Sukkoth in Transjordan.[50] Yadin suggests that Bir-Hadad had brought his army to Sukkoth in order to reestablish his authority over the southern kingdoms which had been under Aram's domination during his father's reign. Israel would have been one of those kingdoms. Bir-Hadad, according to the text, sent messengers to the king at Samaria (who, if the arguments in the previous chapter are correct, was Joash), demanding submission; the king acceded. But Bir-Hadad pressed Joash, requiring a major payment of tribute which Joash, with the backing of the elders of the city and a prophet, refused. According to Yadin's reconstruction, Bir-Hadad then prepared to move toward Samaria from Sukkoth, along the road leading through the Wadi Far^{c}a, which is quite narrow. Joash, in a bold move, sent out his small army to attack the Aramaeans while their chariotry would be strung out in a line in the wadi. The Israelites were successful, wreaking havoc on the chariotry caught in the narrow defile and defeating the army. Bir-Hadad, however, escaped and returned to Damascus.

[49] Yadin 1955: 333–41. Yadin places this chapter in the period of Ahab, but this does not affect his interpretation of the mechanics of the battle.

[50] Vv 12 and 16 refer to Ben-Hadad drinking בסכות, which is translated in the RSV (and other translations) 'in the booths'. But rendering סכות as a proper name makes sense out of a number of ambiguities in the story.

The following year, intending this time to make sure that the battle with Israel took place on a plain where the chariotry could be used (cf. vv 23–25), Bir-Hadad proceeded toward Samaria by a different route. The battle took place near Apheq, usually identified with the modern town of Fiq on the eastern shore of the Sea of Galilee.[51] The Israelites won this battle as well, and the Aramaeans, including Bir-Hadad, fled into the town of Apheq. Joash, rather than killing Bir-Hadad, released him after making a treaty with him in which land taken from his father by Hazael was to be returned to Israel and economic concessions in the city of Damascus itself were given to Israel. This was an extraordinary change of fortune, one that must have taken both the Aramaeans and the Israelites quite by surprise. It appears that the victory in the two battles was won by bold and imaginative leadership by the king of Israel over a numerically superior force. Bir-Hadad, who had received a substantial empire from his father, was apparently unable to maintain the military superiority that was necessary to keep it.

The prophecy of Elisha in 2 Kings 13 refers to three battles to be won by Joash, and these two battles fulfill most of the prediction. But the third battle is not accounted for by these events. Miller has suggested (see chap. 5) that the account of the battle of Ramoth-Gilead in 1 Kings 22 probably mixes the third victorious battle against Bir-Hadad with the battle of Ramoth-Gilead during the reign of Hazael in which Joram was wounded.[52] Miller assumes, correctly, that the original account of the third battle of Joash ended with a victory over Aram, since that was the point of the story of Elisha's prophecy.[53]

Unfortunately, the date of these battles is unknown. 2 Kings does not indicate when in the sixteen year reign of Joash these events occurred. The three battles described in 1 Kings 20 and 22 took place over a period of five years (if the reference to the three-year hiatus between the battle of Apheq and the battle of Ramoth-Gilead [1 Kgs 22:1] is accurate). It is possible that the southern states began to break away from Damascus soon after the death of Hazael, or perhaps after Adad-nirari's

[51] Cf. Yadin 1955: 341. But see Miller 1968: 339–40, for an alternate identification.

[52] Cf. Miller 1968: 340–41; and Miller 1966: 444–45.

[53] Miller 1968: 341.

attack on Aram. But this need not be the case, since Bir-Hadad's vassals may not have been aware early in his reign that Aram was weakening, and that there was an opportunity for them to rebel successfully against it. The evidence from the Zakkūr inscription shows that Bir-Hadad was, at the time of the events described on that stela, considered the chief ruler of Syria. This would probably have been during the early part of his reign, and the revolt of Israel may have occurred only after Bir-Hadad's defeat at Ḥazrak. The exact chronology of events will remain indeterminate until further evidence comes to light.

The third source of information for Bir-Hadad's reign is the Zakkūr inscription, referred to several times previously.[54] It was found in 1903 at the town of ʾAfiz, some 45 km. southwest of Aleppo, and was published in 1907.[55] The surviving portion of the stela stands slightly more than 2 m. high. A relief originally surmounted the inscription, but most of it has not survived. The inscription began on the front of the stela, continued on the left side, where the top thirty or so lines are missing due to the loss of the upper portion of the stela, and then concluded on the right side, where only two lines are preserved.[56]

The stela was dedicated to the god Iluwer (presumably the patron deity of ʾApiš, the ancient name of ʾAfiz[57]) by Zakkūr, the king of Hamath and Luʿaš, in thanksgiving for the god's support against an enemy coalition that had besieged Zakkūr in Ḥazrak (the Hadrach of Zech 9:1), the capital city of Luʿaš. Zakkūr apparently was not a legitimate successor to the throne of Hamath, since he does not give any genealogical information

[54] First published by Pognon (1907: 156–78; photographs, pl. IX and X; facsimiles, pl. XXXV and XXXVI). See also *KAI* #202. On the vocalization of the name of this king, which has been found on an Assyrian boundary stela written ᴵ*za-ku-ri*, see Millard 1978: 23.

[55] The location of the findspot of the Zakkūr inscription was withheld by Pognon, who hoped to return to the site and perhaps find more pieces of the stela. He was never able to do so, however, and on his death the location of the findspot was divulged by Dussaud 1922a: 175–76.

[56] See Pognon 1907: 156–58 and pl. IX and X. Cf. also Kraeling 1918: 100.

[57] On the name Iluwer, see *KAI* 2. 206. For ʾApiš on the Zakkūr stela, see Side B, line 11, and see the note, *KAI* 2. 210.

about himself on the inscription, but merely states that Baᶜlšamayn had made him king. His name is Aramaic, while the name of the last known predecessor of Zakkūr, Irḫulena, is non-Semitic, and this too suggests a dynastic change. After brief introductory remarks, the inscription describes the siege against Ḥazrak. Lines 4–7 read, "And Bir-Hadad the son of Hazael brought together against me [six/seven]-teen kings: Bir-Hadad and his army, Bir-Gūš (i.e., the king of Bīt-Agūsi) and his army, the [ki]ng of Que and his army, the king of ᶜUmq and his army, the king of Gurgu[m and] his [ar]my, the king of Samᵓal and his a[rm]y, and the king of Meliz [and his army] . . ." At this point the stela is broken, but it has been suggested that two or three more kings were listed in the same manner, before the final seven kings are summarized at the end of line eight, "seve[n kings and their army(?)]." The names which are preserved include only Damascus from south of Hamath, while all the other states were from northern Syria and Anatolia.[58] This coalition built a siege wall and a moat around Ḥazrak and waited for the city to fall. Zakkūr then says that he prayed to Baᶜlšamayn, who answered him with an oracle of support through prophets (lines 11–16). Unfortunately, nothing of how the siege was broken is known, for that information was apparently located in the upper left section of the stela, which has been lost. However, there are several interesting things about this inscription to consider.

From a historical perspective, questions which are of great interest include: (1) Why did the coalition, which represents such a wide area, attack Zakkūr? (2) When did this event take place? (3) How was the siege broken?

Two suggestions have been brought forward to answer the first question. The first proposal is that Hamath, which apparently gave in to Assyrian pressure under the repeated attacks of Shalmaneser III and thus by 841 began following a pro-Assyrian foreign policy, had continued to follow this policy. There is no reference in Assyrian sources to a campaign against Hamath

[58] On the number sixteen or seventeen, cf. Kraeling 1918: 99–100 (he reconstructs seventeen). Dupont-Sommer 1949: 46; Gibson 1975: 8, 14–15 (the latter two scholars reconstruct sixteen). The seven undistinguished kings were presumably very minor ones, perhaps vassal kings under one of the more powerful rulers of the coalition.

from 845 through the reign of Adad-nirari III. Thus, it is possible that the reason for the rise of this new coalition and its attack on the king of Hamath was to remove it as a major pro-Assyrian government. No matter when the inscription and the events it describes are dated, the siege must have taken place during a time when the Assyrian threat was perceived to be rather limited, and the fact that the states listed in lines 4–7 are known (from the inscriptions of Adad-nirari III) to have been open antagonists of the Assyrians makes this suggestion quite plausible.[59]

The second proposal accents the fact that Zakkūr was the king of two states, Hamath and Luᶜaš. It has been suggested that Zakkūr, who at first was the king only of Hamath, managed to take control of the neighboring state of Luᶜaš, thus creating a large, new power in Syria, one that was important enough to threaten the major states around it, especially Damascus and Bīt-Agūsi (whose capital was Arpad). Thus, the coalition was formed to attack and weaken this new threat to the balance of power in Syria.[60]

In fact, both of these suggestions may be right. The expanding power of a pro-Assyrian state in central Syria would have been a cause for concern to states such as Damascus and Bīt-Agūsi, regardless of which proposal may more accurately reflect the political situation.

As noted above, Jepsen interpreted the list of allies on the Zakkūr Stela as a list of Bir-Hadad's vassals in northern Syria and Anatolia.[61] This conclusion cannot be drawn from the inscription alone. In fact, the text itself suggests that Bir-Hadad and the king of Arpad were kings of approximately equal power in the alliance. In the list of kings in the alliance, the first two are named (Bir-Hadad and Bir-Gūš, the latter being the dynastic name of the kings of Bīt-Agūsi/Arpad), while the others are identified only as 'the king of X'. The duality of leadership suggested by this is reminiscent of the constant pairing of Hadad-ᶜiḏr of Damascus and Irḫulena of Hamath in the inscriptions of Shalmaneser III. The power of Arpad during this period

[59] Cf. Kraeling 1918: 98; Millard 1973: 163–64; Shea 1978: 109–10; *KAI* 2. 209.

[60] Cf. M. F. Unger 1957: 86; Dupont-Sommer 1949: 47.

[61] Jepsen 1941–45: 168.

may be seen in the fragmentary inscriptions of Adad-nirari III which describe Atar-šumki, the king of Arpad, and the coalition that he had gathered against the Assyrians.[62] It is probable that Damascus and Arpad participated in the attack on Zakkūr as equals, much in the way that Damascus and Hamath (and perhaps Israel) had functioned as approximate equals during the mid-ninth century.

The date of the siege of Ḥazrak is problematical. Estimates have ranged from before 805 to as late as 772 B.C.E. The proposal that the siege occurred before 805 appeared mostly in early treatments of the inscription.[63] Dhorme and Meyer, for instance, put the date before Adad-nirari's campaign against Damascus, since they believed that Marᵓī was the successor of Bir-Hadad. Dupont-Sommer also assumed that the event must have taken place before Assyria returned to Syria in 805. Lipinski and Jepsen, because they assumed that Zakkūr was rescued from the siege by the arrival of Adad-nirari, suggested 796, the date of the campaign to Manṣuate, as the most likely time.[64] Gibson and de Vaux preferred an unspecified date (Gibson sometime between 790 and 780, de Vaux sometime before Assyrian intervention at Ḫatarikka [Ḥazrak] in 772.)[65] Lidzbarski, Millard, and Kraeling have opted for the year of the campaign of Aššur-dan to Ḫatarikka, 772 (mentioned in the eponym canon), as the most probable date.[66] The assumption behind this conclusion is that Aššur-dan came to Ḫatarikka to intervene in the siege.

Of these proposals, the first (before 805) and the last (772) must be rejected. The first relies on two assumptions which were rejected above: (1) that Marᵓī was a successor of Bir-Hadad III, and (2) that Adad-nirari's campaign against Damascus was in his fifth year (806/5). The other proposal, that the siege should be connected with the campaign of Aššur-dan to

[62] See Millard and Tadmor 1973: 58–61; Millard 163–64.

[63] See Dhorme 1910: 184; Meyer 1931: 343–45; Dupont-Sommer 1949: 47–48; Cook 1929: 376.

[64] See Lipinski 1971a: 397–98; and Jepsen 1941–45: 170.

[65] Gibson 1975: 7; de Vaux 1967a: 81.

[66] Kraeling (1918: 101–2) has a very logical scenario of the events that is quite impressive, even if not conclusive. See also Millard 1973: 163–64; Lidzbarski 1909–15: 3. 8–9. For the Aššur-dan eponym, see *RLA* 2: 430.

Ḥazrak in 772, is certainly incorrect, because it is now known that Bir-Hadad was no longer on the throne by 773 (see below). After eliminating these two proposals, however, the date of the siege of Ḥazrak still cannot be pinpointed any closer than sometime during the first quarter of the eighth century.

The third important but unanswered question is: how did the siege end? How was Zakkūr saved? The most common suggestion is that the siege was broken by the arrival of the Assyrians, who came to the aid of their loyal vassal.[67] Lipinski notes that lines 2–3 on side B read ²[ ]*lrkb w lprš* ³[ ]*mlkh bgwh* '. . . for chariots and horse . . . its king in its midst' and interprets this as implying that the siege was broken by the forces of an allied king. But the lack of context and the vagueness of these two fragmentary sentences does not make this interpretation compelling.[68] While the hypothesis of Assyrian intervention is perhaps the most plausible, it is not the only one. The fact that Zakkūr emphasizes the active role of Baᶜlšamayn in saving him could mean that some more unusual event, such as an epidemic breaking out in the camp or the lifting of the siege for some other circumstantial reason, may have occurred.[69]

The sources for Bir-Hadad's reign have been described and the problems in each noted, as well as the present impossibility of placing them into chronological order. Perhaps finds in the future will help solve some of these problems. What can be said now, however, is that the sources clearly indicate the deteriorating condition of the political power of Aram–Damascus. The three extant sources all describe defeats of Bir-Hadad—in north Syria, among his dependencies in the south, and on one occasion even at Damascus itself. It is clear that Bir-Hadad was not able to perpetuate the position of leadership that his two famous predecessors, Hadad-ᶜiḏr and Hazael, had been able to maintain.

[67] See Kraeling 1918: 98; Cook 1929: 376; *KAI* 2: 209; Millard 1973: 163–64; Jepsen 1941–45: 170; Shea 1978: 109–10.

[68] Lipinski 1971a: 398. These lines could as easily refer to the enemy forces.

[69] Unsuccessful sieges were rather common. Cf. particularly the stories of the dispersion of the Aramaean army in 2 Kings 7 and the unsuccessful siege of Jerusalem by Sennacherib in 2 Kgs 18:13–19:37. In both of these cases the lifting of the siege is attributed to divine intervention.

With the loss of the southern part of Hazael's empire, Damascus was beginning a decline that would result in a reversal of its relationship with Israel.

ARAM DURING THE SECOND QUARTER OF THE EIGHTH CENTURY

How long Bir-Hadad III ruled or if he survived Joash (ca. 782) is unknown.[70] Whether he lived into the reign of Jeroboam II of Israel or not, the fortunes of Damascus continued to decline into the second quarter of the eighth century. For this period only the sketchiest of information from Assyrian and biblical sources exists.

In 773 B.C.E. the Assyrians attacked Damascus again. Until recently the only known reference to this expedition was in the eponym canon's terse phrase *a-na* ^{URU}*di-maš-qa* 'to Damascus'.[71] But some further details are now available from an as yet unpublished stela found at Pazarcik in Turkey.[72] This stela was erected during the reign of Shalmaneser IV (ca. 782–772 B.C.E.) by a powerful western governor (*turtānu*) named Šamši-ilu, who apparently was in charge of the whole of Assyria's interests in the West.[73] The inscription refers to a campaign against the land of Imerīšu (Aram), which must be the one referred to in the eponym canon for the year 773. It lists the tribute which Šamši-ilu took from the king of Imērišu and, most importantly, it gives the name of the king, a previously unattested ruler of Damascus called Ḫadiānu.[74] The information in the Pazarcik stela concerning the booty taken from Ḫadiānu's palace is unfortunately all that is known of this king. There is insufficient evidence to determine if he was the direct successor of Bir-Hadad III, but the appearance of his name as king of Aram in 773 at least sets a limit for the length of the reign of Bir-Hadad.

[70] Kraeling (1918: 102) suggested rather fancifully that Bir-Hadad died during the course of the siege of Ḥazrak. But there is absolutely no evidence for this. Cf. also M. F. Unger 1957: 88.

[71] *RLA* 2: 430.

[72] On the Pazarcik Stela, see preliminarily Hawkins 1982: 399–401, 405; and Winter, 1981: 123. Winter's article is an extremely important contribution to the study of the art forms of Aram-Damascus, an area that is only just beginning to be explored.

[73] On Šamši-ilu, see Hawkins 1982: 404–5.

[74] On the etymology of the name Ḫadiānu, see above, pp. 104–7.

The other source of information for the second quarter of the eighth century again is the book of 2 Kings and its account of the reign of Jeroboam II of Israel (ca. 782–748 B.C.E.). This period was one of the more prosperous ones in the history of Israel. 2 Kgs 14:23–29, however, only gives a very sketchy account of this reign, although it is enough to indicate that the military revival that had begun under Joash continued apace. V 25 describes the extent of Jeroboam's realm as follows: "It was he who returned the border of Israel from Lebo͗-Hamath[75] to the Sea of the Arabah." The extension of Israel's domination to the north is reiterated in v 28, which reads, "Now the rest of the affairs of Jeroboam and all that he did and his might and how he fought and how he returned Damascus and Hamath, that belonged to Judah, into Israel [לִיהוּדָה בְּיִשְׂרָאֵל], are they not written in the book of the chronicles of the kings of Israel?" It has been considered doubtful that Israel could have gained ascendancy over Hamath at this time, nor are all convinced that Damascus became part of Israelite territory again, as it had been in the time of David and Solomon. One suggestion which avoids this difficulty has been to emend the text to read something like this: אֲשֶׁר נִלְחַם אֶת־דַּמֶּשֶׂק וַאֲשֶׁר הֵשִׁיב אֶת־חֲמַת יהוה בְּיִשְׂרָאֵל 'how he fought with Damascus and how he turned away the wrath of Yahweh from Israel'.[76] There is no textual evidence for this reconstruction in the versions, and while the text of the MT is difficult, it is not so obviously corrupt that the meaning is obscured. Such a wholesale emendation is an unreliable way to escape a difficulty. The key question is how reliable the assertion is that Israel gained dominance over Damascus and Hamath. As for Hamath, it is doubtful that Israel ever had more than a relationship of parity with it. The reference to Lĕbô͗-Ḥămāth in 14:25 as the northern border of Israel's real sphere of interest makes more sense if Hamath was not actually controlled by Israel, since Lĕbô͗-Ḥămāth was located at the southernmost boundary of Hamath. That Hamath's pro-Assyrian policy was breaking down during this period, thus permitting an alliance with a southern state such as Israel, is suggested by the fact that three times between 772 and 755 B.C.E. the eponym canon lists

[75] See North 1970 for a comprehensive discussion of the proposals for understanding the name Lĕbô͗-Ḥămāth.

[76] See Gray 1970: 616. The reading was first proposed by Burney (1903: 320–21).

campaigns against Ḫatarikka (Ḥazrak) in the northern part of Hamathite territory.[77]

Damascus, however, may well have been a vassal state during the reign of Jeroboam. It is possible that Aram had not been able to free itself from the subjugation originally brought about by Joash (as recorded in 1 Kings 20, according to the reconstruction above), and thus Israel's domination of Damascus during the reign of Jeroboam may simply have been a continuation of the situation as it had stood from the time of the battle of Apheq. There are, however, some indications that Joash's control over Aram was far from complete or permanent and that Damascus was in fact independent from Israelite control during much of the period between its defeat at Apheq and the time when Jeroboam came to dominate southern Syria. It should be noted that, although the account of the battle of Apheq (1 Kgs 20:26–34) ends with the subjugation of Bir-Hadad, it is apparent that this was not the final battle between Aram and Israel under Joash, since a third battle presumably followed some three years later (see above, pp. 168–69). The fact that a third battle occurred indicates that the treaty arrangements made at the end of the battle of Apheq were quickly broken by Aram. Unfortunately, the results of the third battle are not known, although 2 Kgs 13:19 implies that Israel gained some sort of victory, perhaps rather modest. In addition, 2 Kgs 14:28 attributes a resubjugation of Damascus to Jeroboam, which also indicates that for some period of time Aram had become free of Israelite domination. When during the course of his long reign Jeroboam gained control of Damascus is unknown, since 2 Kings 14 provides no chronological information on the subject. Whatever the case, Israel certainly was the dominant power in southern Syria during the second quarter of the eighth century; during part and probably most of that time it controlled Aram as its vassal.[78]

The only other potential reference to Aram–Damascus from the middle part of the eighth century may be found in the

[77] The years of the campaigns against Ḥazrak are 772, 765, and 755. See *RLA* 2: 430.

[78] M. F. Unger (1957: 91–92) prefers to see Damascus as a province of Israel, as it was under David, rather than simply a vassal. Perhaps the most extreme view of the extent of Jeroboam's power may be found in Haran 1967.

treaty between Bir Gaᵓyah of a country named כתך and Matiᶜᵓil, the son of ᶜAttar-samak (Atar-šumki of the Adad-nirari III inscriptions), the king of Arpad, found at Sefîreh in northern Syria.[79] On Stela I, Face A, lines 5–6, there are references to ארם כלה 'all Aram' and to כל עלי ארם ותחתה 'all upper and lower Aram'. There may also be a reference to ארם כלה on Face B, lines 3–4, although only the first two letters are preserved there.

There has been considerable discussion about what these phrases signify, especially since the context of the names is not entirely clear. Mazar assumed that the reference to 'all Aram' designated all of Syria, which he believed had gained that name during the time when all of Syria had been a unified kingdom under the control of Damascus.[80] Mazar also thought that the rather fragmentary lines on Face B, lines 9–10, were a description of the borders of 'all Aram'. His reconstruction of these lines, on which he based his proposed Damascene empire, has been effectively challenged by Fitzmyer and Naaman.[81] Fitzmyer suggests that the geographical description in I B 9–10 delineates the empire of Matiᶜᵓil of Arpad, which he believes covered much of Syria. In this scheme, 'all Aram' refers to the kingdom of Arpad, rather than Damascus.[82] Naaman puts forward a very different reconstruction of these two lines and suggests that they describe the borders of Aram–Damascus, not Arpad or all of Syria, and that all of the geographical names in these lines are to be located south of Hamath. In proposing this, Naaman insists that the name Aram, which elsewhere in West Semitic inscriptions of the ninth and eighth centuries refers to the kingdom of Damascus, does so here as well.[83] However,

[79] For the Sefîreh inscriptions, see Fitzmyer 1967. The two sections which may mention Aram–Damascus are Sf I A 1–6 and B 1–12.

[80] Mazar 1962: 116–19.

[81] Fitzmyer 1967: 62–65; and Naaman 1978: 220–24.

[82] Most commentators have suggested that the city name of Damascus may be restored in line 10, although only a *qop* is preserved on the stela. If Fitzmyer's understanding of these lines is correct, and if Damascus is named as one of the boundaries of Arpad's empire, then Arpad had expanded enormously by the mid-eighth century, when this treaty was made with Ktk. One should remain skeptical about the restoration of *dmśq* in this line.

[83] Naaman 1978: 221–24. Naaman, however, ignores the use of the unmodified name Aram for Zobah in 2 Samuel 10 and was unaware of the new reading of the Bir-Hadad Stela.

Naaman's interpretation fits very poorly in the context of the treaty between *ktk* and Arpad. Why should this treaty delineate so carefully the borders of a land not directly involved in the covenant? Naaman's reconstruction of these lines must therefore remain doubtful. "Aram" is a rather elusive name, with considerably variant connotations, because of the widespread dispersion of the peoples known by that name. There is insufficient evidence, then, to connect the references to 'all Aram' and 'all upper and lower Aram' in the Sefîreh treaty with Aram–Damascus.[84] It is much more likely that the terms refer to the Aramaean states in northern Syria that were dominated by Arpad.

The state of affairs in which Israel dominated Aram–Damascus probably only lasted until the death of Jeroboam II (ca. 748). At that time a power struggle broke out in Samaria, and during this period of instability, Aram presumably was able to reestablish its independence from Israel, as well as some measure of its former importance. During the last phase of the history of Aram–Damascus, the two states appear to have viewed one another as equals.

THE FINAL YEARS OF INDEPENDENT ARAM

During most of the first half of the eighth century, Assyria had been fairly weak, but this ended when Tiglath-Pileser III (745–727 B.C.E.) took the throne. His administrative reforms laid the foundation for the climactic period of the Assyrian empire that would last for about a century.[85] His policy of annexation of territories into Assyria, the setting up of Assyrian governors over these provinces, and the mass deportation of populations of rebellious states led in 732 B.C.E. to the end of the Aramaean state headed by Damascus. It is during the reign of the last king of Damascus, in whose time the city was conquered by Tiglath-Pileser, that the sources for Aram once again reappear.

Little of the reign of this final king, who is called Reṣîn in the Hebrew Bible, may be reconstructed, since most of the

[84] Nor can we accept Naaman's suggestion that the king of Damascus at the time of the treaty was one Muṣuri, which Naaman reads in Sf I A 5. See Naaman 1978: 225–26, note c.

[85] On the reforms of Tiglath-Pileser III, see conveniently Saggs 1962: 116–19.

sources deal only with the final few years before the fall of Damascus. Information on this period is once again found in the Hebrew Bible, especially 2 Kgs 15:37, 16:5–9, and Isa 7:1–9,[86] and in the inscriptions of Tiglath-Pileser.

Unfortunately, the annalistic inscriptions of Tiglath-Pileser III are preserved in a fragmentary state. Unlike the annals of other kings of Assyria, the Tiglath-Pileser texts were not found *in situ*, for they had been removed from the walls of Tiglath-Pileser's palace by Esarhaddon, who used some of them in his own palace, with the original face turned toward the wall; some of the stones even had been cut down to fit smaller places along the wall.[87] The fragmentary nature of the inscriptions, compounded by the fact that the slabs were found out of sequence and that several different versions of the annals were carved on different walls, has made piecing the annals together a very difficult task.[88] The problem was further compounded by the fact that Rost, who published the standard collection of the inscriptions of Tiglath-Pileser, presented the annals in an eclectic text whose lines were numbered consecutively in the transliteration and translation volume, with no indications of laqunae and movement from one slab to another.[89] Several chronological problems were thus obscured. But great progress has been made over the past fifteen years, especially due to the efforts of Hayim Tadmor, whose studies of the texts have been in preparation for a new edition of the inscriptions. A much clearer understanding of the way in which the stone annals slabs were set up in the palace, the number of versions of the annals that are attested, and the different styles of presentation used in the palace, all help clear up several problems that have plagued the study of this period for nearly a century.[90]

[86] Several other passages from this period mention Damascus, including 2 Kgs 16:10–18, which describes Ahaz's visit to Damascus to pay homage to Tiglath-Pileser and the altar that he saw there. Isaiah 8 and 9 contain prophecies from the period of the Syro-Ephraimite War, but they give little historical information. The same may be said about Isa 17:1–3.

[87] For an excellent account of the discovery of the inscriptions and the subsequent copying of the texts, see Tadmor 1968: 168–72.

[88] Cf. Tadmor 1968: 175–76, for a discussion of the problems.

[89] Rost 1893. See again Tadmor 1968: 175–86.

[90] See, for example, Kraeling 1918: 118; M. F. Unger 1957: 95; Cook 1929: 380. Perhaps the most significant improvement in under-

The etymology of the name of the last king of Damascus is quite transparent. In the Hebrew Bible the name is given as רצין. In the early part of this century, it was thought that this name appeared in the annals of Tiglath-Pileser as *ra-ṣun-nu*. However, in 1948 Benno Landsberger suggested that the Akkadian version of the name was to be read as *ra-ḫi-a-nu*, rather than *ra-ṣun-nu*.[91] He proposed that the Akkadian was attempting to reproduce Aramaic *raᶜyān*. Etymologically, this meant that the name was based on the Proto-Semitic root **rḏy* 'to be pleased with'. In some Imperial Aramaic inscriptions (ca. 700–300 B.C.E.), as well as in Biblical Aramaic and later dialects, the phoneme *ḏ* was written with the *ᶜayin*. In Hebrew it was written with a *ṣade*. Thus, Aramaic *raᶜyān* would come into Hebrew as *raṣyān*, or in more Hebraized form as *raṣyōn*, the former being fully consistent with the orthography of the name as it is found in the biblical text.[92] The Masoretic vocalization, which took the *yod* as a vowel marker, may easily be disregarded.

standing the Tiglath-Pileser texts has been with regard to a subject not directly related to this one—that of the so-called "Azriyau episode," which has been discussed extensively since the publication of the Tiglath-Pileser annals. Rost 1893: Annals, lines 103–19, were understood to refer to a coalition headed by King Azariah of Judah that fought against Tiglath-Pileser in northern Syria. Among the considerable discussions of this episode probably the best is Tadmor 1961a. However, after the publication of this article, Tadmor discovered that the purported fragment of an annals slab was not a slab at all, but a clay tablet. Naaman (1974a) studied the tablet and found that it did not belong to the period of Tiglath-Pileser at all, nor did it refer to an Azriyau of Yaudi, but rather was part of a tablet of Sennacherib relating to Hezekiah of Judah. This basically spells the end of the idea that Azariah led a great anti-Assyrian coalition and was the most powerful king of Syria–Palestine of that time. An Azriyau is mentioned in the annals, in Rost 1893: lines 123 and 131, but his country is not preserved. This recent development has been very helpful in giving a clearer picture of the kingdom of Judah during this period.

[91] Landsberger 1948: 1. 66–67, n 169. The sign *ṣun* = *ḫi* + *a*. According to the most recent edition of Labat 1976, the sign which was thought to have the value *ṣun* (#404) is no longer to be given that value. The only value given for *ḫi* + *a* is *ḫá*.

[92] The name must have been misunderstood as Reṣîn before large numbers of *matres lectionis* were inserted into the text, since we would have expected רציון had the name been fully Hebraized, much like חזיון from *ḥazyān*.

There was only one slight problem with this analysis: as far as is known presently, etymological ḍ was not written with an ʿ*ayin* in eighth-century Aramaic script. All Aramaic inscriptions from this period represent etymological ḍ with a *qop*.[93] This, however, was not a serious obstacle to Landsberger's suggestion; the grapheme used to indicate this sound changed over the years, but the sound must have remained distinct, and the scribes who wrote the Akkadian texts with Raḍyān's name were aware of its pronunciation and attempted to represent it as best they could in the Akkadian script. Proof that Landsberger's reading of the name was correct was provided by a stela of Tiglath-Pileser found in Iran and published in 1973.[94] In column II, line 4, the name occurs as *ra-qi-a-nu*. This is clearly an Akkadian spelling of the name from the written Aramaic form רקין, which is the form expected from this period.[95] So the name of this king was Raḍyān, spelled רקין in Old Aramaic and רצין in Hebrew, a hypocoristic name, derived from the verb meaning 'to be pleased with'.

The date Raḍyān came to the throne of Damascus is unknown, but there is evidence that he was a usurper. In the fragment published as Annals lines 191–210, an account is given of Tiglath-Pileser's capture of the town of Ḫādara, which is described as [URU]*ḫa-a-da-ra* É AD-*šú ša* ¹*ra-ḫi-a-ni* KUR *šá* ANŠE.NÍTA-*šú-a-a* [*a-šar*] *i-*ʾ*-al-du*, 'the city of Ḫādara, the ancestral house of Raḍyān the Ša-imērišu-ite, [the place] where he was born'.[96]

[93] For example, the word for 'land', *ʾ*arḍ* in Proto-Semitic, ארץ in Hebrew, is spelled ארק in Old Aramaic inscriptions.

[94] Levine 1972b: 11–24.

[95] See Levine 1972b: 18, for the transcription of col. two. See Fig. 2 for the cuneiform. Levine suggests that the name of this king "provides the earliest example of the interchange of *q* for ʿ in Aramaic." He is assuming that the scribes who wrote the inscriptions reading *ra-ḫi-a-nu* had Aramaic texts before them that read *r*ʿ*yn*. While this is possible, since it is not certain when and where the change in representing ḍ took place, it is not demonstrable that such was the case at all, if the scribes in Kalaḫ were familiar enough with Aramaic to know how the name was to be pronounced and tried to reproduce it in the Akkadian. It is possible that the scribe who worked on the stela found in Iran was not familiar with Aramaic names and simply transcribed the consonants as they were written.

[96] Rost 1893: 1. 34–35. Rost's line numbers for the annals will be referred to throughout this section. The lines here are 205–206 in the

This presumably means that Raḏyān was not of the royal house in Damascus, although it is not certain whether he was of the royal family (a different line) or whether he was a complete outsider. The earliest references to him are in three lists of those who brought tribute to Tiglath-Pileser in the years around 738. Two of these lists may be dated specifically to 738, while the third one appears to come from a year either shortly before or after. The first two have long been known and appear in Rost's version of the Annals as lines 83–91 (which are rather fragmentary)[97] 150–157 (which are virtually intact).[98] These two lists were thought for some time to represent two separate payments of tribute, the former in the third year of Tiglath-Pileser (743 B.C.E.) and the latter in the eighth year.[99] Tadmor, however, has shown that they are actually parallel accounts of the same rendering of tribute and that this event occurred in 738. The date is especially clear in the case of the second list, which occurs in a long fragment of thirty-six lines (Rost lines 123–159) which also refers to the settling of exiles in the town of Ulluba, which was conquered by Tiglath-Pileser in 739. Furthermore, the list of tributary states is followed in line 157 by 'In my ninth year of reign . . .', clearly indicating that the events described previously belong to the eighth year.[100]

The third list is found on the Iran Stela and is very similar to the other two lists, particularly the completely preserved list in lines 150–157, except that Inilu of Hamath is not mentioned in the Iran Stela (Rost lines 151–152), and the Iran Stela refers to king Tubaʾil (I*tu-ba*-DINGIR) of Tyre, rather than Hiram (*ḫi-ru-um-mu*), as rendering tribute. The variation in the name of the king of Tyre suggests that this tribute list comes from a different year. But the fact that the names of the other kings are the same also indicates that it must have been compiled at about the same time. Levine suggested that since Hiram of Tyre brought tribute to Tiglath-Pileser in 738, and since Tiglath-Pileser's campaign into Persia, which was the occasion of the erection of the Iran Stela, occurred in 737, the list on the stela must date to

annals transcription, lines 11–12 of pl. XXII in the cuneiform volume (i.e., vol. 2).

[97] Rost 1893: 1. 14–16; 2. pl. XIII, XIV.

[98] Rost 1893: 1. 26–27; 2. pl. XV.

[99] See Kraeling 1918: 109, 114; Rost 1893: 1. xxi, xxiv.

[100] See Tadmor 1961a: 257–58.

737; Hiram, then, must have died and been followed by a short-lived king, Tubaʾil.[101] Cogan has pointed out the difficulties of this view, since a Hiram of Tyre was on the throne in 734–732, according to another inscription of Tiglath-Pileser, ND 4301 + 4305.[102] Thus, either there was a rapid change of kings during these years (Hiram—to 738; Tubaʾil—ca. 737–734; another Hiram—734), or, as Cogan suggests, the list on the Iran Stela comes from a slightly earlier tribute, and the Hiram of 738 is the same king as the one on the throne in 734. The question has not been resolved, but it is clear that this list, like the other two, must be dated very close to 738.[103]

During the next three years (737–735 B.C.E.) Tiglath-Pileser was involved in campaigns to the north and east. It was during this time that a new coalition of states, apparently with Raḏyān of Damascus at its head, was formed and rebelled against Assyria. This coalition, made up of at least the states of Aram, Israel, and Tyre, is referred to in the Hebrew Bible, and its formation set the stage for the last act of the story of Aram-Damascus.

2 Kgs 15:37 and especially 16:5–9, along with Isaiah 7:1–9, provide the information that the combined partners of Aram and Israel attacked Judah and besieged Jerusalem. The reason for this act of hostility is not mentioned in the texts, but it has been assumed, with good reason, that it had something to do with Judah's pro-Assyrian (or at least lack of an anti-Assyrian) stance. It has usually been supposed that Aram and Israel were seeking to depose Ahaz, who supported this policy, and replace him on the throne with a person called "the son of Ṭābʾēl" in Isa 7:6, perhaps a member of the royal family who supported the anti-Assyrian coalition or maybe simply a puppet king unrelated to the Davidic Dynasty.[104] In spite of a recent attempt to

[101] See Levine 1972b: 23, and especially Levine 1972a.

[102] Cogan 1973. The inscription ND 4301 + 4305 is published in Wiseman 1956: 122–26.

[103] One of these tributes, which according to the Assyrian inscriptions included Menahem of Israel, is apparently referred to in 2 Kgs 15:19–20.

[104] For this understanding of the Syro-Ephraimite War, see, for example, Kraeling 1918: 116–17; M. F. Unger 1957: 99; Bright 1972: 272; Noth 1960: 259–60.

The attempt to discover the identity of Ṭābʾēl and his son has led to considerable speculation. Kraeling (1918: 115) thought that the son

suggest that the background of this war was a purely local struggle, with Aram and Israel trying to remove Judean influence east of the Jordan,[105] the former view seems to fit with the evidence best.

Raḏyān and Peqah of Israel besieged Jerusalem, presumably sometime in 735–734, but were unable to capture the city. 2 Kgs 16:7–8 describes Ahaz's reaction to the situation: he sent messengers and a large gift to Tiglath-Pileser, asking for help against Aram and Israel and affirming his own loyalty to Assyria. In so doing he was ignoring Isaiah's assurance that the allies could not take Jerusalem and would be destroyed without Ahaz's action (Isa 7:4–9, 16; 8:4). The author of Kings rather naively assumed that Tiglath-Pileser received Ahaz's message and decided to help Judah (2 Kgs 16:9). It is clear, however, from Tiglath-Pileser's inscriptions, that the campaigns which he

---

of Ṭābʾēl was Raḏyān, and that Ṭābʾel was the predecessor of Raḏyān on the throne of Damascus. Albright (1955) proposed that Ṭābʾēl should be understood as the name of a Transjordanian state (on the basis of a letter from Nimrud, dating to the reign of Tiglath-Pileser, which refers to one Ayanur the Ṭābʾēlite—^{ID}*Aya-nu-ri* KUR *ṭa-ab-i-la-a-a*). The son of Ṭābʾēl, according to Albright, was a prince of Judah whose mother was from Ṭābʾēl. Mazar (1957: 236–37) links Ṭābʾēl with the Tobiad family, an important noble Judean family which had extensive estates in Transjordan and which had great influence during the Second Temple Period. Oded (1972: 161–62) leans towards Mazar's view and, in any case, is certain that the son of Ṭābʾēl was closely related to Judah, perhaps a member of the royal family. While this may be true, a major part of Oded's argument is as follows: "It is hardly conceivable that the allies should have tried to impose on the people of Judah, who were devoted to the House of David, a king who was completely strange to them and to the nobles of Jerusalem" (p. 161). It is doubtful, however, that two kings who usurped the throne would have been overly concerned about continuing the Davidic line. All of the suggestions referred to here are speculative and no certainty concerning the identity of the son of Ṭābʾēl can yet be reached.

Vanel (1974: 17–24) has recently proposed that Ṭabʾēl was the king Tubaʾil of the Tiglath-Pileser stela from Iran. This is impossible. The Akkadian form *tu-ba-ìl* is certainly meant to render Phoenician אתבעל, Ittobaʿl, a common royal name at Tyre and Sidon. See the rendering of the name of Ittobaʿl of Sidon in Sennacherib's Annals (Chicago Prism), Col. II: 47, 51: ^{I}*tu-ba-ʾa-lum* (Luckenbill 1924: 30, 169). Cf. also Katzenstein 1973: 129.

105 Oded 1972.

waged in southern Syria and Palestine in 734–732 involved plans that were considerably more complex than the author of this passage supposed.

In 734 Tiglath-Pileser returned to western Syria. The sources for the campaigns of 734–732 are not presented in chronological order, but rather in geographical order, thus making a detailed description of what took place in each of the three years impossible. The eponym chronicles are of some help, in that they list the destinations of the campaigns as: 734—to Philistia; 733—to Damascus; 732—to Damascus.[106]

Apparently, Tiglath-Pileser's first thrust was down the Mediterranean coast, taking such towns as Byblos, Ṣimirra, Arqa, and others.[107] Tyre, which was a member of the anti-Assyrian league, surrendered to Tiglath-Pileser, and Hiram its king brought a handsome tribute.[108] Tiglath-Pileser annexed a number of these coastal territories and placed his own officials in some of the towns.[109] He then continued south to Gaza, which he seized, while its king, Ḫānūn, fled to Egypt. Gaza was annexed and the Assyrian king set up a stela of victory at the River of Egypt (ND 400:18).

The following year Tiglath-Pileser turned his attention directly to Aram and Israel. Two years of intense fighting, 733 and 732, brought Aram to its knees, and it was incorporated into the Assyrian provincial system. Israel was slightly more fortunate. The offending king, Peqah, who had been the ally of

[106] Sources for the campaigns of 734–732 are as follows: (1) Layard 1851: #72b–73a = Rost 1893: annals lines 191–210 (this text overlaps (3), below). (2) Layard, #66 = Rost lines 211–228. (3) Layard #29b = Rost lines 229–240. (4) Rawlinson 1861–1909: 3. pl. 10, #2 = Rost, Kleinere Inschriften #I, pp. 78–83. (5) ND 400, published in Wiseman 1951: 21–24. (6) ND 4301 + 4305, published in Wiseman 1956: 124–26. See Tadmor 1968: 185–86; and Cazelles 1978: *71–*72.

[107] See Rost 1893: 1. 78, lines 2–4.

[108] This is described in ND 4301 + 4305: rev. 5–8 (Wiseman 1956: 125), and also, apparently, in the fragmentary lines of ND 400: 1–7, which seem to refer to Tyre, since there is a reference in line 3 to "in the midst of the sea I trod them down." This passage then goes on to describe the surrender of the king of the location that was being attacked (see line 4).

[109] Rost 1893: 1. 78, lines 4–5 indicates that those areas that were annexed into the empire were divided into six provinces. Note also ND 400: 9.

Raḏyān, was murdered by Hoshea at the time when Tiglath-Pileser was attacking Israelite territory. Hoshea then immediately surrendered to the Assyrian king and pledged his loyalty. Tiglath-Pileser claims in his inscriptions that he appointed Hoshea to the throne, although it is clear that he merely confirmed Hoshea's position and allowed him to remain in it as a vassal.[110] The northern part of Israelite territory was incorporated into the Assyrian empire, however, and divided into three provinces: Megiddo, including Galilee; Dor, along the coast; and Gilead.[111] Hoshea was left to rule only the area around Samaria (2 Kgs 15:29).

For the fall of Aram, only a fragmentary account drawn from the inscriptions of Tiglath-Pileser and 2 Kgs 16:9 are available as evidence. The most complete picture of these events is found in the above-mentioned fragment, Layard #72b–73a = Rost Annals lines 191–210. The description of the capture of Aram seems to begin as early as line 195, although this is not certain, since no names are preserved in the section from 195–204. Lines 205–209 record the following: [205]"[ ]The city of Ḫādara, the ancestral house of Raḏyān, the Ša-imērišu-ite, [206][the place where] he was born, I besieged and conquered. 800 prisoners together with their property, [207][ ]their oxen, their small cattle I took as booty. 750 prisoners of war from the city of Kuruṣṣa, [208][X prisoners of war] from the city of Irmaia, 550 prisoners of war from the city of Mituna I took as booty. 591 cities [209][ ]of sixteen districts of the land of Ša-imērišu I destroyed, like mounds after a flood."

Thus Aram fell. Few details of the capture of the capital city have been preserved.[112] The only certain reference to this event

[110] See Rost 1893: 1. 80, lines 17–18; and 2 Kgs 15:29–30.

[111] See Abel 1938: 2. 103–4; and Forrer 1920: 59–62.

[112] It is quite possible that the fragmentary lines 201–204 described the capture of Damascus. Note the reference in line 204 to the "orchards without number" which were cut down by the Assyrians.

A possible reference to the aftermath of the capture of Damascus may occur in a tablet found at Kalaḫ in 1952. This very badly damaged tablet, ND 2381, is a letter from one Uḫati, who seems to have been charged with sending some of the booty from Damascus to Assyria. Unfortunately, very little of the text can now be read. See Saggs 1955: 138 and pl. XXXII. It is uncertain exactly when this letter was written (see p. 153).

is the laconic entry in 2 Kgs 16:9, which reads: "The king of Assyria went up to Damascus and captured it and took it into exile [to Qir],[113] but Raḏyān he killed."

There is one other reference to the battle against Damascus, although it provides very little actual information about the event. It is found in the inscription of Bir-Rākib, a king of Yaʾdiya/Samʾal, who set up a statue in honor of his father, Panammū.[114] Panammū, according to the inscription, was a faithful vassal of Tiglath-Pileser and accompanied the latter on several of his campaigns. It appears from the text that Panammū died during the course of the campaign against Damascus, perhaps in a battle at Damascus itself. Tiglath-Pileser and all the camp of the Assyrians mourned deeply for Panammū (lines 16–17). Then, after a broken passage at the end of line 17, it is stated that Tiglath-Pileser "set up a stela for him along the road and brought my father across from Damascus to Assyria." No details of the battle are given.

One interesting piece of information that can be gained from the fragmentary Assyrian texts is the location of the southern boundary of Aram at the time of its incorporation into the empire. Tadmor has reconstructed the reading of some lines which refer to this, with the aid of three fragmentary inscriptions.[115] His reconstruction reads as follows: [*māt Bīt*] ^{m}*Ḫazaʾili rapšu ana siḫiršu ultu š*[*ad Lab*][*na*]*na adi libbi* ^{URU}*Galʾaza u* ^{URU}*Abil* [*akka*] *ša pāṭi māt Bīt* ^{m}*Ḫumria ana miṣir māt Aššur utirra šutrešēja bēlē-piḫāti elišunu aškun*.[116] This may be translated: "The wide land of Beth Hazael in its entirety, from Mt. Lebanon as far as the town of Galʾaza (probably = Gilead/Ramoth-Gilead)[117] and the town of

[113] The reading 'to Qir' is somewhat problematic. It does not appear in most manuscripts of the LXX (except, of course, the Hexaplaric versions, led by A). The Lucianic recension, found in boc_2e_2, has the reading απωκισεν την πολιν, which suggests a reading העיר in the Vorlage. The reference to Qir may be a gloss under the influence of the prophecy in Amos 1:5, "and the people of Aram shall go into exile to Qir."

[114] For the text, see *KAI* #215. See also Landsberger 1948: 69–72; Gibson 1975: 76–86.

[115] Tadmor 1962: 114–18. The three inscriptions are Rawlinson 1861–1909: 3. pl. 10, #2, lines 5–8; ND 4301 + 4305, lines rev. 2–4; and K2649, lines 1–4 = Rost, Kleinere Inschriften, #III, p. 86.

[116] Tadmor 1962: 118.

[117] See Tadmor 1962: 118–19.

Abilakka (= Abel-Beth-Maacah?)[118] which are on the border of the land of Beth Omri, I restored to the territory of the land of Assyria. Officials of mine I placed over them as governors." If this reconstruction is correct, and the towns of Galᵓaza and Abilakka are correctly identified, then some idea of the extent of Aramaean control in the final years of Aram's existence is gained. Although Israel under Jeroboam II had expanded considerably at Damascus's expense, it is clear that, by the last years of Raḏ̣yān's reign, Aramaean dominance had been reinstituted in several areas that had been under Damascus's control previously. Ramoth-Gilead was once again a border town between Aram and Israel. And, if Abilakka is to be identified with Abel-Beth-Maacah, then Aramaean control had also returned to the southern Biqâᶜ.

The capture of Aram by Tiglath-Pileser III in 732 was the end of the independent state of Aram. Damascus became the capital of an Assyrian province, while the rest of the land of Aram was carved into other provinces, probably following some of the lines of the districts referred to in Tiglath-Pileser's inscription (Annals, line 209). The names of these provinces were Hauran, Qarnini, Manṣuate, and Ṣubite (= Zobah).[119]

The known kings of Aram during the last century of its existence were:

Hazael	ca. 844/42—ca. 800
Bir-Hadad III	early eighth century
Ḥadiānu	second quarter of eighth century
Raḏ̣yān	mid-eighth century—732

118 See Tadmor 1962: 115.

119 On the provinces created from the kingdom of Aram, see Abel 1938: 2. 102–3; and Forrer 1920: 62–63. See also Aharoni and Avi-Yonah 1968: map 148.

EPILOGUE

IT SEEMS WORTHWHILE, in closing this historical study of earliest Damascus, for us to make a few general observations that may be drawn from the foregoing research.

When we look at the evidence that has been preserved about the area of Damascus from the second millennium B.C.E., what appears most clearly from it is the fact that the land of ʾĀpum/Upi was quite insignificant from a political point of view. The references to this area in the Egyptian and the Hittite sources indicate that the area was of note only because it happened to be on the boundary of the spheres of influence of the major powers of the day. What evidence we have seems to indicate that Damascus shared in the culture of and held the same kind of status as the other tiny and insignificant city-states of the area of Canaan (such as Jerusalem, Gezer, Shechem, etc., in the Amarna Letters), rather than belonging to the circle of the larger, more important states to the north (Qatna, Qadesh, Yamḫad).

It was only toward the end of the tenth century B.C.E. that Damascus, now capital of a state called Aram, became a significant political and cultural entity. Although we lack native sources from Aram-Damascus itself, the information preserved in Assyrian and Israelite sources is enough to assure us of the substantial influence that this state had on the political situation of the time. In its relations with the Syrian states to the north, it is clear that, particularly during the ninth century, Aram was considered one of the leading, and often *the* leading state of the Levant. The Assyrians themselves were well aware that Aram was one of the major obstacles to their expansion into the West.

From the biblical sources it has become clear that Aram became the chief political rival of the northern kingdom of Israel and that the conflicts between these two countries had a major impact on both states. Although little actual space was given to the relations between Israel and Aram by the authors of the books of Kings, it is clear from what is recorded there that the two nations were in almost constant conflict and rivalry for supremacy in the southern Levant. During most of the time from the beginning of the ninth century to the beginning of the eighth, Aram was clearly the dominant military power in the south, and at times Israel was under its control (for example, in the days of Bir-Hadad I and of Hazael). But at other times during the ninth century, Israel was able to hold its own (such as during the days of Ahab, when Israel and Aram, under Hadad-ᶜiḏr, were allies against the Assyrians). With the turn of the eighth century, Aram's power began to wane and Israel was able to throw off the dominance of Aram and indeed, for a time, to turn the tables and gain a degree of dominance over Aram. With the rise of the Assyrian threat once again under Tiglath-Pileser III, however, Aram and Israel joined together in alliance one last time to fight the common enemy, an enemy they could not defeat. It is clear from all of this that during the two centuries between the time that Rezon broke away from Solomon's empire and the capture of Damascus in 732, the stories of Israel and Aram were often closely linked, in war, in alliance, or in conquest. What effects the links had with reference to cultural influences between the two can only be speculated on because of the regrettable lack of archaeological and written sources from Aram. Some day new information may surface that will allow us to begin discerning those influences.

For some two centuries, then, Aram–Damascus had been a major political force in the Levant, sometimes, in fact, the dominant power in the area. After its incorporation into the provincial system of the Assyrian empire, its role in politics was greatly diminished. When in 720 B.C.E. a number of western states and provinces gathered together in a revolt against Sargon II of Assyria, Damascus appears only as a minor partner in the undertaking. For Damascus, there would be centuries of relative obscurity ahead. But from this time onward, Damascus would never again be an insignificant city. Although the drift of political fortune would be long in flowing back toward this great oasis, the city, with its water, its strategic location along the great trade routes, would survive and thrive as it waited patiently for new days of glory that would eventually come its way.

BIBLIOGRAPHY

Abel, F.-M.

1938 *Géographie de la Palestine*. Two Volumes. Paris: Librairie Lecoffre.

Aharoni, Y.

1953 "The Land of ᶜAmqi," *IEJ* 3: 153–61.

1979 *The Land of the Bible: A Historical Geography*. Revised Edition. Trans. from the Hebrew by A. F. Rainey. Philadelphia: Westminster.

Aharoni, Y. and M. Avi-Yonah.

1968 *The Macmillan Bible Atlas*. New York / London: Macmillan.

Ahituv, S.

1978 "Economic Factors in the Egyptian Conquest of Canaan," *IEJ* 28: 93–105.

AHw Soden, W. von. *Akkadisches Handwörterbuch*. 3 volumes. Wiesbaden: Otto Harrassowitz, 1965–83.

Albright, W. F.

1934 *The Vocalization of the Egyptian Syllabic Orthography*. New Haven: American Oriental Society.

1941 "The Land of Damascus between 1850 and 1750 B.C." *BASOR* 83: 30–36.

1942 "A Votive Stele Erected by Ben-Hadad I of Damascus to the God Melcarth," *BASOR* 87: 23–29.

1945 "The Chronology of the Divided Monarchy of Israel," *BASOR* 100: 16–22.

1955 "The Son of Tabeel (Isaiah 7:6)," *BASOR* 140: 34–35.

1960 *The Archaeology of Palestine*. Baltimore: Penguin.

1961 "Abram the Hebrew: A New Archaeological Interpretation," *BASOR* 163: 36–54.

1968 *Yahweh and the Gods of Canaan*. Garden City: Doubleday; reprinted, Winona Lake, Ind.: Eisenbrauns, 1978.

1969 *Archaeology and the Religion of Israel*. Fifth Edition. Garden City: Doubleday.

1975a "The Amarna Letters from Palestine." Pp. 98–116 in *The Cambridge Ancient History*, II/2. Ed. by I. E. S. Edwards, *et al.* Cambridge: Cambridge University.

1975b "Syria, the Philistines, and Phoenicia." Pp. 507–36 in *The Cambridge Ancient History*, II/2. Ed. by I. E. S. Edwards, *et. al.* Cambridge: Cambridge University.

Aldred, C.

1975 "Egypt: The Amarna Period and the End of the Eighteenth Dynasty." Pp. 49–97 in *The Cambridge Ancient History*, II/2. Ed. by I. E. S. Edwards, *et al.* Cambridge: Cambridge University.

Alt, A.

1929 "Das System der assyrischen Provinzen auf dem Boden des Reiches Israel," *ZDPV* 52: 220–42.

ANET[3] *Ancient Near Eastern Texts Relating to the Old Testament.* Third Edition. Ed. by J. B. Pritchard. Princeton: Princeton University, 1969.

ARM II

1941 Jean, C.-F. *Archives royales de Mari II.* Paris: Paul Geuthner.

ARM IV

1951 Dossin, G. *Archives royales de Mari IV.* Paris: Imprimerie nationale.

ARM VII

1957 Bottéro, J. *Archives royales de Mari VII.* Paris: Imprimerie nationale.

ARM XIV

1974 Birot, M. *Archives royales de Mari XIV.* Paris: Paul Geuthner.

ARMT XVI/1

1979 Birot, M., J.-R. Kupper, O. Rouault, *Archives royales de Mari XVI/1: Répertoire analytique.* Paris: Paul Geuthner.

ARMT XXII

1983 Kupper, J.-R. *Documents administratifs de la salle 135 du palais de Mari.* Paris: Association pour la diffusion de la pensée francaise.

Astour, M. C.

1971 "841 B.C.: The First Assyrian Invasion of Israel," *JAOS* 91: 383–89.

Avi-Yonah, M., ed.

1975–78 *Encyclopedia of Archaeological Excavations in the Holy Land.* Four Volumes. Englewood Cliffs: Prentice-Hall.

Begrich, J.
1929 *Die Chronologie der Könige von Israel und Juda*. Tübingen: J. C. B. Mohr.
Bilgiç, Emin.
1945–51 "Die Ortsnamen der 'kappadokischen' Urkunden im Rahmen der alten Sprachen Anatoliens," *AfO* 15: 1–37.
BIN IV
1927 Clay, A. T. *Babylonian Inscriptions in the Collections of James B. Nies, IV*. New Haven: Yale University.
Biran, A.
1980 "Tell Dan—Five Years Later," *BA* 43: 168–82.
Birnbaum, S.
1954–57 *The Hebrew Scripts*. Two Volumes. London: Palaeographia.
Boling, R. C.
1975 *Judges*. Anchor Bible. Garden City: Doubleday.
Bordreuil, P., and J. Teixidor
1983 "Nouvel examen de l'inscription de Bar-Hadad," *Aula Orientalis* 1: 271–76.
Bottéro, J.
1981 "L'ordalie en Mésopotamie ancienne," *Annali della Scuola Normale, Superiore di Pisa (Classe di lettere e filosofia)* III: 1005–67.
Breasted, J. H.
1906 *Ancient Records of Egypt: Historical Documents*. Four Volumes. Chicago: University of Chicago.
Bright, J.
1972 *A History of Israel*. Second Edition. Philadelphia: Westminster.
Brinkman, J. A.
1968 *A Political History of Post-Kassite Babylonia, 1158–722 B.C.* Rome: Pontifical Biblical Institute.
1978 "A Further Note on the Date of the Battle of Qarqar and Neo-Assyrian Chronology," *JCS* 30: 173–75.
Brooke, A. E. and N. McLean and H. Thackeray.
1930 *The Old Testament in Greek*. Two Volumes. Cambridge: Cambridge University.
Buccellati, G.
1967 *Cities and Nations of Ancient Syria*. Rome: Istituto di Studi del Vicino Oriente.
Burney, C. F.
1903 *Notes on the Hebrew Text of the Book of Kings*. Oxford: Oxford University.

CAD Gelb, I. J., *et al. The Chicago Assyrian Dictionary*. Chicago: The Oriental Institute, 1955–.

Caminos, R.

1954 *Late-Egyptian Miscellanies*. London: Oxford University.

Campbell, E. F.

1964 *The Chronology of the Amarna Letters*. Baltimore: Johns Hopkins.

1965 "The Ancient Near East: Chronological Bibliography and Charts." Pp. 281–93 in *The Bible and the Ancient Near East* (Festschrift W. F. Albright). Ed. by G. E. Wright. Garden City: Doubleday; reprinted, Winona Lake, Ind.: Eisenbrauns, 1979.

Cauvin, J.

1972 *Réligions néolithiques de Syro-Palestine*. Paris: Librairie d'Amerique et d'Orient.

1978 *Les premiers villages de Syrie-Palestine du IXème au VIIème millénaire avant J.C.* Lyon: Maison de l'Orient.

Cauvin, M. C.

1974 "Outillage lithique et chronologie à Tell Aswad (Damascène, Syrie)," *Paléorient* 2: 429–36.

1975–77 "Outillage lithique et chronologie de Tell Ghoraifé C (Damascène, Syrie)," *Paléorient* 3: 295–304.

Cazelles, H.

1969 "Une nouvelle stèle d'Adad-nirari d'Assyrie et Joas d'Israël," *CRAIBL*: 106–17.

1978 "Problèmes de la guerre syro-ephraimite," *EI* 14: 70*–78*.

Charpin, D.

1983 "Temples à découvrir en Syrie du nord d'après des documents inédits de Mari," *Iraq* 45: 56–63.

Clay, A. T.

1909 *Amurru, Home of the Northern Semites*. Philadelphia: Sunday School Times.

1919 *The Empire of the Amorites*. New Haven: Yale University.

Cogan, M.

1973 "Tyre and Tiglath-Pileser III," *JCS* 25: 96–99.

Contenau, G.

1924 "L'Institut français d'archéologie et d'art musulmans de Damas," *Syria* 5: 203–11.

Contenson, H. de.

1967 "Troisième campagne à Tell Ramad, 1966: rapport préliminaire," *AAAS* 17: 17–24.

1968 "Rapport préliminaire sur les fouilles à Tell al-Khazzami en 1967," *AAAS* 18: 55–62.
1969a "Quatrième et cinqième campagnes à Tell Ramad, 1967–68: rapport préliminaire," *AAAS* 19: 25–30.
1969b "Sixième campagne de fouilles à Tell Ramad en 1969: rapport préliminaire," *AAAS* 19: 31–35.
1970 "Septième campagne de fouilles à Tell Ramad en 1970: rapport préliminaire," *AAAS* 20: 77–80.
1971 "Tell Ramad, a Village of Syria of the 7th and 6th Millennia B.C." *Archaeology* 24: 278–85.
1972 "Tell Aswad. Fouilles de 1971," *AAAS* 22: 75–84.
1973 "Chronologie absolue de Tell Aswad (Damascène, Syrie)," *BSPF* 70: 253–56.
1974 "Huitième campagne de fouilles à Tell Ramad en 1973: rapport préliminaire," *AAAS* 24: 17–24.
1975a "Les Fouilles à Ghoraifé en 1974," *AAAS* 25: 17–24.
1975b "Ghoraifé et la chronologie du néolithique damascenien," *AAAS* 25: 183–84.
1976a "Nouvelles données sur le Néolithique précéramique dans la région de Damas (Syrie) d'après les fouilles à Ghoraifé en 1974," *BSPF* 73: 80–82.
1976b "Précisions sur la stratigraphie de Tell Aswad (Syrie)," *BSPF* 73: 198–99.
1977–78 "Tell Aswad. Fouilles de 1972," *AAAS* 27–28: 205–15.

Contenson, H. de, and W. J. van Liere.
1964 "Sondages à Tell Ramad en 1963: rapport préliminaire," *AAAS* 14: 109–24.
1966 "Seconde campagne à Tell Ramad, 1965: rapport préliminaire," *AAAS* 16: 167–74.

Cook, S. A.
1929 "Israel and the Neighboring States." Pp. 354–87 in *The Cambridge Ancient History*, III. Ed. by J. B. Bury, S. A. Cook, and F. E. Adcock. Cambridge: Cambridge University.

Copeland, L.
1975 "The Middle and Upper Paleolithic of Lebanon and Syria in the Light of Recent Research." Pp. 317–50 in *Problems in Prehistory: North Africa and the Levant*. Ed. by F. Wendorf and A. E. Marks. Dallas: Southern Methodist University.

Courtois, J. C.
1973 "Prospection archéologique dans la moyenne vallée de l'Oronte (el Ghab et er Roudj—Syrie du nord-ouest)," *Syria* 50: 53–99.

Cross, F. M.
1969 "Epigraphic Notes on the Ammān Citadel Inscription," *BASOR* 193: 13–19.
1972a "The Stele Dedicated to Melcarth by Ben-Hadad of Damascus," *BASOR* 205: 36–42.
1972b "An Interpretation of the Nora Stone," *BASOR* 208: 13–19.
1973 *Canaanite Myth and Hebrew Epic*. Cambridge: Harvard University.

Cross, F. M., and D. N. Freedman.
1952 *Early Hebrew Orthography*. New Haven: American Oriental Society.

Dearman, A. J., and J. M. Miller
1983 "The Melqart Stela and the Ben-Hadads of Damascus: Two Studies," *PEQ* 115: 95–101.

Degen, R.
1969 *Altaramäische Grammatik der Inschriften des 10.–8. Jh. v. Chr.* Wiesbaden: Franz Steiner.

Dever, W. G.
1970 "The 'Middle Bronze I' Period in Syria and Palestine." Pp. 132–63 in *Near Eastern Archaeology in the Twentieth Century*. Ed. by J. A. Sanders. Garden City: Doubleday.
1973 "The EB IV–MB I Horizon in Transjordan and Southern Palestine," *BASOR* 210: 37–63.
1976 "The Beginning of the Middle Bronze Age in Syria-Palestine." Pp. 3–38 in *Magnalia Dei: The Mighty Acts of God* (Festschrift G. E. Wright). Ed. by F. M. Cross, W. E. Lemke and P. D. Miller. Garden City: Doubleday.

Dhorme, P.
1910 "Les pays bibliques et l'Assyrie," *RB* 7: 179–99.

Donner, H.
1970 "Adadnirari III. und die Vasallen des Westens." Pp. 49–59 in *Archäologie und Altes Testament* (Festschrift K. Galling). Ed. by A. Kuschke and E. Kutsch. Tübingen: J. C. B. Mohr.

Dossin, G.
1938 "Les archives épistolaires du palais de Mari," *Syria* 19: 105–26.

1939 "Les archives économiques du palais de Mari," *Syria* 20: 97–113.
1954 "Le royaume de Qatna au XVIIIe siècle avant notre ère d'après les 'Archives royales de Mari'," *Bulletin de l'Académie royale de Belgique*: Classe de lettres 40: 417–25.
1954–55 "Le sceau-cylindre de Dêr-Khabiyeh," *AAAS* 4–5: 39–44.
1957 "Kengen, pays de Canaan," *RSO* 32: 35–39.
1958 "L'Ordalie à Mari," *CRAIBL*: 387–92.

Drower, M. S.
1973 "Syria c. 1550–1400 B.C." Pp. 417–525 in *The Cambridge Ancient History*, II/1. Ed. by I. E. S. Edwards, *et al.* Cambridge: Cambridge University.

Dunand, M.
1939 "Stèle araméenne dédiée à Melqart," *Bulletin du Musée de Beyrouth* 3: 65–76.
1942–43 "A propos de la stèle de Melqart du musée d'Alep," *Bulletin du Musée de Beyrouth* 6: 41–45.

Dupont-Sommer, A.
1949 *Les Araméens*. Paris: A. Maisonneuve.

Dussaud, R.
1922a "La stèle araméenne de Zakir au Musée du Louvre," *Syria* 3: 175–76.
1922b "Le temple de Jupiter Damascénien et ses transformations aux époques chrétienne et musulmane," *Syria* 3: 219–50.

Edel, E.
1950 "KBo I 15 + 19, ein Brief Ramses' II. mit einer Schilderung der Kadešschlacht," *ZA* 49: 195–212.
1953a "Die Stelen Amenophis' II. aus Karnak und Memphis," *ZDPV* 69: 97–176.
1953b "Weitere Briefe aus der Heiratskorrespondenz Ramses' II.: KUB III 37 + KBo I 17 und KUB III 57." Pp. 29–63 in *Geschichte und Altes Testament* (Festschrift A. Alt). Tübingen: Verlag J. C. B. Mohr.
1966 *Die Ortsnamenlisten aus dem Totentempel Amenophis III*. Bonn: Peter Hanstein.

Edgerton, W. F. and J. A. Wilson.
1936 *Historical Records of Ramses III: The Texts in Medinet Habu, Volumes I and II*. Chicago: University of Chicago.

Edzard, D. O.
1970 "Die Keilschrift briefe der Grabungskampagne 1969." Pp. 49–62 in *Kāmid el-Lōz—Kumidi: Schriftdokumente aus Kāmid el-Lōz*. D. O. Edzard, *et al.* Bonn: Rudolf Habelt.

1976 "Ein Brief an den 'Grossen' von Kumidi aus Kāmid al-Lōz," *ZA* 66: 62–67.
1981 "Ein neues Tontafelfragment (Nr. 7) aus Kāmid al-Lōz," *ZA* 70: 52–54.

Eissfeldt, O.
1960 "Review of *A History of Israel* by John Bright," *JBL* 79: 369–72.
1965 *The Old Testament: An Introduction*. Trans. from the German by P. R. Ackroyd. New York: Harper and Row.
1975 "The Hebrew Kingdom." Pp. 537–605 in *The Cambridge Ancient History*, II/2. Ed. by I. E. S. Edwards, *et al.* Cambridge: Cambridge University.

Elat, M.
1975 "The Campaigns of Shalmaneser III against Aram and Israel," *IEJ* 25: 25–35.

Elisseeff, N.
1965a "Dimashk." Pp. 277–91 in *Encyclopaedia of Islam*. New Edition. Ed. by B. Lewis, C. Pellat and J. Schacht. London: Luzac.
1965b "Ghuṭa." Pp. 1104–06 in *Encyclopaedia of Islam*. New Edition. Ed. by B. Lewis, C. Pellat and J. Schacht. London: Luzac.

Ephᶜal, I.
1971 "URU*Ša-za-e-na* = URU*Sa-za-na*," *IEJ* 21: 155–57.

Falkner, M.
1957 "Studien zur Geographie des alten Mesopotamien," *AfO* 18: 1–37.

Faulkner, R. O.
1942 "The Battle of Megiddo," *JEA* 28: 2–15.
1947 "The Wars of Sethos I," *JEA* 33: 34–39.
1975 "Egypt: From the Inception of the Nineteenth Dynasty to the Death of Ramesses III." Pp. 217–51 in *The Cambridge Ancient History*, II/2. Ed. by I. E. S. Edwards, *et al.* Cambridge: Cambridge University.

Fitzmyer, J. A.
1967 *The Aramaic Inscriptions of Sefîre*. Rome: Pontifical Biblical Institute.

Forrer, E.
1920 *Die Provinzeinteilung des assyrische Reiches*. Leipzig: J. C. Hinrichs'sche.

Gaál, E.
1978 "*Mātu ša imērīšu* as a Translation from Hurrian," *Révue hittite et asianique* 36: 43–48.

Gardiner, A. H.
1905 *The Inscription of Mes*. Leipzig: J. C. Hinrichs'sche.
1911 *Egyptian Hieratic Texts: Series I: Literary Texts of the New Kingdom. Part I: The Papyrus Anastasi and the Papyrus Koller, Together with the Parallel Texts*. Leipzig: J. C. Hinrichs'sche.
1947 *Ancient Egyptian Onomastica*. Oxford: Oxford University.
1960 *The Ḳadesh Inscriptions of Ramesses II*. Oxford: Oxford University.
1964 *Egypt of the Pharaohs*. London: Oxford University.

Garelli, P.
1963 *Les Assyriens en Cappadoce*. Paris: Adrien Maisonneuve.

Garrod, D. A. E.
1962 "An Outline of Pleistocene Prehistory in Palestine-Lebanon-Syria," *Quaternaria* 6: 541–46.

Gelb, I. J.
1944 *Hurrians and Subarians*. Chicago: University of Chicago.
1961 "The Early History of the West Semitic Peoples," *JCS* 15: 27–47.
1968 "The Word for Dragoman in the Ancient Near East," *Glossa* 2: 93–104.

Gelb, I. J., P. M. Purves, and A. A. MacRae
1943 *Nuzi Personal Names*. Chicago: University of Chicago.

Gerstenblith, P.
1983 *The Levant at the Beginning of the Middle Bronze Age*. ASOR Dissertation Series 5. Winona Lake, Ind.: ASOR/Eisenbrauns.

Gibson, J. C. L.
1975 *Textbook of Syrian Semitic Inscriptions, Volume II: Aramaic Inscriptions*. Oxford: Clarendon.

Ginsberg, H. L.
1970 "Abram's 'Damascene' Steward," *BASOR* 200: 31–32.

Giveon, R.
1969 "Thutmosis IV and Asia," *JNES* 28: 54–59.

GKC Kautzsch, E. *Gesenius' Hebrew Grammar*. Second English Edition. Rev. by A. E. Cowley. Oxford: Clarendon, 1963.

Goetze, A.
1929a "Die Pestgebete des Muršiliš," *Kleinasiatische Forschungen* 1: 161–251.
1929b "Zur Schlacht von Qadeš," *OLZ* 32: 832–38.
1933 *Die Annalen des Muršiliš*. Mitteilungen der Vorderasiatisch-aegyptischen Gesellschaft 38. Band. Leipzig: J. C. Hinrichs'sche.

1941 "Is Ugaritic a Canaanite Dialect?" *Language* 17: 127–38.
1953 "An Old Babylonian Itinerary," *JCS* 7: 51–72.
1975a "The Struggle for the Domination of Syria (1400–1300 B.C.)." Pp. 1–20 in *The Cambridge Ancient History*, II/2. Ed. by I. E. S. Edwards, *et al.* Cambridge: Cambridge University.
1975b "Anatolia from Shuppiluliumash to the Egyptian War of Muwatallish." Pp. 117–29 in *The Cambridge Ancient History*, II/2. Ed. by I. E. S. Edwards, *et al.* Cambridge: Cambridge University.
1975c "The Hittites and Syria (1300–1200 B.C.)." Pp. 252–73 in *The Cambridge Ancient History*, II/2. Ed. by I. E. S. Edwards, *et al.* Cambridge: Cambridge University.

Gordon, C. H.
1952 "Damascus in Assyrian Sources," *IEJ* 2: 174–75.

Gray, J.
1970 *I and II Kings: A Commentary*. London: SCM.

Grayson, A. K.
1972–76 *Assyrian Royal Inscriptions*. Two Volumes. Wiesbaden: Otto Harrassowitz.
1976 "Studies in Neo-Assyrian History: The Ninth Century B.C." *Bibliotheca Orientalis* 33: 134–45.
1982 "Assyria: Ashur-dan II to Ashur-Nirari V (934–745 B.C.)." Pp. 238–81 in *The Cambridge Ancient History*, III/1. Ed. by John Boardman, *et al.* Cambridge: Cambridge University.

Greenfield, J. C.
1976 "The Aramean God Rammān/Rimmōn," *IEJ* 26: 195–98.

Gröndahl, F.
1967 *Die Personennamen der Texte aus Ugarit*. Rome: Pontifical Biblical Institute.

Gurney, O. R., and J. J. Finkelstein
1957 *The Sultantepe Tablets I*. London: British Institute of Archaeology at Ankara.

Güterbock, H. G.
1956 "The Deeds of Suppiluliuma as Told by His Son, Mursili II," *JCS* 10: 41–68; 75–98; 107–30.

Hachmann, R.
1970 "Kāmid el-Lōz—Kumidi." Pp. 63–94 in *Kāmid el-Lōz—Kumidi: Schriftdokumente aus Kāmid el-Lōz*. D. O. Edzard, *et al.* Bonn: Rudolph Habelt.

Haldar, A.
1962 "Hobah." Pp. 615–16 in vol. 2, *Interpreter's Dictionary of the Bible.* Ed by G. A. Buttrick, *et al.* Nashville: Abingdon.
Hallo, W. W.
1964 "The Road to Emar," *JCS* 18: 57–88.
Haran, M.
1967 "The Rise and Decline of the Empire of Jeroboam ben Joash," *VT* 17: 266–97.
Harris, J. E. and K. R. Weeks.
1973 *X-Raying the Pharaohs.* New York: Charles Scribner's Sons.
Haupt, P.
1909 "Midian und Sinai," *ZDMG* 63: 506–30.
1915 "Die 'Eselstadt' Damaskus," *ZDMG* 69: 168–72.
Hawkins, J. D.
1982 "The Neo-Hittite States in Syria and Anatolia." Pp. 372–441 in *The Cambridge Ancient History,* III/1. Ed. by John Boardman, *et al.* Cambridge: Cambridge University.
Hayes, J. H. and J. M. Miller, eds.
1977 *Israelite and Judean History.* Philadelphia: Westminster.
Hayes, W. C.
1971 "The Middle Kingdom in Egypt." Pp. 464–531 in *The Cambridge Ancient History,* I/2. Ed. by I. E. S. Edwards, *et al.* Cambridge: Cambridge University.
1973a "Egypt: From the Death of Ammenemes III to Seqenenre II." Pp. 42–76 in *The Cambridge Ancient History,* II/1. Ed. by I. E. S. Edwards, *et al.* Cambridge: Cambridge University.
1973b "Egypt: Internal Affairs from Tuthmosis I to the Death of Amenophis III." Pp. 313–416 in *The Cambridge Ancient History,* II/1. Ed. by I. E. S. Edwards, *et al.* Cambridge: Cambridge University.
Helck, W.
1960 "Die ägyptische Verwaltung in den syrischen Besitzungen," *MDOG* 92: 1–13.
1971 *Die Beziehungen Ägyptens zu Vorderasien im 3. und 2. Jahrtausend v. Chr.* Second Edition. Wiesbaden: Otto Harrassowitz.
Hours, F.
1975 "The Lower Paleolithic of Lebanon and Syria." Pp. 249–71 in *Problems in Prehistory: North Africa and the Levant.*

Ed. by F. Wendorf and A. E. Marks. Dallas: Southern Methodist University.

Hours, F., L. Copeland, and O. Aurenche
1973 "Les industries paléolithiques du Proche-Orient, essai de corrélation," *L'Anthropologie* 77: 229–80.

Hrouda, B.
1958 "Waššukanni, Urkiš, Šubat-Enlil: Ein Beitrag zur historischen Geographie des nördlich Zweistromlandes," *MDOG* 90: 22–35.

Hulin, P.
1963 "The Inscriptions on the Carved Throne-Base of Shalmaneser III," *Iraq* 25: 48–69.

James, T. G. H.
1973 "Egypt: From the Expulsion of the Hyksos to Amenophis I." Pp. 289–312 in *The Cambridge Ancient History*, II/1. Ed. by I. E. S. Edwards, *et al.* Cambridge: Cambridge University.

Jean, C. F.
1938 "Excerpta de la correspondance de Mari, *Révue des études sémitiques*: 128–32.

Jepsen, A.
1941–45 "Israel und Damaskus," *AfO* 14: 153–72.
1970 "Ein neuer Fixpunkt für die Chronologie der israelitischen Könige?" *VT* 20: 359–61.

Jirku, A.
1918 "Der assyrische Name des Königs Benhadad III. von Damaskus," *OLZ* 21: 279.

Kader, J. A. el-
1949 "Un orthostate du temple de Hadad à Damas," *Syria* 26: 191–95.

KAI
1969–73 Donner, H., and W. Röllig. *Kanaanäische und Aramäische Inschriften*. Three Volumes. Wiesbaden: Otto Harrassowitz.

Katzenstein, H. J.
1973 *The History of Tyre*. Jerusalem. Schocken Institute for Jewish Research.

KB Koehler, L. and W. Baumgartner, *Lexicon in Veteris Testamenti Libros*. Second edition. Leiden: E. J. Brill, 1958.

Kenyon, K.
1971a *Royal Cities of the Old Testament*. New York: Schocken Books.

1971b "Syria and Palestine c. 2160–1780: The Archaeological Sites." Pp. 567–94 in *The Cambridge Ancient History*, I/2. Ed. by I. E. S. Edwards, *et al.* Cambridge: Cambridge University.

1973 "Palestine in the Middle Bronze Age." Pp. 77–116 in *The Cambridge Ancient History*, II/1. Ed. by I. E. S. Edwards, *et al.* Cambridge: Cambridge University.

1979 *Archaeology in the Holy Land*. Fourth Edition. London: Ernest Benn.

Kinnier-Wilson, J. V.

1962 "The Kurbaʾil Statue of Shalmaneser III," *Iraq* 24: 90–115.

Kitchen, K. A.

1962 *Suppiluliuma and the Amarna Pharaohs*. Liverpool: Liverpool University.

1965 "Theban Topographical Lists, Old and New," *Orientalia* 34: 1–9.

1967 "Review of *The Chronology of the Amarna Letters* by E. F. Campbell," *JEA* 53: 178–82.

Klengel, H.

1965–70 *Geschichte Syriens im 2. Jahrtausend v. u. Z.* Deutsche Akademie der Wissenschaften zu Berlin, Institut für Orientforschung, no. 40. Three Volumes. Berlin: Akademie Verlag.

1977 "Das Land Kusch in den Keilschrifttexten von Amarna." Pp. 227–32 in *Aegypten und Kusch* (Festschrift F. Hintze). Ed. by E. Endesfelder, *et al.* Berlin: Akademie Verlag.

Knudtzon, J. A.

1915 *Die El-Amarna-Tafeln*. Leipzig: J. C. Hinrichs'sche, 1915. Reprinted Aalen: Otto Zeller, 1964.

Kochavi, M.

1981 "The History and Archeology of Aphek-Antipatris: A Biblical City in the Sharon Plain," *BA* 44: 75–86.

Kochavi, M., P. Beck, and R. Gophna.

1979 "Aphek-Antipatris, Tel Poleg, Tel Zeror, and Tel Burqa: Four Fortified Sites of the Middle Bronze Age IIA in the Sharon Plain," *ZDPV* 95: 121–65.

Kraeling, E. G. H.

1918 *Aram and Israel*. New York: Columbia University.

Kupper, J. R.

1948 "Nouvelles lettres de Mari relatives à Ḫammurabi de Babylone," *RA* 42: 35–52.

1957 *Les nomades en Mésopotamie au temps des rois de Mari.* Paris: Société d'édition "Les Belles Lettres."
1973 "Northern Mesopotamia and Syria." Pp. 1–41 in *The Cambridge Ancient History,* II/1. Ed. by I. E. S. Edwards, *et al.* Cambridge: Cambridge University.

Kuschke, A.
1966 "Die Biqâ^{c}, ihre altorientalischen Siedlungen und Verkehrswege." Pp. 15–30 in *Kāmid el-Lōz: 1963/64.* Ed. by R. Hachmann and A. Kuschke. Bonn: Rudolf Habelt.
1981 "Das Land Amqu: Neue Beobachtungen und Fragen," *EI* 15: 39*–45*.

Kuschke, A., and M. Metzger
1972 "Kumidi und die Ausgrabungen auf Tell Kāmid el-Lōz," *VTS* 22: 143–73.

Labat, R.
1976 *Manuel d'épigraphie akkadienne.* Paris: Paul Geuthner.

Laessøe, J.
1959 "A Statue of Shalmaneser III, from Nimrud," *Iraq* 21: 147–57.

Lambert, W. G.
1967 *Babylonian Wisdom Literature.* Oxford: Clarendon.

Landsberger, B.
1948 *Sam$^{\supset}$al: Studien zur Entdeckung der Ruinenstaette Karatepe.* Ankara: Türkischen Historischen Gesellschaft.

Layard, A. H.
1851 *Inscriptions in the Cuneiform Character from Assyrian Monuments.* London: Harrison and Son.

Lemaire, A.
1984 "Le stèle araméenne de Bar-Hadad," *Iraq* 46: 337–49.

Levine, L. D.
1972a "Menahem and Tiglath-Pileser: A New Synchronism," *BASOR* 206: 40–42.
1972b *Two Neo-Assyrian Stelae from Iran.* Toronto: Royal Ontario Museum.

Lewy, J.
1952 "Studies in the Historic Geography of the Ancient Near East," *Orientalia* 21: 265–92; 393–425.
1961 "Amurritica," *HUCA* 32:31–74.

Lidzbarski, M.
1909–15 *Ephemeris für semitische Epigraphik.* Three Volumes. Giessen: Alfred Töpelmann.

Liere, W. J. van.
1963 "Capitals and Citadels of Bronze-Iron Age Syria in their Relationship to Land and Water," *AAAS* 13: 109–22.
1966 "The Pleistocene and Stone Age of the Orontes River (Syria)," *AAAS* 16: 8–29.
Liere, W. J. van and H. de Contenson
1963 "A Note on Five Early Neolithic Sites in Inland Syria," *AAAS* 13: 175–209.
Lipinski, E.
1969 "Le Ben-Hadad II de la Bible et l'histoire." Vol. 1, pp. 157–73, in *Proceedings of the Fifth World Congress of Jewish Studies*. Ed. By Pinchas Peli. Jerusalem: R. H. Hacohen.
1971a "The Assyrian Campaign to Manṣuate, in 796 B.C., and the Zakir Stela," *AION* 31: 393–99.
1971b "ᶜAttar-hapeš, the Forefather of Bar-Hadad II," *AION* 31: 101–04.
1971c "Note de topographie historique: Baᶜli-Raᵓši et Raᵓšu Qudšu," *RB* 78: 84–92.
1975 *Studies in Aramaic Inscriptions and Onomastics*. Leuven: Leuven University.
Liverani, M.
1967 "Contrasti e confluenze di concezioni politichi nellᵓetà di el-Amarna," *RA* 61: 1–18.
1974 "La royauté syrienne de l'âge du Bronze Récent." Pp. 329–56 in *Le palais et la royauté: archéologie et civilisation*. XIXe Rencontre assyriologique internationale. Ed. by P. Garelli. Paris: Paul Geuthner.
1975 "Communautés de village et palais royal dans la Syrie du IIème Millénaire," *Journal of the Economic and Social History of the Orient* 18: 146–64.
1979a "Pharaoh's Letters to Rib-Adda." Pp. 3–13 in *Three Amarna Essays by Mario Liverani*. Trans. from the Italian by M. L. Jaffe. Malibu: Undena.
1979b "Social Implications in the Politics of Abdi-Aširta of Amurru." Pp. 14–20 in *Three Amarna Essays by Mario Liverani*. Ed. and Trans. from the Italian by M. L. Jaffe. Malibu: Undena.
Loretz, O.
1974 "Zu LÚ.MEŠ SA.GAZ.ZA *a-bu-ur-ra* in den Briefen von Tell Kāmid el-Lōz," *UF* 6: 486.

Luckenbill, D. D.
1924 *The Annals of Sennacherib.* Chicago: University of Chicago.
1926–27 *Ancient Records of Assyria and Babylonia.* Two Volumes. Chicago: University of Chicago.

Lundquist, J.
1984 "Iron II Found at Tell Qarqur," *ASOR Newsletter* 35.3: 1–3.

Maiberger, P.
1970 "Die syrischen Inschriften von Kāmid el-Lōz und die Frage der Identität von Kāmid el-Lōz und Kumidi." Pp. 11–21 in *Kāmid el-Lōz—Kumidi: Schriftdokumente aus Kāmid el-Lōz.* D. O. Edzard, *et al.* Bonn: Rudolf Habelt.

Malamat, A.
1950 "Concerning the Assyrian Name of Damascus," *Tarbiz* 22: 64 [Hebrew].
1958 "The Kingdom of David and Solomon in its Contact with Egypt and Aram Naharaim," *BA* 21: 96–102.
1960 "Hazor 'the Head of all Those Kingdoms'," *JBL* 79: 12–19.
1963 "Aspects of the Foreign Policies of David and Solomon," *JNES* 22: 1–17.
1965 "Campaigns to the Mediterranean by Iahdunlim and Other Early Mesopotamian Rulers," *Assyriological Studies* 16: 365–73.
1970 "Northern Canaan and the Mari Texts." Pp. 164–77 in *Near Eastern Archaeology in the Twentieth Century* (Festschrift N. Glueck). Ed. by J. A. Sanders. Garden City: Doubleday.
1971 "Syro-Palestinian Destinations in a Mari Tin Inventory," *IEJ* 21: 31–38.
1973 "The Aramaeans." Pp. 134–55 in *Peoples of Old Testament Times.* Ed. by D. J. Wiseman. Oxford: Clarendon.

Mallowan, M. E. L.
1966 *Nimrud and its Remains.* Two Volumes. London: Collins.

Mazar, B.
1957 "The Tobiads," *IEJ* 7: 137–45; 229–38.
1961 "Geshur and Maacah," *JBL* 80: 16–28.
1962 "The Aramean Empire and its Relations with Israel," *BA* 25: 98–120.
1968 "The Middle Bronze Age in Palestine," *IEJ* 18: 65–97.

1970 "Canaan in the Patriarchal Age." Pp. 169–87 in *The World History of the Jewish People, Volume II: Patriarchs*. Ed. by B. Mazar. Jerusalem: Massada.

McCarter, P. K.

1974 "'Yaw, Son of Omri': A Philological Note on Israelite Chronology," *BASOR* 216: 5–7.

1980 *I Samuel*. Anchor Bible. Garden City: Doubleday.

Meissner, B.

1933 "Die Keilschrifttexte auf den steinernen Orthostaten und Statuen aus dem Tell Ḥalâf." Pp. 71–79 in *Auf Fünf Jahrtausenden morgenlandischer Kultur* (Festschrift M. F. von Oppenheim). *AfO Beiheft* 1.

Mellaart, J.

1975 *The Neolithic of the Near East*. New York: Charles Scribner's Sons.

Messerschmidt, L.

1911 *Keilschrifttexte aus Assur historischen Inhalts. Heft I*. Leipzig: J. C. Hinrichs'sche.

Meyer, E.

1931 *Geschichte des Altertums*. Stuttgart: J. G. Cotta'sche.

Michel, Ernst.

1947–52 "Die Assur-Texte Salmanassars III. (858–824)," *WO* 1: 5–20; 57–71; 205–22; 255–71; 385–96; 454–75.

1954–59 "Die Assur-Texte Salmanassars III. (858–824)," *WO* 2: 27–45; 137–57; 221–33; 408–15.

1964 "Die Assur-Texte Salmanassars III. (858–824)," *WO* 3: 146–55.

1967–68 "Die Assur-Texte Salmanassars III. (858–824)," *WO* 4: 29–37.

Millard, A. R.

1973 "Adad-nirari III, Aram, and Arpad," *PEQ* 105: 161–64.

1978 "Epigraphic Notes, Aramaic and Hebrew," *PEQ* 110: 23–26.

Millard, A. R., and H. Tadmor.

1973 "Adad-nirari III in Syria: Another Stele Fragment and the Dates of His Compaigns," *Iraq* 35: 57–64.

Miller, J. M.

1964 *The Omride Dynasty in the Light of Recent Literary and Archaeological Research*. Unpublished dissertation, Emory University.

1966 "The Elisha Cycle and the Accounts of the Omride Wars," *JBL* 85: 441–54.

1967a "Another Look at the Chronology of the Early Divided Monarchy," *JBL* 86: 276–88.
1967b "The Fall of the House of Ahab," *VT* 17: 307–24.
1968 "The Rest of the Acts of Jehoahaz (I Kings 20, 22:1–38)," *ZAW* 80: 337–42.
1969 "Geshur and Aram," *JNES* 28: 60–61.
1974 "The Moabite Stone as a Memorial Stela," *PEQ* 106: 9–18.

Morgenstern, J.
1940 "Chronological Data of the Dynasty of Omri," *JBL* 59: 385–96.

Moscati, S.
1959 "The 'Aramaean Ahlamu'," *JSS* 4: 303–07.

Müller, W. M.
1893 *Asien und Europa nach altägyptischen Denkmälern.* Leipzig: Wilhelm Englemann.

Munn-Rankin, J. M.
1956 "Diplomacy in Western Asia in the Early Second Millennium B.C." *Iraq* 18: 68–110.

Naaman, N.
1974a "Sennacherib's 'Letter to God' on His Campaign to Judah," *BASOR* 214: 25–39.
1974b "Syria at the Transition from the Old Babylonian Period to the Middle Babylonian Period," *UF* 6: 265–74.
1975 *The Political Disposition and Historical Development of Eretz-Israel According to the Amarna Letters.* Unpublished dissertation, Tel-Aviv University, [Hebrew].
1976 "Two Notes on the Monolith Inscription of Shalmaneser III from Kurkh," *Tel Aviv* 3: 89–106.
1978 "Looking for KTK," *WO* 9: 220–39.

Noordtzij, A.
1907 "2 Samuel 8, 3–6," *ZAW* 27: 16–22.

North, R.
1970 "Phoenicia-Canaan Frontier "Lĕbô'" of Ḥama," *Mélanges de l'Université Saint-Joseph* 46: 71–103.

Noth, M.
1955 "Das deutsche evangelische Institut für Altertumswissenschaft des Heiligen Landes Lehrkursus 1954," *ZDPV* 71: 1–59.
1956 "Das deutsche evangelische Institut für Altertumswissenschaft des Heiligen Landes Lehrkursus 1955," *ZDPV* 72: 31–82.

1960 *The History of Israel.* Second Edition. Trans. from the German by P. R. Ackroyd. New York: Harper and Row.
1972 *A History of Pentateuchal Traditions.* Trans. from the German by B. W. Anderson. Englewood Cliffs: Prentice-Hall.

Nougayrol, J.
1956 *Le Palais royal d'Ugarit IV.* Paris: Imprimerie nationale.

O'Callaghan, R. T.
1948 *Aram Naharaim: A Contribution to the History of Upper Mesopotamia in the Second Millennium B.C.* Roma: Pontificium Institutum Biblicum.

Oded, B.
1972 "The Historical Background of the Syro-Ephraimite War Reconsidered," *CBQ* 34: 153–65.

Olmstead, A. T.
1931 *History of Syria and Palestine.* New York/London: Charles Scribner's Sons.

Oppenheim, A. L.
1956 *The Interpretation of Dreams in the Ancient Near East. Transactions of the American Philosophical Society* 46: 3.

Osten, H. H. von der.
1956 *Svenska Syrienexpeditionen I: Die Grabung von Tell eṣ-Ṣaliḥiyeh.* Lund: C. W. K. Gleerup.

Otten, H.
1955 *Keilschrifttexte aus Boghazköi VIII.* Berlin: Gebr. Mann.

Page, S.
1968 "A Stela of Adad-nirari III and Nergal-ereš from Tell al-Rimah," *Iraq* 30: 139–53.
1969 "Joash and Samaria in a New Stela Excavated at Tell al-Rimah, Iraq," *VT* 19: 483–84.

Parpola, S.
1970 *Neo-Assyrian Toponyms.* Neukirchen-Vluyn: Neukirchener.

Parr, P.
1968 "The Origin of the Rampart Fortifications of Middle Bronze Age Palestine and Syria," *ZDPV* 84: 18–45.

Parrot, A.
1953 *Archéologie mésopotamienne.* Two Volumes. Paris: Albin Michel.

Pavlovsky, V. and E. Vogt.
1964 "Die Jahre der Könige von Juda und Israel," *Biblica* 45: 321–47.

Pervès, M.
1945 "Notes sommaires de préhistoire Syro-Libanaise," *BSPF* 42: 201–09.

Pettinato, G.
1979 *Catalogo dei testi cuneiformi di Tell Mardikh-Ebla (Materiali epigrafici di Ebla I).* Napoli: Istituto universitario orientale de Napoli.
1981 *The Archives of Ebla: An Empire Inscribed in Clay.* Garden City: Doubleday.

Pinches, T. G.
1882 "On a Cuneiform Inscription Relating to the Capture of Babylon by Cyrus and the Events which Preceded and Led to it," *Transactions of the Society of Biblical Archaeology* 7: 139–76.

Pognon, H.
1907 *Inscriptions sémitiques de la Syrie, de la Mésopotamie, et de la région de Mossoul.* Paris: Imprimerie nationale.

Porter, J. L.
1855 *Five Years in Damascus.* Two Volumes. London: John Murray.

Posener, G.
1940 *Princes et Pays d'Asie et de nubie.* Bruxelles: Fondation Égyptologique Reine Elisabeth.
1971 "Syria and Palestine c. 2160–1780: Relations with Egypt." Pp. 532–58 in *The Cambridge Ancient History,* I/2. Ed. by I. E. S. Edwards, *et al.* Cambridge: Cambridge University.

Potut.
1937 "La préhistoire dans la région de Damas," *BSPF* 34: 130–32.

Pritchard, J. B.
1954 *The Ancient Near East in Pictures.* Princeton: Princeton University.

Rainey, A. F.
1976 "KL 72:600 and the D-Passive in West Semitic," *UF* 8: 337–41.

Rasmussen, N.
1897 *Salmanasser den II's Indskrifter.* Kjobenhavn: Nielsen and Lydiches.

Rawlinson, H. C.
1861–1909 *Cuneiform Inscriptions of Western Asia.* Five Volumes. London: R. E. Bowler.

Reade, J. E.
1978 "Assyrian Campaigns, 840–811 B.C., and the Babylonian Frontier," *ZA* 68: 251–60.

Redford, D. B.
1973 "New Light on the Asiatic Campaigning of Horemheb," *BASOR* 211: 36–49.

Richardson, H. N.
1958 "The Historical Reliability of Chronicles," *Journal of Bible and Religion* 26: 9–12.

RLA Ebeling, E., and Meissner, B., eds. *Reallexikon der Assyriologie.* Berlin/Leipzig: Walter de Gruyter, 1932–.

Rost, P.
1893 *Die Keilschrifttexte Tiglat-Pilesers III.* Two Volumes. Leipzig: Eduard Pfeiffer.

Roux, G.
1980 *Ancient Iraq.* Second Edition. Bungay, Suffolk: Penguin.

Rudolph, W.
1952 "Der Aufbau der Asa-Geschichte (2 Chr. XIV–XVI)," *VT* 2: 367–71.

Saggs, H. W. F.
1955 "The Nimrud Letters, 1952—part II," *Iraq* 17: 126–54.
1962 *The Greatness That Was Babylon.* New York: Mentor.

Sasson, J.
1984 "Thoughts of Zimri-Lim," *BA* 47: 110–20.

Sauvaget, J.
1934 "Esquisse d'une histoire de la ville de Damas," *Révue des études islamiques* 8: 421–76.
1949 "Le plan antique de Damas," *Syria* 26: 314–58.

Schedl, C.
1962 "Textkritische Bermerkungen zu den Synchronismen der Könige von Israel und Juda," *VT* 12: 88–119.

Scheil, V.
1900 *Textes Élamite-sémitiques Serie I (Memoires de la Délégation en Perse, II).* Paris: Ernest Leroux.

Schiffer, S.
1911 *Die Aramäer.* Leipzig: J. C. Hinrichs'sche.

Schmitz, F. J.
1978 *Amenophis I.* Hildesheim: Gerstenberg.

Schräder, E.
1889 *Keilinschriftliche Bibliothek, I.* Berlin: H. Reuthers.

Schramm, W.
1973 *Einleitung in die Assyrischen Königsinschriften: II* Leiden/Köln: E. J. Brill.

Schulman, A. R.
1964 "Some Observations on the Military Background of the Amarna Period," *JARCE* 3: 51–69.
1978 "ᶜAnkhesenamūn, Nofretity, and the Amka Affair," *JARCE* 15: 43–48.
Seger, J. D.
1975 "The MB II Fortifications at Shechem and Gezer: A Hyksos Retrospective," *EI* 12: 34*–45*.
Seidmann, J.
1935 *Die Inschriften Adadnirâris II. (Mitteilungen der altorientalischen Gesellschaft, IX).* Leipzig: Otto Harrassowitz.
Sellin, E.
1905 "Melchizedek. Ein Beitrag zu der Geschichte Abrahams," *Neue Kirchliche Zeitschrift* 16: 929–51.
Sethe, K.
1926 *Die Ächtung Feindlicher Fürsten, Völker und Dinge auf altägyptischen Tongefässscherben des Mittleren Reiches.* (Abhandlungen der Preussischen Akademie der Wissenschaften, Jahrgang 1926). Berlin: Verlag der Akademie der Wissenschaften.
Several, M. W.
1972 "Reconsidering the Egyptian Empire in Palestine during the Amarna Period," *PEQ* 104: 123–33.
Shea, W. H.
1977 "A Note on the Date of the Battle of Qarqar," *JCS* 29: 240–42.
1978 "Adad-nirari III and Jehoash of Israel" *JCS* 30: 101–13.
1978–79 "The Kings of the Melqart Stela," *Maarav* 1: 159–76.
Shenkel, J. D.
1968 *Chronology and Recensional Development in the Greek Text of Kings.* Cambridge: Harvard University.
Simons, J.
1937 *Handbook for the Study of Egyptian Topographical Lists Relating to Western Asia.* Leiden: E. J. Brill.
Simpson, W. K., ed.
1973 *The Literature of Ancient Egypt.* New Haven: Yale University.
Skinner, J.
1930 *Genesis.* International Critical Commentary. Edinburgh: T. & T. Clark.
Smith, S.
1929 "The Foundation of the Assyrian Empire." Pp. 1–31 in *The Cambridge Ancient History*, III. Ed. by J. B. Bury, S. A.

Cook and F. E. Adcock. Cambridge: Cambridge University.

Soggin, J. A.
1970 "Ein ausserbiblisches Zeugnis für die Chronologie des Jĕhô'āš/Jô'āš, König von Israel," *VT* 20: 366–68.

Speiser, E. A.
1951 "'Damascus' as *Ša-imērišu*," *JAOS* 71: 257–58.
1964 *Genesis*. Anchor Bible. Garden City: Doubleday.

Tadmor, H.
1961a "Azriyau of Yaudi." Pp. 232–71 in *Studies in the Bible*. Scripta Hierosolymitana 8. Ed. by C. Rabin. Jerusalem: Magnes.
1961b "Que and Musri," *IEJ* 11: 143–50.
1962 "The Southern Border of Aram," *IEJ* 12: 114–22.
1968 "Introductory Remarks to a New Edition of the Annals of Tiglath-Pileser III," *Proceedings of the Israel Academy of Sciences and Humanities* 2: 168–87.
1969 "A Note on the Saba'a Stele of Adad-nirari III," *IEJ* 19: 46–48.
1973 "The Historical Inscriptions of Adad-nirari III," *Iraq* 35: 141–50.
1975 "Assyria and the West: The Ninth Century and its Aftermath." Pp. 36–48 in *Unity and Diversity: Essays in the History, Literature and Religion of the Ancient Near East*. Ed. by H. Goedicke and J. J. M. Roberts. Baltimore: Johns Hopkins University.
1979 "The Decline of Empires in Western Asia ca. 1200 B.C.E." Pp. 1–14 in *Symposia Celebrating the Seventy-Fifth Anniversary of the Founding of the American Schools of Oriental Research*. Ed. by F. M. Cross. Cambridge: ASOR.

Tarn, W. W.
1964 *Alexander the Great*. Boston: Beacon.

TCL XIV
1928 Thureau-Dangin, F. *Textes cunéiformes du Louvre, XIV: Tablettes cappadociennes, deuxième série*. Paris: Paul Geuthner.

TCL XX
1936 Lewy, J. *Textes cunéiformes du Louvre, XX: Tablettes cappadociennes, troisième série, deuxième partie*. Paris: Paul Geuthner.

Thiele, E. R.
1965 *The Mysterious Numbers of the Hebrew Kings*. Revised Edition. Grand Rapids: William B. Eerdmans.

Thomas, D. W., Ed.
1961 *Documents from Old Testament Times.* New York: Harper and Row.
Thompson, H. O., and F. Zayadine.
1973 "The Tell Siran Inscription," *BASOR* 212: 5–11.
Thubron, C.
1967 *Mirror to Damascus.* Little, Brown & Co.
Thureau-Dangin, F., *et al.*
1931 *Arslan-Tash.* Two Volumes. Paris: Paul Geuthner.
Tocci, F. M.
1960a "Damasco e *ša imērišu,*" *RSO* 35: 129–33.
1960b *La Siria nell'età di Mari.* Roma: Centro di Studi Semitica.
Turner, G.
1968 "The Palace and Batiment aux Ivoires at Arslan Tash: A Reappraisal," *Iraq* 30: 62–68.
Unger, E.
1916 *Relief-stele Adadniraris III. aus Sabaʾa und Semiramis.* Publicationen der kaiserlich osmanischen Museen 2. Constantinople.
Unger, M. F.
1953 "Some Comments on the Text of Genesis 15:2, 3," *JBL* 72: 49–50.
1957 *Israel and the Aramaeans of Damascus.* Grand Rapids: Zondervan.
Vanel, A.
1974 "Tâbe'él en Is. VII 6 et le roi Tubail de Tyr," *VTS* 26: 17–24.
Vattioni, F.
1969 "Frustula epigraphica," *Augustinianum* 9: 366–69.
Vaux, R. de.
1967a "La chronologie de Ḫazaël et de Benhadad III, rois de Damas." Pp. 75–82 in *Bible et Orient.* Paris: Éditions du Cerf. Originally published in *RB* 43 (1934): 512–18.
1967b "Les prophètes de Baal sur le Mont Carmel." Pp. 485–97 in *Bible et Orient.* Paris: Éditions du Cerf. Originally published in *Bulletin du Musée de Beyrouth* 5 (1941): 7–20.
1978 *The Early History of Israel.* Trans. from the French by D. Smith. Philadelphia: Westminster.
Virolleaud, C.
1941 "Cinq tablettes accadiennes de Ras-Shamra," *RA* 38: 1–12.

Ward, W. A.
1961 "Egypt and the East Mediterranean in the Early Second Millennium B.C." *Orientalia* 30: 22–45; 129–55.
Watzinger, C. and K. Wulzinger.
1921 *Damaskus: Die Antike Stadt.* Wissenshaftliche Veröffentlichungen des deutsch-türkischen Denkmalschutz-Kommandos, Heft 4. Berlin/Leipzig: Walter de Gruyter.
Weidner, E. F.
1923 *Politische Dokumente aus Kleinasien.* Leipzig: J. C. Hinrichs'sche; reprinted, Hildesheim: Georg Olms, 1970.
1926 "Die Annalen des Königs Aššurdan II. von Assyrien," *AfO* 3: 151–61.
1958 "Die Feldzüge und Bauten Tiglatpilesers I." *AfO* 18: 342–60.
Weippert, M.
1978 "*Jau(a) mār Ḫumrî*—Joram oder Jehu von Israel?" *VT* 28: 113–18.
Weiss, H.
1985 "Tell Leilan on the Habur Plains of Syria," *BA* 48: 6–34.
Whitley, C. F.
1952 "The Deuteronomic Presentation of the House of Omri," *VT* 2: 137–52.
Wilhelm, G.
1973 "Ein Brief der Amarna-Zeit aus Kāmid el-Lōz (KL 72:600)," *ZA* 63: 69–75.
Winter, I. J.
1981 "Is There a South Syrian Style of Ivory Carving in the Early First Millennium B.C.?" *Iraq* 43: 101–30.
Wirth, E.
1971 *Syrien: Eine geographische Landeskunde.* Darmstadt: Wissenschaftliche Buchgesellschaft.
Wiseman, D. J.
1951 "Two Historical Inscriptions from Nimrud," *Iraq* 13: 21–26.
1953 "Texts and Fragments," *JCS* 7: 108–09.
1956 "A Fragmentary Inscription of Tiglath-Pileser III from Nimrud," *Iraq* 18: 117–29.
Wright, G. E.
1971 "The Archaeology of Palestine from the Neolithic through the Middle Bronze Age," *JAOS* 91: 276–93.

Wright, G. R. H.
1968 "Temples at Shechem," *ZAW* 80: 1–35.

Wutz, F.
1933 *Die Transkriptionen von der Septuaginta bis zu Hieronymus.* Stuttgart: W. Kohlhammer.

Yadin, Y.
1955 "Some Aspects of the Strategy of Ahab and David (I Kings 20; II Sam. 11)," *Biblica* 36: 332–51.
1972 *Hazor: The Head of All Those Kingdoms.* Schweich Lectures, 1970. London: Oxford University.
1975 *Hazor: The Rediscovery of a Great Citadel of the Bible.* New York: Random House.

Yeivin, S.
1956 "The Extent of Egyptian Domination in Hither Asia under the Middle Kingdom," *EI* 4: 37–40 [Hebrew].
1967 "Amenophis II's Asianic Campaigns," *JARCE* 6: 119–28.

Zimmern, H.
1909 "Benhadad." Pp. 299–303 in *Assyriologische und Archaeologische Studien* (Hilprecht Anniversary Volume). Chicago: Open Court.

GEOGRAPHICAL NAMES INDEX

PERSONAL NAMES INDEX

BIBLICAL REFERENCES INDEX